....

Good Deeds
&
Gunboats

....

Good Deeds & Gunboats

TWO CENTURIES OF AMERICAN-CHINESE ENCOUNTERS

HUGH DEANE

CHINA BOOKS & PERIODICALS · SAN FRANCISCO

We are grateful to the following publishers for their kind permission to quote from the following works: *Book of Songs,* by Arthur Waley. Grove Press, 1960. *The Cantos of Ezra Pound.* Reprinted by permission of New Directions Publishing Corporation. Copyright © 1948 by Ezra Pound. *Collected Poems, Nineteen Sixteen to Nineteen Seventy,* by Conrad Aiken. Oxford University Press, 1970. *Eisenhower: Volume 2, The President,* by Stephen E. Ambrose, Simon and Schuster, 1984. Copyright © 1984 by Stephen E. Ambrose. Excerpt from "Burying Ground by the Ties" from *New and Collected Poems, 1917–1982* by Archibald MacLeish. Copyright © 1985 by the Estate of Archibald MacLeish. Reprinted by permission of Houghton Mifflin Co. Excerpt from *The American Inquisition,* by Stanley I. Kutler. Copyright © 1982 by Stanley I. Kutler. Reprinted by Permission of Hill and Wang, a division of Farrar, Straus and Giroux, Inc. *In Exile from the Land of Snows,* by John Avedon. Random House, 1984. Copyright © by John Avedon, 1976, 1984. *Frank N. Meyer, Plant Hunter in Asia,* by I. S. Cunningham. Copyright © 1984, published by Iowa State University Press, Ames, Iowa. *In Search of History,* by Theodore H. White. Copyright © 1978 by Theodore H. White. Reprinted by permission of Harper & Row, Publishers, Inc. *Personae,* by Ezra Pound. Copyright © 1926 by Ezra Pound. Reprinted by permission of New Directions Publishing Corporation. *Reminiscences,* by General of the Army Douglas MacArthur. McGraw-Hill Book Company. Copyright © Time-Warner Inc. *A Secret War: Americans in China, 1944–45,* by Oliver J. Caldwell. Southern Illinois University Press, 1972. Copyright © 1972 by Oliver J. Caldwell. *Sailing Through China,* by Paul Theroux, illustrated by Patrick Procktor. Text copyright © 1983 by Paul Theroux. Illustrations copyright © 1983 by Patrick Procktor. *The United States and China in the Twentieth Century,* by Michael Schaller. Oxford University Press, 1979. *Yangtze Patrol: The U.S. Navy in China,* by Kemp Tolley. Copyright © 1976, U.S. Naval Institute, Annapolis, Maryland.

Cover design by Rick Wong
Text Design by Laurie Anderson

Copyright © 1990 by Hugh Deane

This edition copublished with New World Press, Beijing, China

Library of Congress Catalog Card Number: 90-81149

ISBN 0-8351-2378-2

Printed in the United States of America by CHINA
BOOKS
& Periodicals, Inc.

For Our Daughter,

Winifred Deane Goldblatt

—called Frou by family and friends

CONTENTS

FOREWORD

In this book Hugh Deane spreads before us a rich tapestry: vivid in color, varied in pattern, and surprising in details.

Perhaps it was to be expected, as the China-born son of missionaries, that I should have thought of American-Chinese encounters more in terms of missionary activity. Certainly the missionaries had an effect in China. But perhaps more important to this story was their effect in the United States: shaping the American perception of China, inventing "the loss of China," chilling the American response to China's revolution.

Another commonly remembered thread was American business. "Oil for the lamps of China" and "400 million customers." The business did not come up to those early expectations; but at least we had the self-congratulatory pleasure of having sponsored the Open Door doctrine in China.

Mr. Deane shows us that there is much, much more to the story of American involvement in China. Turn, I suggest, to the Table of Contents for an overview of his all-encompassing reach. Here is a brief sample: Samuel Shaw, Frederick Ward, Ezra Pound, Mark Twain, Frank Meyer, Joseph Stilwell, Agnes Smedley, Koji Ariyoshi, Douglas MacArthur, Paul Robeson, John William Powell. Many others are there—Edgar Snow and Evans Carlson, for example—who do not have chapters of their own. We find poet and singer, plant hunter and road builder, soldiers and sailors, journalists and publishers, students and revolutionaries, prisoners of war and rescued aviators, opium merchants and soldiers of fortune, diplomats and practitioners of covert operations, enemies and friends.

One important addition that Mr. Deane has been able to make to the story, partly no doubt because he was there, are incidents relating to the period of our alliance with China in World War II—and also to the time of our bitter hostility in Korea.

Not all our author's subjects liked the Chinese and China; and not all were on what he (and I) would consider the right side. He is wise to be realistic: the history of our relations, both as nation states and as peoples, has had sharp ups and downs. Nonetheless, there seems to be a sort of chemistry between Americans and Chinese that favors friendship. During America's self-imposed isolation from China in the 1950s and 1960s, the American people were far ahead of their timid officials and politicians in favoring a return to the traditional friendship. Hence the overwhelming popularity of President Nixon's "opening to China."

Mr. Deane himself could be a case study of this chemistry of American-Chinese friendship. His first contact with China was as a Harvard student when he spent his junior year at Lingnan University in Canton [Guangzhou]. He doesn't tell us what led him to make this—for that time quite unusual—venture; but his life since then has shown that it had a lasting effect. After graduating from Harvard he returned to China as a journalist for several years during China's Resistance War against Japan. Following war duty as an officer in naval intelligence, he returned to journalism and was in China in 1945 and 1949. During the years when direct contact was not possible, he kept up his interest and wrote widely on China affairs and American policy. When times changed for the better, he was a founder of the US-China Peoples Friendship Association, has taken an active role in non-governmental relations, and has made many trips to China. He writes from broad experience and intimate knowledge.

Although these histories of American-Chinese encounters necessarily relate to the past, it is surely the hope of our author that knowledge of them will help to smooth the encounters of the future. I heartily share this hope.

The potential benefits and gains of cooperation between China and the United States are so broad and so clear that definition seems superfluous. The pursuit of world peace, protection of the environment, economic development, health and medicine, population control, food production and living standards, technical exchange, the cross-fertilization of arts and literature—all these are part of our common cause of humanity. Our great population and rich resources require us to be major partners on spaceship Earth. It is a cliché that cooperation needs understanding, and will be facilitated by—if not dependent on—friendship.

So what of the future? I am optimistic. It certainly will not all be smooth and easy. Some of the problems will be on the Chinese side. China's long authoritarian political history, and present governance by a Marxist party which is trying to carry out and accommodate itself to a very rapid process of economic liberalization and growth, have brought about a difficult period of tension and adjustment. The Chinese have a great capacity for common sense, moderation, and compromise. They will find a way out of their present situation, and it will be better than the past. But it will develop from their own character and experience; it will never be a carbon copy of Western free enterprise and American democracy. The need for us Americans is to accept that fact, and to be patient.

Perhaps it is only by looking at the past that we can see how things have changed. The nature and basis of our relations with China have fundamentally altered, and that is good.

I have spoken already of American smugness about "our" Open Door doctrine for China. Today, China is following her own open door policy. It is far wider than ever before. And it is being carried by China's own volition, for her own interest and benefit (though we also benefit in many ways in addition to business). On my first trip back to China, in 1971, the strongest first impression, almost tangible in what I saw and sensed in the people around me, was that China "had stood up."

Another way of looking at this is that there are literally millions of people in China today studying English—many times more than ever before. And there are probably hundreds of thousands of Chinese whose work puts them in contact with foreign travelers and businessmen—again, many times more numerous than in the old days. But all these people are studying and speaking "proper" English. In seven visits and extensive travel in China since 1971 I have not heard a single Chinese speak pidgin English. Thank goodness!

It is also a fact that we know much more about each other than in the past. Many of us have had contact with some of the many thousands of Chinese scholars (perhaps as many as twenty thousand at any one time) who have studied at American universities in recent years. Local chapters of the US-China Peoples Friendship Association have done great work in helping numbers of these scholars make their adjustment to a confusing and very different society.

There are also far more American students in China. In Mr. Deane's student days there were only two universities in China—Yenching in what was then called Peiping, and Lingnan in Canton—that had programs for American students. Both programs were small and operated for only a few years; and both universities were missionary institutions—hence under foreign administration. I have lost track of the numerous Chinese—100 percent Chinese—universities and institutions that today are operating various kinds of study programs for American and other foreign students.

It is reasonable to hope that both these waves of students—Chinese in America, and Americans in China—are seeds for a fruitful future. Although that early contingent of Americans in China were few in number, I know of at least three (two besides Mr. Deane) who went on to achieve distinction in American-Chinese relations. One was Fulton Freeman, who studied at Lingnan; the other was John P. Davies, who was at Yenching. Both made their careers in the American Foreign Service. And both, in varying degrees, were victims of McCarthyism. It would be interesting to know the full story of what became of all that band of pioneering American students in China.

Friendship, obviously, is a two-way street. Mr. Deane tells us of many Americans who have contributed in different ways to friendship with China. Some of them have done it in unpopular ways or at unpopular times—and have paid a price. McCarthyism has just been mentioned. Mr. Deane himself was blacklisted in his journalist profession and had to support himself for a time by managing a laundromat. In China the numbers involved were far greater, and the periods of fierce nationalism and anti-Americanism even more intense. Some day I hope to read a book like this written from the Chinese side. When that day comes, we will know that the friendship of the American and Chinese peoples is on an even firmer footing.

JOHN S. SERVICE
Oakland, California
1987

AUTHOR'S PREFACE

Szuma Chien observed centuries ago that "though death befalls all men alike, it may be weightier than Mount Tai or lighter than a feather." Mao Zedong quoted this in his 1944 essay, "Serve the People."

Between my typewriter and these printed pages weighty deaths have occurred. In October 1987 Rewi Alley invited me to dinner at No. 1 Tai Ji Chang. The only other guest was Dr. Ma Haide. I was honored to dine and converse with them but painfully aware of their weakened health. Rewi was frail and ate very sparingly, despite Ma's urging. Ma himself could no longer eat with his usual gusto. Rewi died in December shortly after his ninetieth birthday and Ma, his closest friend, died a year later. He had just turned seventy-eight.

Rewi's last energies were largely devoted to the revival of the Chinese Industrial Cooperatives, the movement which added the term "Gung Ho" to our language. A worthy cause—Chinese economics and politics would be well served by a national network of cooperatives democratically managed by their members. The movement which is Rewi's legacy has made some progress since I wrote my chapter on the subject and a supportive International Committee has been formed. Rewi and his associate Lu Guangmien decided I should be a vice chairman and I hope to justify their confidence in me.

I met Dr. Ma (born George Hatem in Buffalo, New York) in Edgar Snow's books and in person in 1973. Encounters over the years strengthened my admiration for him. My tribute to him was published in *China Daily* of December 16, 1988 and in the Spring 1989 issue of the *US-China Review*. But Ma would wish to be memorialized by efforts in behalf of his last great cause, the eradication of a disease of the poor, leprosy.

Su Kaiming—Frank Su to his many American friends—was the first editor of my manuscript and offered both encouragement and very helpful criticisms. I deeply regret that he did not live to see the published book. He left us his own admirable book, *Modern China: A Topical History*, to which I turn often for information and insights.

In writing the section on Agnes Smedley and Lu Xun (pp. 99–106) I was helped by articles by Janice R. and Stephen MacKinnon. Their impressive biography, *Agnes Smedley: The Life and Times of an American Radical*, was published in 1988. The result of fourteen years of the most searching investigation and writing, their book is worthy of its subject, the best kind of American. They conclude that Smedley's lifelong task "was to communicate the desperate, endless nightmare of poverty and ignorance. Her goal was the overthrow of these two dragons. Her life was a battle, without truce or compromise, to that end." I reviewed the book for *China Daily* (March 11, 1989) and the *US-China Review* (Spring 1989).

An updating note on the section on Lingnan/Zhongshan (pp. 213–219): In November 1987 I attended a reunion, rich in nostalgia, of the 1936–37 Lingnan exchange students in San Francisco. In May, leading a tour group, I again visited Zhongshan, bringing a gift of books for the new library and a report on the reunion. We had an afternoon of realistic discussion of progress and problems with faculty members of the growing university, which had revived ties with Harvard, the University of California, and other foreign academic institutions. I was pleased to learn that the old university name of Lingnan would be given to a college that would be part of the university.

At Zhongshan I did not have an opportunity to meet Professor Arnold Xiangze Jiang, historian and author of the admirable work, *The United States and China* (Chicago University Press, 1988). I regret that by the time his book came to my attention my own manuscript was completed, but I am pleased that our views very often coincide. Drawing on both Chinese and Western sources, he argues forcefully that self-interest outweighed friendship in the minds of those shaping Washington's policy, and that invariably the U.S. supported reactionary Chinese regimes. And he points to the illusions that undermined U.S. decisions and strategies.

A well-attended and useful two-day conference celebrating the fiftieth anniversary of Edgar Snow's *Red Star Over China* was held in Beijing in June 1988. I presented a paper on Snow's persuasive rejoinders to his critics which was published in the American edition of the *Beijing Review* (September 19, 1988). My chief source was the rich collection of Snow papers at the University of Missouri, Kansas City.

The idea of the book came in conversation over lunch in the Xi Yuan Hotel in 1985. Chen Xiuzheng of New World Press was there and receptive. I am most obliged to her and others at New World Press and I am grateful that China Books & Periodicals in San Francisco agreed to be the copublisher. My thanks to editor Bob Schildgen and his colleagues.

I am honored that John S. Service took the time to write an eloquent and wise foreword that adds to the usefulness of the book.

New York City
May 1989

I
....

Sweet and Sour

THE US-CHINA RELATIONSHIP
IN PERSPECTIVE

In 1771, four years before the outbreak of the American Revolution, a member of the American Philosophical Society argued that the colonies could gain much by emulating the ancient land of China. "Could we be so fortunate as to introduce . . . the arts of living and improvements in husbandry, as well as their native plants, America might in time become as populous as China."

The China reached in 1784 by the *Empress of China* and the other trading ships that followed swiftly in her wake was generally seen as a formidable power and held in respect. Captain Amassa Delano, an early trader in seal skins and a collateral forebear of President Franklin Delano Roosevelt, wrote that "China is the first for greatness, riches and grandeur of any country ever known."

But the outward appearance of strength and serenity concealed inner decay and disintegration. China's pyramidal society, in which a landed elite lived in refined comfort and splendor on the surplus produced by an industrious peasantry, was showing signs of cyclical decline. The impact of the traders and opium traffickers from the West interacted with and exacerbated the internal causes of social

1

dissolution, which were linked to the rapid growth of population. The opium trade, in which Americans quickly joined the British, drained China of silver. (In 1839 alone no less than 5.3 million pounds of the drug were brought to China.) Later imports of British textiles and other manufactures had a devastating effect on China's cottage industries. The Opium War of 1840–42, initiated by the British in furtherance of trade generally and the opium bonanza in particular, exposed China's military weakness and its anachronistic view of itself as the civilized center of an otherwise barbarian world, and began a Chinese century of defeat, exploitation and humiliation. The Anglo-Indian assault added a new word to the English language—*loot*, from the Hindi and Sanskrit.

The "unequal treaties" forced upon China by foreign powers and the division of much of China into Western enclaves and "spheres of influence" turned China into what Sun Yat-sen later termed a "hypocolony," the colony of many nations. "Today we are the poorest and weakest nation in the world . . . ," the revolutionary nationalist wrote. "Other men are the carving knife and serving dish, we are the fish and the meat."

Foreign flags flew over the concessions—areas in coastal or river ports in which Western powers exercised virtual sovereignty. Moreover, foreigners everywhere in China were subject only to their own national laws, even if their offenses were committed against Chinese. This system of legal exceptionalism was called "extraterritoriality," or "extrality" for short. A young American employed as a bank teller in a Chinese port described the situation this way: "If a Chinaman does not at once make room for me in the street I would strike him forcibly with my cane in the face. . . . Should I break his nose or kill him, the worst that could happen would be that he or his people would make complaints to the Consul, who might impose the fine of a dollar for the misdemeanor, but I could always prove that I had just cause to beat him."

American, British, and other foreign naval ships patrolled China's coast and inland waters, and Western army units were stationed in selected cities. The United States garrisoned Tianjin with the 15th Infantry and stationed Marines in Shanghai, where the American residents also formed a volunteer militia. Consortia of Western financiers and entrepreneurs—forerunners of today's multi-national corporations—took advantage of diplomatic muscle to extract railroad construction rights and other profitable deals. China was forbidden to raise import duties above 5 percent, assuring a protected market for Western dumping of consumer goods on China.

But from the onset China's plight engendered resistance by the more principled members of its elite and by the people themselves. During the First Opium War, peasants from over a hundred villages gathered at Sanyuanli near Guangzhou (Canton) to take on a marauding British force, but the clash was halted by the intervention of Chinese officials. Such incidents gave rise to the popular saying of the time that "the people fear the officials, the officials fear the foreign devils, and the foreign devils fear the people."

Meanwhile, the atrophying Qing dynasty was confronted with one rebellion after another—uprisings by anti-Qing secret societies, rebellions by minority peoples and religious sects against the oppressive rule of the officialdom, and, finally, the greatest upheaval of them all, called in the West, the Taiping Rebellion. It swept north out of southern China in 1851 and raged for fifteen years. Thomas Taylor Meadows, a perceptive English observer of the time, wrote that "of all peoples, the Chinese are the most rebellious and the least revolutionary." But as he himself came to know, the Taiping Revolution differed from the peasant uprisings that had merely contributed to the replacement of one dynasty by another.

The Taiping Revolution had genuine revolutionary aspects. Visions of a changed society as well as of national power and respect motivated its leadership, which drew some of its inspiration from a militantly interpreted Christianity. Its grander agrarian and other reforms largely remained on paper, but its prohibitions of opium smoking, prostitution, concubinage, and foot binding were strictly enforced. Foreign as well as Chinese witnesses testified to the moral rectitude, proud bearing, and administrative justice of the rebels, though various forms of corruption set in as the devastating civil war (which took perhaps twenty million lives) lengthened.

An American adventurer from Salem, Massachusetts, Frederick Townsend Ward, organized a mercenary force to repel the Taiping Revolutionaries in the Shanghai area. American merchants in Shanghai were not averse to buying tea from the rebels, but their typical view was expressed by Albert Heard of Augustus Heard and Company: "I think it would be better for the benefit of China and humanity, to say nothing of cotton goods, to exterminate the whole party."

The Taiping Revolution was defeated by its own mistakes and weaknesses and by foreign intervention, but one of its legacies included the inspiration of future generations of young Chinese in their own struggle to bring about a new China. Sun Yat-sen, Zhu De, and Mao Zedong were among those who drew lessons from the experiences of the Taipings. When the triumph of China's revolution finally came in 1949, it had a convoluted and bloody history—of plots that failed, of reforms betrayed, of uprisings crushed, of death and agony beyond calculation, and of the past studied and heeded.

The great Chinese diaspora of the nineteenth century had a painful American chapter. Hundreds of thousands of Chinese left their country as laborers, called "coolies," and were taken in the holds of ships to Malaya, Chile, Peru, Cuba, British Guiana, South Africa, and Hawaii and California. The mortality rate during voyages was often 10 percent and sometimes as high as 25 percent. In the United States, young men from Guangdong and Fujian met the American need for cheap labor to open up the West. By 1869, nine-tenths of the workers in the Union Pacific Railroad construction gangs were Chinese. But when the transcontinental railroads were built and hard times set in, unemployment—and some instances of strike-breaking on the part of the immigrants—stimulated racist prejudice, and Chinese were subjected to insults, discriminatory laws, theft of property, beatings, even lynchings. The Chinese presence was said to create unfair competition for jobs and to menace the purity of Caucasian blood. The Yellow Peril was born, and also the telling phrase, "a Chinaman's chance."

A report prepared by J. Ross Browne in 1868 as he departed to assume the post of Minister to China included these observations:

> In nearly every large city and settlement [in California], where the Chinese live in considerable numbers, they have been the object of mob violence, their houses sacked and burned, and their persons subjected to violence. In San Francisco and Sacramento these outrages have been repeated. . . . Bands of white desperados have been organized for the express purpose of robbing and killing Chinese. Over one hundred unsolved murders, and over one million dollars' worth of unrecovered stolen gold dust, attest to the extent of their depredations and the injustice of our courts.

Chinese in general became the target of obloquy.[1] Charles H. Phelps, editor of *The Californian*, a lively magazine which accepted Mark Twain's early writings, declared that the "parchment-skinned pagans" were "morally and mentally dead," and that the world would continue as usual and miss nothing if an astronomical body were to wipe out all 400 million of the "human ants."

To Senator James G. Blaine, candidate for the presidency in 1884, the issue was whether "the Mongolian" or the Anglo-Saxon race "would possess the Pacific Coast." And the *Anthropological Review* asserted in 1866 that "as the type of the Negro is foetal, that of the Mongol is infantile. And in strict accordance with this we find their government, literature and art are infantile also. They are beardless children, whose life is a task, and whose chief virtue consists in unquestioning obedience."

The Chinese did have staunch and eloquent defenders who cited democratic principles and religious precepts, as well as the evident good character and industry of most Chinese residents, but these defenders were in the minority. Letters to California editors on the question of barring further Chinese immigration ran two to one in favor of the ban. Agitation for an end to Asian immigration was taken up by politicians and organized labor and the Exclusion Act became federal law in 1882. Chinese would not be eligible for naturalization until 1943 when China was widely perceived as being America's junior partner in the war against Japan and its Axis allies. In that year Congress allowed 105 Chinese annually to become U.S. citizens.

In the years before this minor concession, however, the trickle of arriving students, returning residents, visitors with proper visas, and even diplomats was subjected to harassment and ill-treatment on inappropriately named Angel Island in the middle of San Francisco Bay. Physical abuse sometimes accompanied repeated interrogations. Sun Yat-sen himself suffered this kind of reception. Publication of the abuses in China led to a boycott of American products in Guangzhou and nearby places in 1905.

Many years later a ten-person delegation from the People's Republic of China visited Angel Island. After viewing the isolation cells and reading poems and desperate scribbling on the walls, Li Xin,

---

1. A witness testifying before the Joint Congressional Committee to Investigate Chinese Immigration said in 1876: "The Chinese are inferior to any race God ever made. . . . There are none so low. I believe that the Chinese have no souls to save, and if they have, they are not worth the saving."

director of the Institute of Modern History in Beijing, wrote these lines:

> Drifting thousands of miles,
>   a thousand grievances;
> Breasts filled with anger,
>   walls filled with poems.
> A different era,
>   the present is better than the past,
> However treat not history
>   as fictional tales.

Ceremonial speeches by American diplomats and some academic treatises to the contrary, the United States diplomatically reacted as negatively to China's struggle to maintain its independence in the face of the imperialist assault as it did to the quest for social justice by its non-Caucasian and Asian minorities. Throughout the nineteenth and into the twentieth century, America pursued a policy described by Owen Lattimore as "Me Too," and by others as "hitchhiking imperialism." It successfully insisted that the concessions and rights wrung from the Qing dynasty by the guns of Britain, France, and other powers be extended to it, sometimes with a bonus. It was Britain's junior partner—"country cousin," some put it. The basic China decisions were made in Whitehall, and British banks financed the American merchant houses in the treaty ports.

Albert Heard of Heard and Company wrote to his senior partner in Boston in 1860: "You needn't be surprised if we become half English, living as we do under her protection, and witnesses to her great power in every emergency." Heard and Company dealt in opium to sustain its cash flow.

The opening of Japan by Commodore Perry's "Black Ships" in 1853–54 was viewed by Perry and others as just the start of an extension of American power to the Far East. Taiwan—called Formosa by the West—should be American, Perry argued, as did Peter Parker, medical missionary turned imperialist diplomat. "I believe Formosa and the world will be better for the former coming under a civilized power," Parker, then commissioner (equivalent of minister), said in a dispatch to the State Department. But the internal frontier was still absorbing American energies and the civil war over secession and slavery was still to be fought. The Manifest Destiny of the time faded.

Destiny manifested itself compellingly once more in the last years of the century, by which time industrialization had created a demand for foreign markets and built the navy.

China inspired in Americans feelings of benevolence, often alloyed with paternalism. John K. Fairbank of Harvard has commented that China became "our favorite charity." Such sentiments gave strength to a sustained missionary effort. The number of missionaries, about half of them American, rose from eighty-one in 1858 to over six thousand by 1936. By then they had converted some 960,000 Chinese to one or another of the Protestant sects and nearly two million to Catholicism. Some converts were just "rice Christians," but the enduring faith of others survived persecution during the Cultural Revolution of 1966–76 and founded a wholly Chinese-run Christian community. And the dimes collected at Sunday services over the decades and the grants from such philanthropists as the Rockefellers built schools, universities and hospitals which structurally still serve China today.

But in the main the missionaries were allies of the imperialism which had forced the Chinese to admit them. They served the China policies of their home governments in the nineteenth century as interpreters, advisers, negotiators, intelligence gatherers, and apologists. Those who were martyred served one last time as pretexts for extravagant demands for retribution.

Most missionaries approved of China's successive defeats in the Sino-Japanese War (1894–95) and the Boxer Rebellion as being for its own good. Moreover, they were thrilled by their country's entry into the imperialist competition. Anna Seward Pruitt, a southern Baptist in Shandong and mother of Ida Pruitt, provided her household with American flag napkin rings and lapel buttons.

The American minister to China in the 1890s, Charles Denby, thus acknowledged missionary support: "For nearly a century our missionary men and women have labored to carry our prestige, our language, and our commerce into China. . . . If we turn them adrift, our national fame will be dimmed. It cannot be doubted that by their disappearance our commerce would greatly suffer, and our diplomacy would lose its chief support."

Living in spacious houses in walled compounds and attended by ample staffs of servants, most missionaries were not unduly discomfited by the squalor and cruelties that came through to them. They took care to stay on the good side of the local authorities and did not allow their specific complaints to become a challenge to the status quo. Theodore Roosevelt, whose word for Chinese was "Chink," observed gratefully that "their work helped to avert revolutionary disturbances in China." To him, the Chinese were "an immoral, degraded and worthless race."

In the 1890s the YMCA and YWCA began social programs in China, but the movement overall stressed conversion of members of the elite and was short on social concerns until the 1920s. Then the swift rise of revolutionary forces stirred it to undertake preventive reforms. Hand in hand with the fervor of a drive to "Win China for Christ" went support for patchwork reforms calculated to counter the appeal of the radicals in the impoverished countryside. Villagers were invited to instructive talks, festivals, and sports contests; urged to take more baths, brush their teeth (a brochure explained how), dig deeper wells, and whitewash the walls of their houses; and to learn how to read a minimum number of characters. But the essential source of peasant misery, exploitation by an alliance of landlords, moneylenders and officials, was sidestepped by reformers with links to the Kuomintang regime.

Then there were the American philanthropies. What was called Rural Reconstruction, for example, was handsomely financed by the Rockefellers. Liberal reformers, missionaries, and Chinese worked for it with dedication, but achieved no more than the similar Green Revolution of the 1960s in other parts of Asia. Missionaries also contributed advice and respectability to Generalissimo Chiang's cherished New Life Movement, which propagated a mixture of Confucian and Christian precepts as part of the counterrevolutionary effort. In this movement, missionaries found themselves working alongside Chiang's fascist Blue Shirts.

Chiang Kai-shek was persuaded to convert to Methodism (the quip was that there was Methodism in his madness), a move which helped him win a legion of missionary apologists. Some missionaries did speak out against the corruption, cruelty, incompetence, and reactionary character of the Kuomintang as the evidence accumulated, but others wrote and made radio broadcasts in defense of it. They persisted even while it was tottering, and joined the pro-Chiang China Lobby in the United States. When in 1949 the State Department invited missionary organizations to send in regular intelligence reports on local conditions, all but one or two agreed.

The YWCA, almost alone among missionary groups, followed a different course. While its male counterpart kept on the good side of the authorities and cooperated with them, the YWCA attempted programs addressed to genuine social ills, in particular to the needs of working-class Chinese women. The Americans Maud Russell and Talitha Gerlach and many of the Chinese staff naturally identified with the causes of the Chinese Revolution and served it.

In 1898 Stephen Crane, best known as the author of *The Red Badge of Courage* and a poet who influenced Ezra Pound and the imagists, took up his pen to satirize imperialist use of missionary martyrdom. Months earlier Germany had seized Qingdao and Jiaozhou Bay in retribution for the slaying of two Catholic missionaries. Crane's response was a three-act skit titled *The Blood of the Martyr*. At Qingdao, with an anchored squadron in the background, Prince Henry of Prussia discusses with an aide the arrival of more missionaries:

> *Prince Henry:* "Send them into every corner of China, and in time we will reap enough martyrs. You see, we need twenty-three more railway concessions and eight more ports. These missionaries are noble people."
>
> *Aide:* "Pardon, Your Highness, but the missionary at Yen Hock has appealed for assistance. He says that the people are about to kill him."
> *Prince Henry:* "The missionary at Yen Hock, eh? Let me think. Isn't Yen Hock in that fertile Fan Tan Valley? . . . Oh, send him a box of cigars and my compliments. Tell him he is the right man in the right place "

One-sided treaties enabled missionaries to work within the matrix of traditional Chinese society under the protection of their own governments. The first of the unequal treaties, the Treaty of Nanjing in 1842, opened up five ports to Britain, gave it Hongkong, and with these territories and concessions opened much of south and central China to British commerce. The Treaty of Wangxia, which followed two years later, gave the United States similar benefits, and then more. Trade prospects were very much on the mind of the negotiator, Caleb Cushing, a Massachusetts politician. Secretary of State Daniel Webster, in his instructions to Cushing, noted that certain American products were being exported to China and added that "to augment these exports . . . is a matter of moment." President Tyler was delighted when the news reached him that Cushing had succeeded in adding sixteen particulars to what the British had obtained. "I thought the President would go off in an ecstasy," his wife wrote.

The Anglo-French victory in the Second Opium War (1856–60) legalized the opium trade (importation of the drug remained legal until 1917, though the trade had long been diminished by poppy cultivation in China itself); opened up the country to the missionaries and the Yangtze to foreign gunboats; added to the number of treaty ports; gave the Western powers control of customs; and imposed huge indemnities on the Qing regime. The United States viewed benignly the Anglo-French assault on Beijing and accepted for itself a full share of the imperialist gains. An American naval vessel came to the rescue of a British ship mired in the mud and taking a pounding from the Dagu Forts near Tianjin. "Blood is thicker than water," the American commander said, as he towed the beleaguered British vessel off the mud flat. He was later commended by the Navy Department.

The closing years of the century were jackal time—Germany, Japan, Russia, and lesser powers joined Britain and France in further inroads, giving credence to the forecast that "The Breakup of China" (a contemporary book title) was indeed imminent. Industrialization and the rationalization of Western banking systems added new dimensions to the imperialist appetite; depression years that extended into the early 1890s fortified arguments that Western industry needed foreign markets. Banking groups pressed loans on China, placing it heavily in debt, and consortia competed for rights to build railroads and open factories and mines.

It was a propitious season for adventurers and con men. A future president of the United States, Herbert Hoover, played a key role in a swindle that gave a foreign, largely British, combine control of the vast Kaiping mines in north China. Hoover came away with a fortune.

Japan, the sole Asian nation at that time able to break out of semi-colonial controls, joined the predators and crushed China in a lightning war. With the Treaty of Shimonoseki in 1895, it secured possession of Taiwan and the Pescadores (Penghu Islands). A former U.S. secretary of state, John W. Foster, grandfather of John Foster Dulles, earned Japan's gratitude by urging the Chinese negotiators, whom he was advising, to yield to Japan's demand for Taiwan. He thought that an American takeover of the island later was very likely. Washington similarly supported Japan's acquisition of Korea in 1910.

The Japanese gains inspired the rival powers and the "great scramble" for concessions followed. Germany took over the superb port of Qingdao, Britain seized Weihaiwei to the north, Russia gained Dalian (Dalny) and Lüshun (Port Arthur, named for a son of Queen Victoria) in what was then Manchuria, and France took over Guangzhou Bay in the far south. The United States became a serious competitor. Its industry was growing at a rapid rate. Petroleum output surged from 221 million gallons in 1870 to 2.7 billion in 1890. By 1900 the U.S. had overtaken Britain in the production of both coal and steel and its rate of growth in the ensuing years was twice that of Britain. At the same time the recurrent depressions seemed to make irrefutable the arguments that overseas outlets for manufactures were essential to prosperity.

By taking the stepping stones of Hawaii and part of Samoa, by its conquest of the Philippines in the Spanish-American War of 1898, and then by its construction of the Panama Canal, which gave its navy easy access to the Pacific, the U.S. readied itself for the competition for Asian markets and influence over China. A rosy assessment of its future in China was part of the reason for the U.S. seizure of the Philippines. Senator Albert Beveridge of Indiana, just returned from the islands, used commercial, racist, and religious arguments in calling for a takeover. He described the Filipinos as "children" who "are not of a self-governing race," and asserted that God "has marked us as His chosen people, henceforth to lead in the regeneration of the world." In a widely publicized speech in the Senate in 1890, Beveridge said:[2]

> The Philippines are ours forever . . . and just beyond the Philippines are China's illimitable markets. We will not retreat from either. We will not repudiate our policy in the archipelago. We will not abandon our opportunity in the Orient. We will not renounce our part in the mission of our race, trustee under God, of the civilization of the world. . . . Most future wars will be conflicts for commerce. The power that rules the Pacific, therefore, is the power that rules the world. And, with the Philippines, that power is and will forever be the American

2. Daniel B. Schirmir and Stephen Rosskamm Shalom, eds., *The Phillipines Reader* (Boston: South End Press, 1987), 23–26. The inimitable Mr. Dooley said of Beveridge's rhetoric "Twas a speech ye cud waltz to." And my hometown paper, *The Springfield Republican*, wrote that Beveridge "talks like a young Attila come out of the West."

Republic. China's trade is the mightiest commercial fact in our future.
. . . We ought to have fifty percent, and we will.

Brooks Adams, brother of Henry Adams, was one of those who
argued vigorously to intellectuals and politicians for an American
surge in China and elsewhere. Theodore Roosevelt was among those
he influenced. A series of books by Captain Alfred T. Mahan of the
U.S. Navy on the role of sea power in American expansionism was
also a major influence on Roosevelt, who saw to it that the Spanish
war was extended to the Philippines.

Margherita A. Hamm, journalist, lecturer, and author, addressed a
more popular audience. She argued that the cause of humanity
limited choices regarding China to these: "a partition among more
civilized nations, as in the case of Africa, annexation as with India,
or a protectorate as with the Malay peninsula." She wrote that
"acting under the invincible laws of national growth, which include
territorial and commercial expansion," the United States had taken
over outlying islands, Hawaii among them, and was then pausing
"like an animal which has eaten a substantial meal," digestion
having to precede further consumption. In the meantime, businessmen
and bankers with an eye on China organized the Committee on
American Interests in China, which shortly became the American
Asiatic Association.

But the United States immediately faced the prospect of a virtual
shutout from a China carved into spheres of influence. In 1899
Secretary of State John Hay responded by proclaiming what became
known as the Open Door policy. In notes to the chancellories he
insisted that all powers be given equal access to China trade and
investment opportunities. The next year, following the suppression of
the Boxer Revolutionaries by foreign troops, Hay asked the powers to
respect China's territorial integrity and sovereignty. The responses to
the notes were either evasive or guarded assurances that did not
reflect real policy.

For many years the Open Door gambit was rhetorically described
as a timely move in defense of China's independence—"a majestic
eagle" has swooped down to save China, one exuberant writer put it.
Actually, it was one more instance of "Me Tooism," and America's
climb to the status of a great power made it still something more.
The not-at-all-modest calculation was that in an open arena of
economic competition, American corporate capitalism could become

the dominant purveyor to China's millions of customers. Some described China as "our India." According to John Hay, "In the field of trade and commerce we shall be the keen competitors of the richest and greatest powers, and they need no warning that in that struggle we shall bring the sweat to their brows." Hay did not take the trouble to send his notes to the yamen handling China's foreign relations.

American commitment to China's territorial integrity was not total. In November 1900 Hay sought a naval base and concession in Fujian Province, but that was in a Japanese sphere of influence, and Tokyo successfully objected.

The Open Door notes signaled a strategy for informal empire that would live for decades. Except incidentally, the United States would not seek overseas possessions but press for a world which would be open to its shipping, its products and its bankers, and it would use the "Big Stick" and "Dollar Diplomacy" in its quest. What historian William Appleman Williams called "imperial anticolonialism" remained central to American policy.

Defeat and humiliation induced Chinese officials and scholars to pursue self-strengthening policies, the objective being to graft Western science and technology onto Confucianism. Their energies culminated in 1898 in a short-lived series of reforms decreed by Emperor Guang Xu—the Hundred Days. The Empress Dowager Ci Xi acted harshly and put an end to them; she ordered the execution of some reformers, and forced others into exile.

The failure of an elitist attempt at reform was followed by the failure of an anti-imperialist uprising. A rural secret society composed of peasants, peddlers, and boatmen, called Yihetuan, or Boxers, in the West, because members practiced martial exercises, took up arms against the foreign presence, first in defiance of German abuses in Shandong, later throughout much of northern China. They killed over two hundred foreigners, almost all of whom were missionaries[3] and, embraced as allies by the Empress Dowager, surged into Beijing and besieged the legation quarter.

Handicapped by naive politics, superstitious illusions, lack of modern weapons, and betrayed by the Qing court, the Boxers were bloodily subdued by a multi-national force that included American

---

3. The Boxers spared certain missionaries and to them they gave large boards to be hung around their necks which instructed Boxer units to give them safe passage. One such board is in the Midwest China Center in St. Paul, Minnesota.

troops. The Stars and Stripes were hoisted on Beijing's city wall and American soldiers joined in the rapine and looting of the city. Mass execution was the lot of the Boxers.

The American troops had been sent from the Philippines and the Republican Party of Massachusetts made much of this evidence of the usefulness of the new possession as a military base. It declared in a leaflet against Democratic presidential candidate William Jennings Bryan in 1900:

> Isn't every American proud of the part American soldiers bore in the relief of Peking? But that would have been impossible if our flag had not been in the Philippines. Gen. Chaffee led two infantry regiments, the Ninth and the Fourteenth, and one battery of the Fifth Artillery to Peking. They did not come direct from the United States; there was not time. . . .[4]

The Boxers were credulous and unsophisticated, but their uprising was a response to real foreign affronts and threats, and was one more reminder that the Chinese people were not supine. The Boxers remained a cautionary memory in the thinking of those foreigners who had an influence on China policies.

The anti-imperialist movement that arose in the United States in the wake of the Spanish-American War was, more accurately, anti-colonial. Its greater part was not critical of the Open Door and economic expansionism abroad, just of the possession of colonies, which was seen as cruel and harmful to democracy. The movement did, however, include some passionate anti-imperialists, among them Mark Twain, one of the handful who spoke out in support of the Boxers.

In the first decades of the new century China gained some of the appurtenances of modernity—railroads and telegraph wires, flickering electricity, textile mills, cities with some resemblance to those in the West. Peasants migrated to the cities and formed a small working class. Classical education tested by the examination system yielded to schools and colleges, some run by missionaries, which taught science and other forms of Western learning. World War I distracted the West and gave Chinese-owned industry a chance to develop.

---

4. Cited in Schirmir and Shalom, *The Philippines Reader*, 32.

Yet the changes mostly exacerbated the growing sense of a profound social crisis. The factors included a peasantry impoverished by rents, taxes, and natural disasters; the destructive clash of warlord armies; the endless foreign exactions; sweatshops and child labor (the dead bodies of seven-year-old silk workers were wrapped in matting and put out with the garbage); and, above all, a corrupt and ineffectual government that kowtowed to the imperialist presence and abused its own people.

The limitations on what seemed to be possible clashed with the rising expectations of students and others who had turned paragraphs in books into convictions and visions. More joined the revolutionary organizations fostered by Sun Yat-sen.

The moribund Qing dynasty, which had tried reform far too late, fell in 1911. The rising in Sichuan against foreign railroad takeovers was one of the immediate causes. A republic, of which Sun Yat-sen himself was the president, was proclaimed in Nanjing. In the U.S. the news generated sympathetic hope, even euphoria. The "sick man of Asia" image of China was transfused by the rosy promise of a democratic dawn.

In April 1913, Secretary of State William Jennings Bryan read to the Wilson cabinet a newspaper report that the Chinese government had appealed to all Christian churches in China to set aside April 27 as a day of prayer that the nation might find wise solutions to its critical problems. President Wilson, according to the diary of Josephus Daniels, "said that he did not know when he had been so stirred and cheered. . . ."

But the promise faded. The 1911 Revolution had not been achieved primarily by Sun Yat-sen's nationalist followers, but by officers of the modernized army and by the last minute turn to it of the provincial elite. The interests of the rebels and those of the foreign powers coincided in a preference for Yuan Shikai, formerly a Qing general, who had crushed the reformers of the Hundred Days, but supported the 1911 turnover as a vehicle which could carry him to power. He was called "China's Strong Man" by the American press. Sun resigned the presidency in favor of Yuan in what he thought were the interests of national unity, but quickly found he had simply abetted a counterrevolutionary turn when Yuan outlawed Sun's party, the original Kuomintang. Woodrow Wilson became a firm supporter of Yuan against the revolutionaries; he refused even to receive Huang Xing, an envoy from Sun Yat-sen, and was able to delay recognition of the republic until May 2, 1913, by which time Chinese politics appeared safely conservative.

Yuan's chief American adviser, Dr. Frank J. Goodnow, professor of constitutional law at Columbia University, abetted Yuan's attempt to establish a new dynasty and place himself on the Dragon Throne. In a memorandum in 1915, Goodnow argued that imperial rule was appropriate because "the intelligence of the people is not high." Yuan's enthronement was proclaimed and vast sums spent on a planned ceremony, but widespread criticism and provincial revolts forced him to back down. He died in June 1916. China broke up into a cacophony of warlords, each with a foreign patron though nominally under a wrangling and weak national government in Beijing. Britain and Russia took advantage of China's weakness to intervene in its peripheral territories, Tibet, Mongolia, and Manchuria.

In 1915, Japan made twenty-one far-reaching demands on China and backed them with an ultimatum. This move recalled ominously the similar demands Tokyo had made on Korea before taking it over. Among them were recognition of Japanese dominance in key areas, joint Sino-Japanese police departments in certain places, and the appointment of Japanese advisers to Chinese ministries. Yuan Shikai generally yielded.

The U.S. reaction approached acquiescence. Secretary of State Bryan's note of March 13, 1915 observed that the U.S. had grounds to object to the demands, but then said that "nevertheless the United States frankly recognizes that territorial contiguity creates special relations between Japan and these districts."

The Versailles Treaty of 1919 brought a second humiliation. Wilson was forced to abandon the anti-colonialist thrust of his own Fourteen Points and joined Lloyd George of Britain, Orlando of Italy, and Clemenceau of France in turning over to Japan the Shandong properties of defeated Germany "and other privileges set forth in the Sino-German Treaty of March 1898." China had joined the Allied Powers and sent thousands of laborers to the Western Front, but this contribution to the Allied war effort was ignored. The American minister to China, Paul Reinsch[5], was among those shocked:

Probably nowhere else in the world have expectations of America's leadership in Paris been raised so high as in China. The Chinese

5. *An American Diplomat in China* (Doubleday, Page, 1922; Taipei: Ch'eng-Wen Publishing Co., 1967), 361.

trusted America. They trusted the frequent declarations of principle uttered by President Wilson, whose words had reached China in its remotest parts. The more intense was their disappointment and disillusionment due to the decisions of the old men that controlled the Peace Conference. It sickened and disheartened me to think how the Chinese people would receive this blow which meant the blasting of their hopes and the destruction of their confidence in the equity of nations.

Reinsch returned to the legation to find he had missed a student protest demonstration—just one of many in Beijing, Shanghai and other cities that gave birth to what is known as the May Fourth Movement. Teams of students explained what was at issue in teach-ins in the streets that won growing support. Workers and merchants joined the chorus of indignation. Protest and study organizations sprang up all over the nation. The ministers agreeing to the Versailles shame were forced to recant. Several were beaten and their residences broken into.

May Fourth broadened into a movement for a new anti-Confucian culture and social justice. It led to new magazines full of ideas that captured the allegiance of students and others to a literature written in the language of the people. And it led to a succession of revolutionary advances: the formation of the Communist Party in 1921; the Kuomintang-Communist alliance forged by Sun Yat-sen; the reorganization of the Kuomintang; the swift growth of unions in the cities and the strikes that showed their power; the organization of peasants in Hunan, Guangdong, and elsewhere; and the Northern Expedition of 1926–27 that brought down the northern warlords.

Disfavor and skepticism characterized most American comments on the dramatic events in China. Senator William E. Borah of Idaho,[6] a maverick Republican, however, was among those who spoke optimistically about China's new turn:

Four hundred million people imbued with the spirit of independence and of national integrity are in the end invincible. There is no power

6. Cited in Dorothy Borg, *American Policy and the Chinese Revolution* (New York: American Institute of Pacific Relations and MacMillan, 1947), 190. In a 1925 speech attacking extraterritoriality and control of Chinese tariffs, Borah said, "There is no place where the blood of helpless children is so covered with dollars and cents as in China."

which can master them or hold them in subjection. Warships and Gatling guns and dead students may mislead some but the forces which determine the action of empires and great nations lie deeper.

The China policy of the United States had two linked aspects. First, it gave its support to warlord regimes in Beijing that were agreeable to helping American enterprise gain access to the China market and investment opportunities. Secondly, the U.S. emerged from World War I as a leading global power and was somewhat more forceful in its relationships with rival imperialists. It sometimes contended, but more often colluded, with Japan, confident, under Presidents Coolidge and Hoover, that its superior economic strength would shape the future favorably and pacifically.

The United States forced a breakup of the Anglo-Japanese alliance at the Washington Conference of World War I victors in 1921–22, and compelled Japan to beat a partial (and temporary) retreat in China. It also obtained from all powers, including China itself, a pledge to respect the principle of the Open Door. By adding its signature reluctantly, the Beijing regime in effect recognized the right of the powers to penetrate and exploit China, provided they did so cooperatively. The principle of cooperation instead of competition was expressed in the formation of the Second International Banking Consortium for China, a new U.S.-British-French-Japanese combination which, it was thought, would eliminate political rivalries growing out of economic competition. But a substantial American effort to gain entry into the Japanese sphere of influence in Manchuria failed.

American exports to China were at once modest and encouraging. A very small percentage of the total, they increased from $16.7 million in 1900 to $26.1 million in 1913, to $138.4 million in 1920, and to $190 million in 1930, but shrank in subsequent years. The essential American conviction that exports and investments abroad were the keys to prosperity continued unshaken, as these views of successive presidencies indicate:

- President William Howard Taft took the trouble to cable Prince Chun, handling the Qing court's foreign affairs, that he had "an intensive personal interest in making use of American capital in the development of China."
- Wilson vetoed a major consortium project of the First International Banking Consortium for China because American

bankers would not have a controlling interest. He promised that the United States "would participate and participate very generously in the opening to the Chinese and to the use of the world the almost untouched and perhaps unrivalled resources of China." He also said: "Our domestic markets no longer suffice. We need foreign markets."[7] Wilson preached Christian peace, but did not hesitate to use American armed forces in support of this conviction.

- Hoover, who had served the Coolidge administration as secretary of commerce, described overseas economic expansion as essential to American wealth, welfare, and stability. He declared that "the hope of our commerce lies in the establishment of American firms abroad distributing American goods under American direction, in the building of direct American financing and, above all, in the installation of American technology. . . ."[8]
- Roosevelt's New Deal policies and reforms aimed at heading off radical change. They went hand in hand with efforts to promote the overseas activities of American business. Roosevelt saw "exportable surpluses" as important for domestic revival and for relieving conditions all over the world that gave rise to revolutions.
- Truman's secretary of state, Dean Acheson, argued: "My contention is that we cannot have full employment and prosperity in the United States without the foreign markets."

As the Kuomintang-Communist armies swept north in the 1926–27 Northern Expedition and a great revolutionary upsurge seemed certain of total victory, those making or influencing American policy were alarmed. Some, among them the American minister to China, John V. A. MacMurray, and the American Chamber of Commerce in Shanghai, clung to support of the warlords and advocated foreign intervention against the Chinese Bolsheviks from the south. The Chamber of Commerce demanded that John B. Powell, editor of the *China Weekly Review*, resign because of his opposition to intervention. The chamber appointed as its Washington representative a pro-Japanese propagandist, George Bronson Rea, later the Washington agent of the Japanese puppet state of

---

7. Cited in William Appleman Williams, *The Contours of American History* (Cleveland and New York: World Publishing, 1961), p. 420.
8. Williams, *Contours*, 429.

"Manchukuo." A faction within the chamber, the Raven Group, worked to make Shanghai a "Free City," separated from China.

But the more sophisticated view that prevailed, that of Secretary of State Frank B. Kellogg, President Coolidge, and Herbert Hoover (who had the power of veto in foreign policy), was that a modicum of Chinese nationalism had to be accepted, that intervention was impractical, and that the best hope for conservatism and business as usual lay with the right wing of the Kuomintang and Generalissimo Chiang Kai-shek, to whom promising overtures had already been made. They foresaw correctly that the Kuomintang and its Red allies were bound to fall out. Most missionary groups and considerable American editorial opinion were in agreement.

That estimate, shared by the British Foreign Office, was justified when, on April 12, 1927, Chiang, with the help of local gangsters in Shanghai (he himself was a member of the Green Gang), turned on the trade unions, which had risen in support of his arriving forces, and massacred thousands of their members and allies. For years terror gripped the cities while the Communists fled to the countryside, survived, and grew.

The U.S. was the first nation to recognize Chiang's Nanjing regime and conceded tariff control to it. Amicable relations followed, helped by Chiang's marriage to Wellesley-educated Soong Meiling (an American sang "Oh, Promise Me" at the ceremony), and his publicized conversion to Methodism. And for a period a majority of Chiang's cabinet members were returned students from the U.S.

But the U.S. did no more than protest Japan's seizure of Manchuria in 1931, which was accompanied by months of terror against patriotic Chinese and Russian Jews. Later in the decade, the U.S. also reacted with restraint to the Japanese push into north China and, initially, even to the invasion of China in July 1937.

On the eve of the Japanese invasion, mutinous officers from the Northeast (Manchuria) and Northwest seized Chiang Kai-shek in Xi'an after killing his bodyguard and forced him to abandon his strategy of trying to appease Japan while pressing efforts to exterminate the Reds, the survivors of the historic Long March. Known as the Xi'an Incident of December 12, 1936, it capped student demonstrations and the growth of a National Salvation Movement in support of resistance to Japanese aggression. Allowed to live, partly because of intercession by Zhou Enlai, Chiang agreed to halt his so-called "bandit annihilation campaigns" against the Communists. An accord was reached which the Communists called the Second United Front.

In the early phase of the war the Nationalist troops fought hard and won occasional victories. But the protracted defense of Shanghai was paid for by enormous casualties, which undermined the KMT's will to further resist. The Japanese occupied the major cities of eastern China and drove the defenders into the undeveloped west. China's capital followed, moving west from Nanjing to Hankou (part of Wuhan), and then further on to Chongqing, in Sichuan on the Yangtze. Japan tried to win over Chiang by diplomacy and stopped military drives against the KMT troops. Resistance to the Japanese became the exception to the rule and the Kuomintang-Communist accord frayed to the point of dissolution. A treacherous assault on the Communist New Fourth Army in Anhui in January 1941, ordered by Chiang, made the war triangular. Kuomintang troops blockaded the Communist base area in the northwest. For Chiang the invasion was a distraction from counterrevolution. He and his aides said again and again that the Japanese were a "skin disease" while the Communists were a "disease of the heart."

American policy changed slowly. The U.S. exported scrap iron and oil to Japan in 1938, but opinion sympathetic to China swelled and Chiang and his wife were *Time* magazine's "Man and Woman of the Year" in 1938 (after centuries "the Chinese people had at last found a leader," *Time* said). Then, in mid-1938, the U.S. began a phase-by-phase embargo on trade with Japan and at the end of the year granted China a loan of $25 million.

The long-standing U.S. policy of seeking understanding with Japan was succeeded by one centered on a wartime and postwar alliance with China—Chiang Kai-shek's China. Roosevelt took seriously the notion that the Philippines were "America's show window in Asia" and saw China as potentially a decisive extension of that success.[9]

The Chiang policy was to count on foreign allies, principally the United States, to defeat Japan, meanwhile building up with American equipment and holding in readiness his armed forces for the postwar task of wiping out the Communists. Consequently, Pearl

9. Michael Schaller in *The United States and China in the Twentieth Century* (New York: Oxford University Press, 1979) writes that Roosevelt became convinced "a strong democratic China would replace the influence of Japan and the European empires, while countering the appeal of revolutionary doctrines among the masses of the East. Another thought expressed during the war by Roosevelt and Harry Hopkins, an advisor, clinched the argument. 'In any serious conflict of policy with Russia, Nationalist China 'would line up on our side.' "

Harbor, which brought the U.S. into the war directly, was a cause for rejoicing in Chongqing. Chiang was so happy he sang an opera aria and played "Ave Maria" over and over on the phonograph.

American ties to the Chiang regime tightened and continued until the civil war of 1946–49 ended in a Communist triumph. After a pause described as "letting the dust settle," Washington embraced the remnant Kuomintang regime on Taiwan and undertook policies calculated to undermine the People's Republic.

Throughout the years of the Japanese war the U.S. poured some hundreds of millions into the Kuomintang treasury, its willingness to do so stimulated by Chiang's calculated threats to make peace with Tokyo. The amount of real resistance thus bought was questionable, and a byproduct was corruption of Washington officials who helped to create a pro-Chiang China Lobby. Chiang's brother-in-law, T. V. Soong, handled the largess.

Secretary of the Treasury Henry Morgenthau, the member of Roosevelt's cabinet most directly involved in China during these early stages of the war, commented that it was difficult to deal with American officials linked to the Chinese. He never knew whether they were working for "Mr. Roosevelt or T. V. Soong, because half the time [they are] on one payroll and the rest of the time . . . on the other."

The Japanese invasion reignited Chinese nationalism, and in vast areas in north and central China linked it to the injustices and aspirations of Chinese society. The triumph of the revolution in the aftermath of the war was at once the result of a profound Kuomintang failure—even in a struggle for national survival it persisted in oppressing and fleecing its own people—and a creative revolutionary strategy of which Mao was the principal architect. A united front, moderate reforms, guerrilla war, and, later, positional war—these were the ingredients which gave birth to the People's Republic. The particulars included decent treatment of the peasants by the Communist Eighth Route and New Fourth armies and a combination of political and military actions that circumscribed the Japanese occupation and created the staging for the civil war.

For American policy a turning point was the recall of General Joseph "Vinegar Joe" Stilwell in 1944. Stilwell had led the struggle not only to retrieve Burma but to develop a genuine military effort against the Japanese. And for that purpose he favored military cooperation with the Communist forces. He saw China with a clarity he shared with such American diplomats as John S. Service and John

Melby—to him Chiang was "The Peanut" or "The Dummy," and the Chongqing regime was "the manure pile." Roosevelt's yielding to Chiang on the issue of Stilwell's recall foretold an abandonment of anything like an even-handed attitude toward the Kuomintang and the Communists. It signaled an all-or-nothing commitment to Chiang and the Kuomintang regime against the Communists. That policy became evident as the defeat of Japan became assured.

In the postwar period American support for Chiang took the form of massive supplies of arms and money, the rushed air and sea transport of Kuomintang troops to cities and strategic areas surrendered by the Japanese before the Communists could take them, the use of U.S. Marines as auxiliaries, and a tainted mediation effort by General George Marshall.

Some fifty-three thousand marines were rushed to China. The Truman administration pretended that their role was simply to assist in the repatriation of Japanese troops, but their real mission was to shoehorn Kuomintang troops into north China, thus keeping cities and lines of communication out of the hands of the Communist forces, which had an overwhelming presence in the countryside. Japanese troops and the forces of the Chinese puppet regime with which the Kuomintang had maintained stealthy contact, also joined this effort.

The First Marine Division, arriving in four days from Okinawa, occupied Tianjin in September 1945 and shortly joined airlifted Kuomintang units in taking over Beijing (Peiping then) and points north. This move gave Chiang's troops access to Manchuria. Teamed up with still-armed Japanese units, the marines guarded bridges and rail lines, freeing Kuomintang troops to take the offensive against Communist guerrillas. In retaliation for being fired on by guerrillas, the marines mortared, machine-gunned, and strafed nearby villages.

On August 25, near Suzhou, an incident took place which added to U.S.-Communist hostility and led to the naming of the ultra-rightist John Birch Society. There, according to historian Michael Schaller, the Communists "clashed with an intelligence party led by army Captain John Birch and a KMT officer. Even the surviving KMT officer attested to the fact that Birch had provoked the Communist troops, who had stopped the party for questioning. Birch had ad- dressed the Communists as 'bandits.' When he was warned by the Kuomintang officer to stop this provocation, Birch reportedly said, 'I want to find out how they intend to treat Americans. I don't mind if they kill me. If they do they will be finished, for America will punish them with atomic bombs.' Since the Communists were certain teams such as that led by Birch were linked to Tai Li (Dai Li) and Nationalist espionage, Birch's macabre wish was fulfilled and he was executed."[10]

The marine actions, and the continuing supply of arms and dollars to the Kuomintang regime, compromised the Marshall Mission. Ostensibly an impartial effort at mediation, General Marshall and his aides actually strove to keep the Generalissimo in power by pressing modest reforms on him and by bringing about Communist participation in the government in safe, minor roles. John Carter Vincent, one of the makers of American-China policy in 1945–46, explained during the McCarran Committee hearings on the Institute of Pacific Relations that his concept was that the Communists would come into the government on a minority basis and that "through support of the Chiang Kai-shek government . . . with help from us we could eventually strengthen the Chinese government enough to eliminate the Communists." "In short," Vincent continued, "the tactic was taking the Communists in, in more ways than one."

Chiang did not have the political self-confidence to agree to this gambit, and Marshall soon ceased even to press it. Truce efforts, which were fleetingly promising, were doomed by Chiang's conviction that a military victory was within his grasp, and by the more realistic optimism of the Communists. By the early summer of 1946, the mission was a failure and civil war was raging.

The Communists were able to move from guerrilla to positional warfare, inflicting a succession of defeats on Chiang's legions, each successively further to the south. Enormous quantities of American arms changed sides. In April of 1949 the Communist forces, now named the People's Liberation Army, crossed the Yangtze and took Nanjing and Shanghai.

As in the case of the French and Russian revolutions, much of the ruling elite had practically abdicated as the civil struggle neared climax. As Lucien Bianco observed, "In the closing days of the conflict, it seemed as if the Chinese ruling classes simply stepped aside." By late fall the Kuomintang's shiny limousines and silken ladies were crossing the strait to Taiwan.

The U.S. aid to Chinese counterrevolution had stopped just short of massive intervention by American armed forces, an impracticality in

---

10. *The U.S. Crusade in China, 1938–1945* (New York: Columbia University Press, 1979), 269.

the wake of World War II and the demand to "bring the boys home."
Secretary of State Dean Acheson stated this view in often-quoted
paragraphs in the White Paper of 1949:[11]

> A realistic appraisal of conditions in China, past and present, leads to
> the conclusion that the only alternative open to the United States was
> full-scale involvement in behalf of a government which had lost the
> confidence of its own troops and its own people. Such intervention
> would have required the expenditure of even greater sums than have
> been expended so far, the command of Nationalist armies by American
> officers and the probable participation of American armed forces—
> land, sea, and air—in the resulting war. Intervention of such scope and
> magnitude would have been resented by the mass of the Chinese
> people, would have diametrically reversed our historic policy, and
> would have been condemned by the American people.

And therefore:

> The unfortunate but inescapable fact is that the ominous result of the
> civil war in China was beyond the control of the government of the
> United States. Nothing that this country did or could have done
> within the reasonable limits of its capabilities could have changed
> that result; nothing that was left undone by this country has
> contributed to it. It was the product of internal Chinese forces, forces
> which this country tried to influence but could not.

On the eve of the proclamation of the People's Republic on October
1, 1949, the *New York Times* described Mao and his associates as a
"nauseous force" and "a compact little oligarchy dominated by
Moscow's nominees." Acheson said the Chinese Communists were
puppets of the Soviet Union and that their government could not pass
the first test of legitimacy. "It is not Chinese," he said.

On October 2, the People's Republic invited all nations to enter into
diplomatic relations with it, but the U.S., unlike Britain and many
other states, refused. In January, the U.S. used its muscle in the

---

11. The White Paper was formally titled *United States Relations with China*,
Department of State Publication 3573, Far Eastern Series 30. Acheson wrote its Letter of
Transmittal to President Truman. The 1095–page document was re-published by
Stanford University Press in 1970.

United Nations to deny, by one vote, China's seat on the Security Council to the People's Republic, and a largely impotent hostility toward China characterized American policy for over two decades.[12]

American interventionism did not go quietly into the overflowing dustbin of history. Farce mixed with venom. Senator Kenneth Wherry had argued that "with God's help" the United States could "lift Shanghai up and up, ever up, until it is just like Kansas City." The Henry Luce publications, *Time* and *Life,* had trumpeted calls for intervention by General Claire Chennault, Stilwell's China adversary, and William Bullitt, a former ambassador to the Soviet Union. Chennault never gave up his notion that air power could prevail. Young Congressman John F. Kennedy denounced what he called the desertion of Chiang and China, "whose freedom we had once fought to preserve. What our young men had saved, our diplomats and President have frittered away." Disloyal and incompetent officials had sold China out, Kennedy charged. And Richard Nixon, later Kennedy's presidential rival, for years was second to none in his denunciations of the People's Republic and Americans accused of being soft on it.

John S. Service, O. Edmund Clubb, and other diplomats who had served in China and reported the turn of events with general accuracy and foresight received the traditional treatment of messengers bringing bad news. Accused of disloyalty and Communist proclivities, they were allotted a major share of the blame for the triumph of the Chinese Revolution. A quip of the time was that four Johns, three of them diplomats, had "lost China"—John S. Service, John Paton Davies, John Carter Vincent, and John Kai-shek. By the end of the inquisition all the Americans who had served as diplomats in China, save two, had been fired or harassed into resigning.

These diplomatic "losers of China" might have recited a seventh-century poetic lament by Chen Tzu-ang:

> The Han court honors clever eunuchs
> The Cloud Pavilion disdains frontier deeds.
> How sad is the envoy on a piebald horse—
> His hair white, whose hero now?

---

12. In January 1950 the Communists took over the barracks compound in Beijing ceded to the United States in an "unequal treaty" following the suppression of the Boxer movement. Washington used that action to widen the split.

Edgar Snow, whose *Red Star Over China* brought the Chinese Communist story to the Americans and the West, found he could no longer publish in the *Saturday Evening Post* or elsewhere and went into exile in Switzerland, as did Charlie Chaplin, also a victim of the McCarthy years. Pearl Buck, author of *The Good Earth* and other novels which portrayed Chinese sympathetically and thus countered the "Fu Manchu" stereotype, was refused the right to keep a campus speaking engagement by Miner Teachers College in Washington, D.C.

Theodore H. White, co-author with Annalee Jacoby of the best-selling *Thunder Out of China*, testified in support of John Paton Davies before the State Department's Security Hearing Board and found out that he had instantly made himself a suspect while in the presence of a "lynching party." At the time White groveled and in later years he was cautious; he finally wrote candidly in his book *In Search of History:*

> I would never again want to be a polemicist or an advocate in a national debate. . . . A self-censorship, imposed not by government but by prudence, circumscribed me—as it circumscribed countless others. . . . I meant to go on writing of politics in America, and clearance of charges meant that I could continue to do so. But I know that from then on and for years I deliberately ignored the dynamics of foreign policy and defense because too much danger lurked there; and for that shirking I am ashamed.[13]

Congressman Kennedy blamed the "Fairbanks and Lattimores" for what he saw as the China debacle, and shortly a swelling chorus was finding American scapegoats responsible for "the loss of China." Senator Joseph McCarthy's scatter-gun demagoguery took in China targets, but the principal witchhunt in connection with China was led by the McCarran Committee (a subcommittee of the Senate Committee on the Judiciary headed by Senator Pat McCarran of Nevada), which seized the files of the Institute of Pacific Relations stored in a Massachusetts barn and used them selectively in support of its thesis that conspiring American scholars had given the Chinese Communists vital assistance.

John King Fairbank, Harvard's eminent China scholar, was not protected from abuse by his reputation and balanced judgments, and was slandered even into the 1980s by conservative writer William F.

---

13. (New York: Harper & Row, 1978), 392.

Buckley. Owen Lattimore of Johns Hopkins University, whom Roosevelt had sent to China as adviser to Generalissimo Chiang, was twice indicted by the Justice Department on flimsy charges of perjury, which eventually were thrown out of court. Lawrence K. Rosinger, a most talented young Sinologist, was driven from the profession and became a hardware store clerk and later a teacher in Detroit. China scholarship became largely the possession of virulent anti-Communists, footnote writers, and sycophants.

Even at the height of the McCarthy period, Maud Russell, who had been executive director of the Committee for a Democratic Far Eastern Policy and kept on going when the committee was forced to disband, and some others across the country dared to speak out for China friendship and understanding. Russell reflected on the trying past in 1975:

> Gone are the days when hecklers, provocateurs and government agents were serious concerns. An initial question at many meetings was "Have security precautions been taken?" No longer does one have to borrow a local car for areas where a New York State license would surely cause danger to the speaker and the audience.[14]

China reaped some side benefits. Targeted Treasury Department economists Solomon Adler and Frank Coe took up residence in Beijing, serving as advisers. Professor Robert Hodes, fired by Tulane University for radical views and opposition to segregation, taught neurophysiology in China for five years.

The Pentagon devised a contingency plan for an invasion of north China, but execution of it was never seriously considered. General MacArthur's call for an assault on China as an extension of the Korean War was seen as impractical and risky even by the Washington generals and led to his downfall in 1951. The commitment of American armed forces to two wars on China's periphery turned out to be adventures beyond the possibility of success. In Korea, Asians fought a great Western army to a standstill, and the United States had to abandon its drive to unify the peninsula by force. In Indochina, revolutionary nationalism was prevailing and the stage being set for the U.S. to suffer its first major

---

14. From a message to the 1975 convention of the US-China Peoples Friendship Association, Chicago.

military defeat, though it would not come for another twenty years. In the meantime, the U.S. poured massive military and economic support into the Chiang regime on Taiwan and did whatever it could to realize its hope and forecast that the People's Republic would be a "passing phase."

The "passing phase" concept was expressed by Walter S. Robertson, a right-wing businessman turned diplomat who had served on the Marshall Mission, eight days after the proclamation of the People's Republic. He thought that "China's ignorant masses" would turn against the Communists. In a letter to Ambassador-at-Large Philip C. Jessup, Robertson said:

> There is logical reason to assume that once they experience the ruthless exploitation and regimentation of Communist power, as they surely will experience it, they will again be restive to follow any leadership that promises relief. . . . Withholding recognition would seem to offer the Chinese people some hope of eventually escaping Communist domination and control.

Robertson was appointed Assistant Secretary of State for Far Eastern Affairs by President Eisenhower, and in January 1957 testified before the House Committee on Appropriations as follows:

> *Rep. Frederick R. Coudert:* Did I correctly understand you to say that the heart of the present policy towards China and Formosa is that there is to be kept alive a constant threat of military action vis-a-vis Red China in the hope that at some point there will be an internal breakdown?
>
> *Robertson:* Yes sir, that is my conception.
>
> *Coudert:* In other words, a cold war waged under the leadership of the United States, with constant threat of attack against Red China, led by Formosa and other Far Eastern groups, and militarily backed by the United States?
>
> *Robertson:* Yes. . . .
>
> *Coudert:* Fundamentally, does not that mean that the United States is undertaking to maintain for an indefinite period of years American dominance in the Far East?
>
> *Robertson:* Yes. Exactly.

In a sweeping directive on CIA covert activities in December 1954, President Eisenhower instructed the agency to "develop underground resistance and facilitate covert and guerrilla preparation" in China and the Soviet Union and their "satellites." In 1957 Secretary of State Dulles said that the U.S. must never recognize the Beijing regime, but rather promote conditions that would bring about its downfall. "We owe it to ourselves, our allies, and the Chinese people to do all that we can to contribute to that passing," he said.

In an aggressive blockade of China's ports between 1950 and 1954, U.S.-supplied ships manned by Kuomintang crews detained, sank, or plundered over five hundred ships, including sixty-seven foreign vessels. The trade embargo and the stamping "Not valid for travel in China" on American passports continued until the change in policy by the Nixon presidency.

The CIA, under the cover name Western Enterprise Inc., established a major base on Taiwan and a forward base on the off-shore island of Quemoy. It organized and equipped intelligence-gathering, sabotage, and battalion-size commando raids on the mainland. Airplane overflights were routine.

CIA operations to foment an uprising in Tibet included raids from Nepal and efforts by agents to promote rebellion, which helped to bring the uprising of 1959 in Tibet. Some fourteen thousand Tibetans were armed and equipped and some were taken to Colorado illegally for training in clandestine operations. The CIA was in charge of these covert operations. "The Dalai Lama would never have been saved without the CIA," according to a high-ranking CIA officer. The bringing down of the U-2 in the Soviet Union in 1960 ended the American attempt to subvert Chinese rule in Tibet. Eisenhower ordered an end, for the sake of American credibility, of operations requiring large-scale overflights and long-range transport plane infiltration.

In 1954, and again in 1958, U.S. support of Kuomintang occupation of the harbor islands of Quemoy and Matsu led to crises. The United States, which had threatened China with a nuclear attack during the latter stage of the Korean War, stockpiled nuclear weapons on Taiwan and supplied Kuomintang troops on Quemoy with eight-inch howitzers capable of firing nuclear shells. Tied to the U.S. by a military treaty, Taiwan served it as an air and transport base in the Indochina war.

Eisenhower had the saving virtue of caution. According to his biographer, Stephen E. Ambrose, five times in 1954 he overruled the recommendations of the National Security Council, the Joint Chiefs of Staff, and the State Department that he intervene against China, even using nuclear bombs:

> First, in April, as the Dien Bien Phu situation grew critical. Second, in May, on the eve of Dien Bien Phu's fall. Third, in late June, when the French said the Chinese air force was about to enter the Indochina conflict. Fourth, in September, when the Chinese began shelling Quemoy and Matsu. Fifth, in November, when the Chinese announced the prison terms for the American fliers.[15]

In both Korea and Vietnam, China was the enemy both in rhetoric and in action. Chinese troops intervened effectively in Korea when the U.S. ignored Beijing's repeated warnings and drove to the Yalu River in the northern frontier. China sent some 50,000 troops into northern Vietnam to construct and maintain railroads and airfields; they suffered significant casualties from air raids, and Chinese anti-aircraft fire brought down American planes. The American interventions both in Korea and Indochina were justified by the U.S. to the world as responses to an inappeasable Chinese appetite for Asian conquest. Just as the Chinese Communists had been perceived as puppets of Moscow, so Beijing was seen as pulling the strings in Korea and Vietnam.

President Lyndon B. Johnson declared in April 1965: "Over this war—and all Asia—is another reality: the deepening shadow of Communist China. . . . The rulers of Hanoi are urged on by Peking." And two years later, Vice-President Hubert Humphrey, a supporter of the war to the end, asserted that "the threat to world peace is militant, aggressive Asian communism, with its headquarters in Peking."

The humiliating defeat in Indochina contributed to the dramatic turn in Sino-American relations initiated by the Nixon administration in 1971. Washington had to reconcile itself to a world of various power centers in which its ability to intervene militarily was limited. And it hoped that Beijing would influence Hanoi and help the U.S. to extricate itself from the Indochina morass. That did not happen, contrary to Vietnam's subsequent allegations, but the gambits of the China visits of the American pingpong players and

---

15. *Eisenhower: Volume Two, The President* (New York: Simon and Schuster, 1984), 229.

Henry Kissinger led to President Nixon's dramatic televised flight to Beijing and the accord set forth in the Shanghai Communique of February 1972. The full diplomatic relations envisaged in that document were established on January 1, 1979.

A mutuality of strategic interests brought the U.S. and China together. China saw the Soviet as a threatening enemy, a conclusion it drew from the enormous Soviet forces along its northern frontier and the increasingly dominant Soviet role in Indochina. Amicable relations with Washington added to China's security and eventually helped to bring about improved relations with Moscow. Washington had a comparable interest in ties with China even if short of alliance.

In both capitals the potential for economic exchange was thoroughly studied. China suffered from technological backwardness, and the American dream of a China market had survived the decades of estrangement. In Yan'an in 1945 Mao told John S. Service that the U.S. and China had mutual interests, including economic interests:

> America needs an export market for her heavy industry. . . . She also needs an outlet for capital investment. China needs to build up light industries to supply her own market and raise the living standard of her people. . . . America is not only the most suitable country to assist this economic development of China; she is also the only country fully able to participate.[16]

Mao and Zhou Enlai offered to visit Washington to discuss U.S.-China relations, but their overture was ignored, and Mao's hopes that the U.S. would stay out of the approaching civil war were dashed.

Overlapping strategic interests continue. U.S.-China trade has developed and a modest amount of American capital has been invested in China. But Beijing and Washington disagree not only about Taiwan, but also about such central issues as peace and disarmament and Third World policies, and the existence of a strong Chinese state has changed the character of economic exchange. How state-to-state relations will develop is problematical.

---

16. Joseph W. Esherick, ed., *Lost Chance in China: The World War II Despatches of John S. Service* (New York: Random House, 1974), 373.

But the reconciliation of the capitals has opened the door in a way Secretary of State John Hay did not foresee. Exchanges of all sorts, and institutional and personal connections and friendships have proliferated; but they are very different from those of the past. They are different because most Americans now perceive that China has indeed "Stood Up," as Mao said at Tiananmen in October 1949.

The American attitude of the past was characterized by wishes to dominate or exploit, by expressions of disrespect or even contempt, or by patronizing "Do Goodism." Steven Levine has observed that the U.S-China relationship historically

> was extremely lopsided. It was founded in the American belief that the United States held the answers to China's problems. This was a manifestation of cultural imperialism. . . . The fundamental structure of the relationship looked at from the American side was the underlying belief that if China were ever to develop and progress, that if China were ever to come out of its state of "backwardness," then China needed the United States. The Chinese lacked the ability or the competence to progress on their own.[17]

Now Americans may not like much of what they see or understand about China, but they do see a bustling society of generally well-fed and well-clothed people and they do know that the China of today was "Made in China." China can learn from the American relationship, but it can pick and choose and say "no" and it has knowledge and experience to share. The Chinese revolution has made a truly reciprocal and amicable relationship between the peoples possible.

That possibility has roots in the past. True friendship has a history. Not all Americans who voyaged across the Pacific to China succumbed to Treaty Port cant, ethnocentrism, and "Do Goodism." Some were educated or reeducated by the evidence of a society in crisis and were moved to sympathize with and be helpful to the courageous groups taking the initiative in struggles to change things.

---

17. Stephen Levine, "Historical Turning Points in US-China Relations," *US-China Review*, July-August 1986. This article is an edited version of a talk by Dr. Levine at the Washington Seminar on US-China Relations sponsored by the US-China Peoples Friendship Association in April 1986.

Among them were missionaries like Joseph Bailie, Spencer Kennard, and the Canadian James Endicott; soldiers like Evans Carlson and Joseph Stilwell; diplomats like the Sichuan-born John S. Service; physicians like George Hatem (Ma Haide); a remarkable sisterhood of YWCA workers, and a hard-working and brilliant group of journalists and writers.

The typewriters in the hands of the journalists and writers made the foremost American contribution to the cause of the Chinese revolution—hundreds of pages of reality, pages that took the aches and aspirations of a different culture across the ocean, pages that served information and opinion then and continue to serve history. Edgar Snow, Helen Foster Snow (Nym Wales), Agnes Smedley, Anna Louise Strong, Jack Belden, Graham Peck, and William Hinton were very different, but shared a common engagement in the struggles of their time.

Publications and organizations were of some help to a cause that was essentially made triumphant by the Chinese people themselves. The *China Weekly Review* in Shanghai published articles by the Snows and Belden and was a progressive influence, especially under the editorship of John W. Powell. Americans launched two short-lived publications at the time of the national crisis brought on by Japanese aggression—the magazines *Democracy* in Beijing and the *Voice of China* in Shanghai. A succession of three organizations have done what they could with limited support and resources. In the 1930s the American Friends of the Chinese People published the periodical *China Today,* and organized demonstrations protesting the export of oil and scrap iron to Japan. During the anti-Japanese war which broke out in 1937, the China Aid Council, supported by anti-fascists who had opposed Franco and by other progressives, raised money for the China Defense League headed by Soong Ching Ling to aid the medical work of Dr. Norman Bethune in the Communist-led liberated areas. In the post-World War II years the Committee for a Democratic Far Eastern Policy published the *Far East Spotlight,* protested American intervention in the civil war, and later campaigned for recognition of the People's Republic, but eventually fell victim to McCarthyism.

An important consequence of the positive turn in U.S.-China relations in 1971–72 was the birth of the US-China Peoples Friendship Association, which grew into a national organization with some sixty-five chapters and six thousand members and which began efforts on behalf of normal diplomatic relations. It publishes the *US-China Review*, and its Center for Teaching About China provides schools and teachers with educational materials.

In a struggle that went on for over a century, the people of China confounded domestic oppressors and foreign enemies with a modest amount of help from foreign friends, a collaboration that testifies to the linked fate of all who live on this

> . . . globe that sails the starry dark.
> Launched as never galleon into nothingness
> Was launched before—as never Noah's Ark
> With such dear lading in such long distress. . . .

II

············

Elaborations

1. Ginseng to Opium: Samuel Shaw, Warren Delano and the Early China Trade

> Businessmen boast of their skill and cunning
> But in philosophy they are like little children.
> Bragging to each other of successful depredations
> They neglect to consider the ultimate fate of the body.
> What should they know of the Master of Dark Truth
> Who saw the wide world in a jade cup . . .
>   CHEN TZU-ANG (656–698)[1]

John Ledyard of Groton, Connecticut was one of two Americans who sailed with Captain James Cook on his fatal last voyage in 1778. His account, published in Hartford in 1783, told of the enormous profits to be had from trading furs in Canton [Guangzhou]. Trade with China was a hopeful prospect in that time of post-war depression and Ledyard was persuasive. He convinced Robert Morris, a rich Philadelphia tea smuggler who had contributed generously to the cause of in-

---

1. This epigraph is borrowed from Michael Greenberg's *British Trade and the Opening of China, 1800–42* (Cambridge: Cambridge University Press, 1969).

37

dependence, and others, who put together $120,000 to send the first American ship to Guangzhou. The 360-ton *Empress of China*—described as "handsome, commodious, and elegant"—cleared New York Harbor on George Washington's fifty-second birthday, February 22, 1784. It carried a letter from Congress asking Chinese and other potentates "of all the good cities and places, whether ecclesiastical or secular" to welcome and assist the visitors from America. The *Empress* dropped anchor off Guangzhou in August. Captain John Green, a former Morris employee who had been released by the Navy to take the command, wrote that he "had the honor of hoisting the first Continental Flagg Ever seen or maid Euse of in those parts."

The *Empress of China* had in its hold some 2,600 pelts, but its principal cargo was thirty tons of ginseng, prized in China as a tonic and aphrodisiac, which was found in the Appalachians and other shady, cool hillsides along the Atlantic seaboard. Samuel Shaw, a Bostonian who had served with distinction in the American revolution (he survived Valley Forge), was the supercargo in charge of selling the ginseng and the remainder of the trade goods (woolens, cotton, lead, pepper) and refilling the hold.

Shaw learned the restrictive regulations imposed by a self-sufficient Chinese imperial regime with very little interest in commerce with the "outer barbarians." Dealing with designated Chinese merchants and compradors (suppliers), he filled the hold of the *Empress* and a smaller Baltimore-bound vessel with 440 tons of tea—large quantities of cheap and hearty black tea and fewer caskets of the green tea favored by connoisseurs. The return cargo also included fifty tons of porcelain (soon to be called china), which was ballast on the voyage and profit on the docks; silks and nankeens (a cloth first made in Nanjing which for decades was superior to any cloth manufactured in Western mills); cinnamon-like cassia; rich home furnishings for Robert Morris; and Shanghai roosters (which became the ancestors of Bucks County chickens). Shaw learned little of China. Like all who came to trade, he was confined to a shorefront enclave of commercial houses (called "hongs" or "factories"); he never entered Guangzhou. He was critical of idolatry and official oppression, but was drawn to much of what he saw and was inclined to look for reasons for faults and imperfections. He found instances of commercial knavery "as elsewhere," but also found the Chinese merchants "as responsible a set of men as are commonly found in other parts of the world." He was perhaps the first among many Americans to catch the China bug—to want to go back again and again. "All we know with certainty respecting China," he wrote in his journal, later published, "is that it has long existed as striking evidence of the wisdom of its government and still continues [to excite] the admiration of the world."

And he strove to bring the Chinese he dealt with to a tolerant view of his new nation and his countrymen, whom the Chinese called "second chop Englishmen" or the "New People." He displayed a map of the thirteen states and found that the Chinese "were not a little pleased at the prospect of so considerable a market for the production of their empire."

Returned to the United States, Shaw served as top assistant to Secretary of War Henry Knox, his wartime commander, but China was in his thoughts, as was the hope for profit. He went back to Guangzhou four times, his status enhanced by congressional appointment as the first American consul, an unpaid post. In 1794, married just six months, he contracted a liver disease in Bombay and died on the voyage home. He was thirty-nine.

The *Empress of China* turned a profit of some thirty thousand dollars, most of which went to Morris. Shaw complained that he hadn't earned "a single guinea." But others were captivated by the potential for profits. A second ship, the *Experiment*, commanded by Stewart Dean, was financed by a New York partnership which included one of the Vanderbilts, and though smaller than the *Empress*, yielded a larger profit. Soon the ports of the American seaboard—Salem, Boston, Providence, Philadelphia, and Baltimore, as well as New York—were sending ships to Guangzhou and other Asian ports either around the Cape of Good Hope or westward around the Horn. Vessels foundered in storms or were overrun by pirates, but the ledgers showed gratifying numbers. In 1801 thirty-one American ships dropped anchor in Whangpoa [Huangpu] off Guangzhou.

A steady American market existed for tea (Americans were drinking it twice a day, according to one observer) and what was not consumed was profitably re-exported to Europe. Easily salable also were silks, all manner of Chinese handicrafts, and especially porcelain. Shaw had served as secretary of the committee which founded the Society of the Cincinnati, composed of Revolutionary War officers, and in Guangzhou he had chinaware emblazoned with its insignia. George Washington paid $150 for a set of 302 pieces.

What to exchange for these was the problem. Supplies of ginseng soon exceeded the demand and the price fell. A search for substitutes followed, the unwelcome alternative being continued payment to the

Chinese in milled Spanish dollars, for self-sufficient China needed few products from the "outer barbarians."

The first important substitute for ginseng was that publicized by John Ledyard—furs. American ships went around the Horn and up the coast to what is now Washington and Oregon and traded brightly colored cloth and trinkets for furs collected by the Indians. Holds filled with tens of thousands of pelts fetched thirty times the purchase price in Guangzhou, where they were used to line the long gowns of the gentry. But the furred animals in the Great Northwest suffered the fate of the beavers in seventeenth century New England and the supply of pelts dwindled.

The next substitutes were seal skins and sandalwood from the South Seas. In a few years American crews slaughtered seals by the hundreds of thousands until their near extinction made them of little commercial interest. Trade in sandalwood was a bonanza that lasted just seven years, with wood collected at a cost of $800 bringing in $80,000 in Guangzhou. The virtual destruction of the sandalwood forests on Fiji ended the trade.

Opium was the solution. Opium imports had long been officially prohibited in China and so the trade had to be the work of smugglers, made practical by the venality of Chinese officials and the fleetness of the small ships that took the drug up the China coast.

Britain's East India Company encouraged the large-scale cultivation of poppies in India and sold the product in China at a huge profit; that profit paid for English tea drinking and helped to finance the Indian empire.

Samuel Shaw initially favored an effort to establish an American ginseng monopoly. He argued that some day ginseng would be "the equivalent of others' mines of silver and gold." But before his early death his thoughts had turned to opium, which, he observed, "could be smuggled with the utmost security."

Determined American merchants worked around British control of Indian opium. Their ships picked up Turkish opium in Smyrna en route to Guangzhou, but their profit was less. The Turkish drug was inferior and was used mainly to adulterate Indian opium. The East India Company lost its monopoly in 1834 and thereafter the Americans were able to get a small piece of the Indian action. During the First Opium War of 1840–42 American merchants stayed neutral, and served the British opium traders as middlemen, exacting superprofits.

During the early 1800s about 3,000 to 5,000 chests of opium, each containing one picul or 133.33 pounds, were smuggled into China. The commerce in the "soother of all sorrows" grew rapidly, to over 35,000 chests in 1831–32 and to 40,000 by 1839–40. The effect on China was pernicious. Millions became addicts and the country was drained of silver, debasing the currency. The pressure on the Qing court in Beijing to take action became explosive. In 1839 an incorruptible and resolute official, Lin Zexu, was sent to Guangzhou as commissioner. His moves to eradicate the opium trade culminated in the public destruction of more than 20,000 chests valued at about $12 million.

Opium was almost the only commodity the British had to trade in China, and London responded to the trade halt with warships and English and sepoy troops. In operations that lasted nearly three years the British inflicted one defeat after another on the courageous but ill-armed Chinese forces, which a foreign merchant publication described as a "wretched burlesque" of military power. Britain forced on China the first of the unequal treaties, the Treaty of Nanjing, in 1842. The expansion of the opium trade was assured, though it was not mentioned in the treaty and was legalized only by the Second Opium War of 1856–60. By the 1860s some 60,000 chests of opium were being dumped into China, earning the traffickers up to $35 million annually.

All of the American merchant houses participated in the opium action with the exception of two: D. W. C. Olyphant & Company of New York, headed by a leading Presbyterian, and Nathan Dunn of Philadelphia, Quaker-influenced.

Russell & Company of Boston was the foremost American trader in opium and the third largest, British or American. Warren Delano II, grandfather of Franklin Delano Roosevelt, was one of the partners and managers responsible for Russell & Company's drug profits. A member of a family with a history of seafaring and mercantile experience, Warren Delano arrived in China in 1833 as a supercargo and junior partner of what was then Russell, Sturgis & Company of Boston and Manila. He was in charge of the Guangzhou operation throughout the Opium War and took skillful advantage of British preoccupations. His personal annual take was around $30,000. Russell & Company had to contribute 1,250 chests to the opium collection ordered destroyed by Commissioner Lin Zexu, but its success in smuggling in some 8,000 chests that year eased the pain. Looking over the books for 1839–40, Edward (Ned) Delano, Warren Delano's brother and associate in Russell & Company, basked in the record of "magnificent profits, the like of which I think cannot again accrue."

The bravery with which Chinese troops and peasant militia fought through the Opium War wrung tributes even from British officers, but the realities were British victories followed by the looting that put the word in the English language. The scene after engagements was hundreds of Chinese bodies, some mutilated. A "horrid butchery," Ned Delano described one such scene near Guangzhou which he visited. The Delanos were occasionally given to anti-British comments, but were essentially supportive. "Great Britain owes it to herself and to the civilized world to knock a little reason into this besotted people," Warren Delano wrote.

And he defended the opium traffic as "a fair, honorable and legitimate trade, and to say the worst of it, liable to no further or negative objections than is the importation of wines, brandies and spirits into the States, England, etc."

In 1846 Delano returned home, invested his riches, and raised a large family, which included daughter Sara, mother of Franklin Roosevelt.

Nearly bankrupted by imprudent investment and the 1857 depression, Delano returned to Hongkong in 1860 and made a second fortune in five years. Thereafter he was able to live in secure comfort in Algonac (of Algonquin origin), his home on the Hudson River. The furnishings ever reminded him of China and he and his wife slept in a Chinese bedstead inlaid with mother-of-pearl. He called himself the staunchest of Republicans and boasted that he would never pay a man more than $1.50 for a day's work because he could always hire immigrants for that amount. He died in 1898. "You can never imagine how deeply grieved I was to hear that my darling grandfather had passed away," the young Franklin wrote to his mother.[2]

Opium profits helped to make Boston a financial center and to capitalize the industrial growth of New England and the mid-Atlantic states, constructing railroads and the mills that hired immigrant women to produce the cheap cotton that could compete even in China. The partners of Russell & Company and other firms and their descendants became the elite—Cabot, Forbes, Perkins, Cushing, Sturgis, Coolidge, Bryant, Higginson, Griswold, Alsop, Paine, Tappan—which continued to run banks, brokerage houses, and industries, and manage Harvard. Their fortunes built handsome clapboard mansions full of artifacts brought in holds from Guangzhou.

Trade with China diminished in mid-century. The opening of the American West and the country's industrial development were more profitable and both China and the United States turned inward and

---

2. Geoffry C. Ward, *Before the Trumpet: Young Franklin Roosevelt, 1882–1905* (New York: Harper & Row, 1985), 199.

fought civil wars. The trade revived but never caught up to the vision and dream of what it could be.

FDR and the White House were silent when a Roosevelt-baiting columnist, Westbrook Pegler, publicized Warren Delano and the drug traffic, but Eleanor Roosevelt, investigating during a visit to Hongkong in 1953, made a partial admission: "I suppose it is true that the Delanos and the Forbeses, like everybody else, had to include a limited amount of opium in their cargoes to do any trading at all."[3]

2. The Young Olmsted in Canton

Herman Melville and Richard Henry Dana, Jr., were just two of the sons of respectable New England families who took to the sea for a voyage or two. Another was Frederick Law Olmsted of Hartford, Connecticut, later the principal designer of Central Park in New York and the nation's premier landscape architect. The Olmsted family naturally picked a China-bound vessel, for Frederick's grandfather Benjamin and two great uncles, Aaron and Gideon, had been shipmasters in the China trade.

Undismayed by a reading of Dana's *Two Years Before the Mast*, Olmsted, twenty-one, sailed from New York's East River aboard the 350-ton bark *Ronaldson* on April 23, 1843. The weather was rough, perilously so on the turn around the Cape of Good Hope, and the treatment of the hands was rough. Often ill, shocked by the brutalities of forecastle life, the young Olmsted had reason to be relieved when on September 9 the *Ronaldson* dropped anchor in Huangpu, twelve miles before Canton [Guangzhou]. He knew very well the lay of land and water, as Captain Warren Fox had set him to making an 800 percent enlarged chart of the Pearl River estuary.

Olmsted's first China experience was frustration. For a month he was kept aboard, his view landward one of rice paddies and a burial ground. The only Chinese he could get close to were the few who drew alongside to inspect the trade goods or supply victuals.

Such encounters started him off with a favorable impression of the Chinese people. He came to admire one called Sam who ran errands for the captain in a small boat, acted as interpreter, and made himself useful on deck or in the cabin. The captain invited him to join the crew as steward and go to America with them. When he refused, the captain doubled his wage offer. But he could not accept, what-

3. Ward, *Before the Trumpet*, 87–88n.

ever the offer, Sam told Olmsted, because he was the only son of an aged man.

Once a wealthy Chinese merchant's elegant craft came alongside and Olmsted was courteously invited aboard. In an essay written much later, probably in 1856, he recalled:

> The cabin was rich with carvings and contained pretty furniture of black wood inlaid with ivory and mother-of-pearl and a number of musical instruments. All these were shown to me in a pleasant way. In a corner there were two gentlemen over a table, playing chess, I think. When we came near them they bowed and smiled and, the servant at this moment bringing the tea things which were placed upon another table, they rose and one of them handed me a cup of tea. Delicious tea it was; they each took a cup with me, then offered me cigarettes and finally waited upon me to the gangway and bowed me over the side with perfectly suave gravity.[4]

But at last Olmsted did get to go ashore—frequently, when the captain discovered he could row. Approaching Guangzhou, he saw the flags of the trading nations over the hongs or factories (warehouses, offices, and residences combined) on the fifteen-acre littoral between the city wall and the water, to which the foreigners were confined. Behind rose two pagodas in the city itself and in the background were the White Cloud Hills. He described himself ashore as swinging along "in tarry trousers, check shirt, with the lanyard of jackknife in place of a cravat, money jacket, etc."

He bought himself a new pair of trousers before calling on Dr. Peter Parker, to whom he had a letter of introduction, and his wife, the former Harriet Colby Webster of Washington, a relative of Daniel Webster. The first medical missionary in China, Dr. Parker treated eye diseases in his ophthalmic hospital established in the foreign enclave in 1835. His wife was the first foreign woman permitted to reside in Guangzhou. "A most agreeable call," Olmsted wrote home.

Olmsted and his mates were warned not to go far from shore and to stick together for common defense in case of trouble with the Chinese. "The Opium War had just ended and British frigates which had brought desolation and more bitter poverty to many a poor household

---

4. Olmsted's "The Real China" was published in *The Papers of Frederick Law Olmsted*, vol. 1, *The Formative Years, 1822–1852* (Baltimore and London, 1977), 187–190. It appeared also in *China and Us* 11, no. 1 (New York) (Winter 1982). The quotation above and those from Olmsted which follow are in *The Papers*, 189–90.

. . . were moored near us," Olmsted wrote in his 1856 account, titled "The Real China." "It was naturally to be supposed that the traditional antipathy of the people to foreigners had been greatly exasperated. . . ."

Despite this very real antipathy, people responded to a young sailor with an open countenance and friendly curiosity in his eyes. On some excursions into the countryside Olmsted and his fellows ran into epithets and jeers and boys threw mud balls at them, but many people were forbearing, courteous, even friendly. Olmsted wrote:

> We rowed wherever inclination led us, hardly ever saying by your leave but taking that for granted. . . . Thus we made our way, often interrupting men and women at their work, into shops and factories, boat-builders' yards and potteries, gardens, cemeteries and houses of worship, even into private homes, seldom receiving the rebuffs and rebukes which I am sure that we deserved, often invited and assisted to gratify our curiosity.

Some encounters were shocking. Presumably after the October 24, 1843 fire, which burned a square mile of the city, two convicted arsonists were put to painful death. Olmsted wrote home that they sat "in stocks, with their tongues cut out, undergoing the pleasant operation of starving to death."

Yet there was much to wonder at and think about—the exotic flora and fauna, the astonishing variety of strange but tasty dishes, the women walking on bound feet—"exactly as if on wooden legs," he wrote home.

Once he looked in a window "and saw an elderly man with great spectacles teaching about twenty little boys. As soon as he observed me, he laid down his book, came forward and throwing open a door, invited me to enter and then proceeded with great cleverness by gesture and example to show me how he taught the boys to read."

On another occasion he went into what seems to have been a Confucian temple.

> Presently, as my eyes became accustomed to the gloom, I saw an old gentleman observing me from a side door. As our eyes met, he bowed and directly came forward and beckoning me to follow him, led the way into a little room where there were piles of books and manuscripts. He laid open one of them which appeared very ancient and showed me that it contained plans of the building and tried in a

gentle, patient way to make me understand something of its origin and purposes.

He could use a very few words of Pidgin-English and, rightly or wrongly, I made out that the object of the structure was to keep the memory green and preserve the sayings of some good man who lived many generations ago.

On December 30, 1843, the *Ronaldson*, laden with tea, cassia (cinnamon) and silk, began a rough voyage home. If it had stayed another five weeks, it would have been joined in the Huangpu anchorage by a squadron of four U.S. Navy vessels which brought Caleb Cushing to exact from China the first of the "Me Too" treaties—giving the United States the rights Britain had won in the Opium War, among them commercial access to five ports.

About the time that Olmsted began his China voyage, Hong Xiuquan failed the imperial examination for the fourth time and returned embittered to his Hakka[5] village outside of Guangzhou. While the *Ronaldson* was on the high seas, Hong read some Christian tracts which started him on the path to leadership of a great revolution—the effort of the Taipings to overthrow the Manchu dynasty and found the kingdom of God on earth.

But if Olmsted missed historical turns, he did get a sense of what the people of China were like. He wrote in his essay on "The Real China":

I suppose that civilization is to be tested as much by civility as anything else, and I have recalled these incidents as illustrations of a personal experience which made a strong impression upon me, tending to a higher estimate of the social conditions of the masses of the Chinese people than, I think, generally prevails.

Olmsted went on to a distinguished career as a journalist and publisher and finally as a pioneering landscape architect and city planner. His monuments include books—now classic studies of the slave-holding South; and parks—Central Park in Manhattan, Prospect Park in Brooklyn, South Park in Chicago, Mount Royal Park in Montreal, and park systems in Buffalo and Boston.

---

5. Descendants of migrants from the north whose language and customs set them apart from their neighbors, who looked down on them.

Throughout his life he kept to a favorable opinion of the Chinese. Operating a gold mine in California in 1863, he voiced a view of them which was very much in the minority. Chinese miners and Chinese immigrants generally were being slandered, exploited, physically abused, and burned out, but to Olmsted they were the most civilized group in the community. The Chinese had nothing to learn from their white neighbors "except new forms of vice and wickedness," he wrote, and made plain how deeply he was saddened by the failure of the whites to treat the Chinese properly. That humane and sensible opinion is also part of Olmsted's legacy.

3. Pioneering Counterinsurgency: Frederick Townsend Ward and the Taiping Revolution

The Taiping Revolution, called in the West the Taiping Rebellion, was in its eleventh year when Fort Sumter was fired on; its doomed army was still in the field when Lee surrendered at Appomattox. The beginning was like a pamphleteer's dream of glory: some Christian tracts thrust into the hand of Hong Xiuquan, a frustrated scholar, on a Guangzhou street first converted a handful, and then— their message preached in a society with feudal ills being compounded by the aggression of the West—fired hundreds and thousands. Out of Guangxi Province, west of Guangzhou, came a crusade waged by peasants and Miao mountain people who prayed before they stormed into battle.

Like the Levellers, the Taipings eyed the earth as well as heaven. They prohibited the use of opium, by which the West was debilitating both the Chinese economy and people. They dispensed a stern justice, but in open courts, and did away with cruel punishments. They forbade prostitution, female servitude, and foot-binding. They took a straight look at Western science and adopted such useful practices as vaccination. And, finding sanctions both in ancient texts and the Bible, they set forth a plan for agrarian communism based on twenty-five-family units and nine land classifications:

> All the fields in the empire must be cultivated by all the people alike . . . so that all the people in the empire may together enjoy the abundant happiness provided by the Great God. . . . Having fields, let them cultivate them together, and when they grow food, let them eat it together. So also with regard to clothes and money, let them use

them in common, so that each may share and share alike, and everyone be equally well fed and clothed.

The rebels captured Nanking [Nanjing] in March 1853, and made it the capital of their Taiping Tianguo—Heavenly Kingdom of Great Peace. They were visited shortly by the British naval ship *Hermes* and the American *Susquehanna*. The Westerners were distressed by the evidences of Taiping nationalism and by the liberties taken with Biblical doctrine, but they noted the proud bearing, devotion, idealism, energy and discipline of the rebels. "It was obvious to the commonest observer that they were practically a different race," Captain Edmund Fishborne of the *Hermes* wrote.

The Americans reported the militant communism the Taipings were practicing, a vaccination program for the people, the exceptional cleanliness of the streets. The Rev. E. C. Bridgman wrote in the *North China Herald* that

> their red and yellow turbans, their long hair, and their silk and satin robes . . . made the Insurgents appear like a new race of warriors. All the people we saw were very well clad, well fed, and well provided for in every way. They all seemed content and in high spirits, as if sure of success.

Twelve years later Manchu [Qing] dynasty armies under Zeng Guofan, backed by the military power of the West, completed the suppression of the Revolution. The Manchus burned the Taiping books and tracts and otherwise tried to assure a monopoly for their own version of events. In most of the subsequent Western histories, too, the Revolution was belittled and twisted. The Taipings were hordes, fanatics, destroyers, perverters of Christianity. Western intervention against them was a benevolence.

What this sort of history notably failed to explain was the memory of the Taipings kept in the villages through the years. To the gentry the Taipings were rabble; Chiang Kai-shek took Zeng Guofan as a model hero. But in the tales, songs, and poems handed down by the peasants, the Taipings were righters of wrongs, champions of the people. One song went:

Bamboo shoots' two ends are yellow
Li Xiucheng[6] is the peasants' leader.

---

6. Li Xiucheng (1823–1864), an outstanding general of the Taiping Revolution.

> The landlords dread him like the King of Hell,
> The peasants love him like a mother.

To American students reading standard texts, the entire "bizarre episode" of the revolution, as Professor Nathaniel Peffer of Columbia called it, was a half-dozen pages. To young Chinese listening in the villages to the stories that made the blood run hot, the Taipings dominated just the day before yesterday.

Sun Yat-sen, born in 1866 as Taiping remnants were being mopped up, as a boy cherished the nickname "Hong Xiuquan the Second." Growing up not far from Hong's birthplace, he learned stories praising the Taipings as revolutionaries as well as anti-Manchu crusaders. Communism "was applied in China in the time of Hong Xiuquan," he told his audience in one of his 1924 lectures on the *San Min Chu I* (Three People's Principles). "His economic system was the real thing in communism and not mere theory."

The Taiping leaders were heroes in tales told by old peasants to Mao Zedong in Hunan, through which the rebels fought on their way in Nanjing. In Sichuan, where the separatist Taiping general Shi Dakai met his bloody end in 1863 after a long march from Jiangxi and scores of battles, the young Zhu De was talked to and stirred by an old weaver who had fought in Shi's army. Peng Dehuai's great uncle was a Taiping veteran.

To them and many others, the Taiping Revolution was proof of the power of an aroused peasantry, a precursor offering strengths to emulate and weaknesses to avoid, a Chinese instance of communism, and, not least, evidence of the implacability of the West.

Frederick Townsend Ward, an adventurer from Salem, Massachusetts, took the timely initiative which began the decisive Western intervention against the Taiping Revolution. Ward, who grew up in a family of shipmasters and ship chandlers, early learned the ways of the sea and was a second mate while still in his teens. Soldiering attracted him. He ran away to enlist in the Mexican War, but was caught, and applied for an appointment to West Point but was turned down. His father sent him to an academy in Norwich, Vermont for two years and there he gained basic military knowledge. In a career marked by rapid changes in employment and locale and little success, he voyaged as first mate on clipper ships (visiting China ports in 1847 and 1851), mined gold in California, and was fleetingly a Texas Ranger, an instructor in the Mexican army and a soldier in the French army during the Crimean War. According to some accounts, he served with the filibuster William Walker, who attempted insurrections in Mexico and Nicaragua, but did not stay with him long.

Ward had just turned twenty-eight when he came to Shanghai in April 1860 in search of fame and fortune, and his timing was perfect.

In the spring and summer of 1860, Taiping armies under Li Xiucheng, titled the Zhong Wang or Loyal King, scored a series of brilliant victories to clear most of east central China of the forces of the Qing dynasty. Shanghai, one of the five treaty ports opened by the Opium War of 1840–42, beckoned. This swiftly developing Western enclave was providing the Manchus with arms, transport and customs revenue. Its capture would give the rebels a door to the West and access to modern arms and perhaps break the strategic impasse that had marked the civil war since the Taiping capture of Nanjing in March 1853.

Ward is believed to have come to China to offer his services to the Taipings, but if so, circumstances in Shanghai quickly changed his mind. Respectable tongues had nothing but ill to say of the rebels, who were even reputed to have made marriage a capital offense. But, more to the point, the moneyed Chinese merchants and bankers, and the Qing officials and their retinues, many of whom had fled before the Taiping advances, were desperate for succor, and for Ward that spelled opportunity. He offered to recruit a mercenary force to defend the city and environs, and a banker-official combine agreed to finance it and pay handsome bonuses for the capture of towns— $45,000 to $133,000 according to size.

Very quickly Ward assembled a band of deserters, adventurers, beachcombers, and drunks, and in July began assaults on Taiping-held towns on the outskirts of Shanghai. After an initial failure he captured Songjiang, thirty miles southwest of Shanghai, in mid-July, but it fell again to the rebels in August.

Ward received a wound that failed to heal properly and after some weeks he went abroad—to Paris, according to one account—for surgery. He was gone until well into 1861.

Li Xiucheng was assured by well-meaning but naive missionaries and by French merchant provocateurs at Suzhou that he would be well received by his fellow worshipers of Jesus in Shanghai, and on August 18, ten days after Ward's last defeat, he approached the city. The Qing garrison in the Chinese walled city adjoining the British, French and American concessions was weak, and Li took with him only a small force consisting largely of his own bodyguard brigade. Composed of Hakka and Han peasants and Miao tribesmen who had early joined the "God Worshipers" in Guangxi and Hunan, these fervent and highly disciplined bearers of Li's green standard had a great record of exhausting marches and swift victories. "One of the finest bodies of men I have ever seen in my life," wrote Augustus F. Lindley (Lin-le), an Englishman who later served the Taipings as an artillery officer and aide to Li.[7]

As this force moved along the paths and canals to Shanghai, Li's orders reminded the Taipings that the Westerners were foreign brethren, like themselves followers of Jesus and the Heavenly Way, and that even if met with hostility they were to abstain from responses in kind and show by their behavior that they came in friendship. Li similarly addressed a friendly communication to the Shanghai foreign community, assuring it that the hoisting of a yellow flag over a structure would bring it immunity from attack.

Forced to fight, the Taipings quickly overran a Qing encampment (and its American-made artillery) outside the walls of the city on the eighteenth and then approached the west gate. British and French units had manned the walls. Then, according to the official British report:

> Troops under Captain Cavanagh destroyed the west gate bridge and "gave the insurgents a rather warm reception from the city wall with rifles and canister." Captain McIntyre's Madras unit brought up mountain guns, passing within a few yards of the Taipings, who, "curious to relate," did not fire a shot. Rebels outside canister range "were treated to shell, thrown time after time into the very middle of their flags." At the south gate marines and Sikhs under Lieutenant O'Grady "gave them another dressing." A Brown Bess "inflicted no small loss on the enemy" and Gunner Deacon of the Royal Artillery worked a Chinese gun "with great success." British and French troops then moved outside the walls to burn the suburbs; "the fires raged outside the west and south gates during the whole of Saturday night." The day ended "with no small loss to the enemy, but without a single casualty report on the foreign side."

7. Lin-le [Augustus F. Lindley], *Ti-ping Tien-kwoh, The History of the Ti-Ping Revolution, Including a Narrative of The Author's Personal Adventures* London: Day & Son, 1866). I have drawn heavily on this admirable work for my account of the Shanghai confrontation. Much of this chapter appeared in an earlier article, "The Taipings at Shanghai: A Note on an Unobserved Civil War Centennial," *Monthly Review*, February 1964. The official British report and the subsequent quote from *Friend of China* are from Lin-le, 275–77, 684.

On Sunday the work of firing the suburbs continued. "Flames sprang up with fearful grandeur" as the French destroyed the hongs of the Chinese wholesale merchants. The British brought up gunboats to rake the Taiping positions.

But on Monday the Taipings approached again. "It was really a curious sight to see them moving along one of the little paths which run parallel to the city walls, each man carrying a little flag, and all moving in Indian file, but in excellent order, and quite calm and steady. On they came without hesitation, perfectly within range. . . ." The Western forces subjected the rebels to a "heavy fire" but "strange to say, scarcely a shot was returned."

The account of the events of the eighteenth and after in the *North China Herald* added to the picture in the official report:

When it was discovered that they were real rebels, orders were given to fire on them. They waved the hand, begged our officers not to fire, and stood there motionless, wishing to open communication and explain their object. No notice was taken of this, but a heavy fire of rifle and grape was kept up on them. . . .

After they had been driven back, the French soldiers rushed frantically among the peaceful inhabitants of the place, murdering men, women and children without the least discrimination. One man was stabbed right through as he was enjoying his opium pipe. A woman, who had just given birth to a child, was bayoneted without the faintest provocation. Women were ravished and houses plundered. . . . Everything was taken away from the poor people, who were trying to escape, and thrown into a heap. . . .

After this sort of work had been going on for some time, the beautiful temple of the "Queen of Heaven" was set on fire by the French.

The burning of the Southern and Western suburbs by the English, and the greater part of the Eastern suburb by the French, has deprived thousands. . . .

When the British and French resumed shelling the next day, the Taipings "stood it for several hours like men of stone, immovable, without returning a single shot," but at length shells from the gunboats "started them fairly."

Ward, on the eve of departure, played a minor role in the Shanghai action. His force was in a sorry state, but he gathered a handful of men and volunteered their services.

On the eighteenth, after they had first been fired on, the rebels encountered a missionary, a Reverend Milne. They sent him to the city with an escort to protect him from stragglers. Once Milne was within the gate, British soldiers shot down the Taiping guards. Major Charles Gordon of the Royal Engineers, later "Chinese Gordon" and Ward's successor, noted basketfuls of rebel heads suspended from the city walls.

Following the Taiping retreat from Shanghai, one of Li Xiucheng's orders was found posted on a village Catholic church:

> Now it is ordained that not the minutest particle of foreign property is to be injured. The veteran soldiers are supposed to be acquainted with the Heavenly religion, that foreigners together with the subjects of the Heavenly dynasty all worship God and equally reverence Jesus, and that all are regarded as brethren. . . .

The British and French commands in Shanghai for some time looked upon Ward's force with professional disdain and with resentment of its open practice of recruiting deserters. Ward was called an upstart, a buccaneer, and a filibuster. Shortly after Ward returned from abroad in the spring of 1861, Admiral Sir James Hope had him seized and confined aboard one of the ships of the British squadron. But with the help of his influential Chinese backers, Ward was able to obtain his release by claiming he was a naturalized Chinese.

The Tianjin treaties, already written at the time of the Shanghai events of August 1860, sealed the doom of the Taipings. The terms strengthened the key Western control of import tariffs, legalized the opium trade (which the victorious rebels would have extirpated), extorted a substantial indemnity, and opened additional areas, including the Yangtze valley, to Western economic penetration. Even as the Taipings were being shot down before the walls of Shanghai, Anglo-French forces in north China were thrusting these concessions down the throat of the Manchu court. A few weeks later they plundered and burned the Yuan Ming Yuan, the old Summer Palace, and its art treasures in what Lord Elgin, in command, later described as "an injudicious method of signalizing the triumph of Western civilization." Ratification of the treaties of Tianjin and Beijing followed.

Many Old China Hand merchants in the treaty ports then and later sought the "Indian solution" of direct British rule of China. Some backed the Taipings for a time for their own purpose—in the hope, not that the rebellion would triumph, but that it would break up China and prepare it for a British takeover. The more practical makers of policy under Lord Palmerston paid heed to Britain's rising manufacturing and financial interests and considered the limits to stretched-out British power and the keenness of Western rivalry in China. The decision was to support a Chinese regime too weak to deny British demands but, it was hoped, strong enough to preserve internal order—which remained the basic policy of the imperial powers, including the U.S. The treaties of Tianjin and Beijing, a triumph of that policy, turned the Taipings into a vexatious obstacle.

On October 24, the very day of the ratification of the British treaties, a missionary correspondent sent a dispatch to the *Times of India* from Shanghai taking note

> of rebels being handed over to the (Qing) imperialists for torture; of Shanghai, with its notorious execution-ground, being held by English and French troops; of a steamer manned by sailors from French ships of war, and loaded with rice, being sent to the relief of Imperialist cities; of English officers and soldiers fortifying cities and mounting guns, and instructing Tartar soldiers in fighting against the rebels; of guns being plundered from the Taipings; of duties being collected for the Imperialists. . . .

Unremitting military pressure limited the ability of the Taipings to carry out agrarian and other reforms. Mistakes and deeply rooted weaknesses had eroded their power by the time the West decided to press its intervention. The civil war seesawed for years. The modern arms of the West finally upset the protracted balance of power in the Yangtze valley.

Ward's contribution was to create a strike force that augmented the relatively small British and French military and naval forces and the Qing contingents and to devise counterinsurgency tactics that were employed with some success. Ward had finally learned he could not fight with riffraff and had been disabused by the Taiping performance of the notion that one European soldier was worth twenty Chinese. On his return in 1861 he organized a new force made up of a Chinese rank and file, American and European officers and drillmasters, a contingent of Filipinos, then called Manilamen, ample artillery, and armed steamers. He clothed the Chinese troops (soon known as "false foreign devils") in Zouave-like uniforms and armed them with a mixture of Prussian and Enfield rifles and Sharp's carbines, some supplied by the British. Good pay was supplemented by looting opportunities.

The Taipings were tactically deft. They were generally well led. They had supporters and spies in all the villages and towns, and they moved surely and fast through the flat riverine countryside about Shanghai. In the words of a contemporary British journalist, "Hunting grasshoppers in a hayfield with fox-hounds would be a more sensible occupation than sending soldiers about a country intersected by a network of creeks, in the expectancy of catching swift-footed and slippery-skinned Taipings."[8]

Ward's knowledge of boats helped him. He assembled fast, shallow-draft and well-armed boats that to some extent offset the Taiping advantage of mobility. The main Taiping weakness was in weapons; they were armed largely with matchlocks, gingalls, and spears. Ward acquired Armstrong guns and other artillery, some through his father, a ships' broker in New York, and used them to batter down town gates and slaughter Taipings from a distance.

Operating in close conjunction with British, French, and Qing forces, Ward undertook to clear out all rebels within a thirty-mile radius of Shanghai. The Taipings resisted with a bravery acknowledged by their enemies. They were resilient, recapturing towns they lost, defeating Ward and later "Chinese Gordon" on a number of occasions. But they suffered enormous casualties and their overall dispositions were weakened.

Ward's force gained in reputation and Ward made himself something of a legend in his own time. He wore a tightly-buttoned frock coat, sometimes a cape, never a uniform; his black hair flowed to his shoulders, and he carried even in battle a rattan stick, never a sword or revolver.

In February 1862 an allied force that included Ward and 600 of his men crushed raw and ill-equipped Taiping levies in several encounters, victory being followed, in the words of one account, "by an orgy of wanton slaughter and pillage." The grateful Qing court heaped honors on Ward, making him a general and a mandarin with peacock's feather and naming his force the "Ever Victorious Army." Ward gained riches and, in partnership with a Chinese banker patron whose daughter he married, he engaged in lucrative commerce.

A critical defeat for the Taipings, but the end for Ward, came in the Ningbo campaign of 1862. Ningbo was the sole treaty port the

---

8. Spence, Jonathan D. *To Change China: Western Advisers in China, 1620–1960* (Boston: Little, Brown, 1969), 67–68.

Taipings had been able to seize and they had hopes that through it they could import the kind of modern arms that were giving their enemies such an advantage. But the British and French saw Ningbo in Taiping hands as a barrier to their penetration of the Yangtze valley, and in May 1862 their warships joined a Manchu fleet and land forces in driving the Taipings out of the city, which was then subjected to the usual pillage and bloodletting.

That summer Ward saw great things in store for him. He drafted plans to expand the "Ever Victorious Army" to twenty-five thousand men, and in August he proposed to the local Qing commander, Li Hongzhang, that his force join in laying siege to Nanjing itself. He asked for equal looting rights in return. But this proposition was ignored, and instead detachments of Ward's army were dispatched to Ningbo, where the Taipings were counterattacking. Ward himself and a thousand men arrived there on September 18. On the twenty-first Ward was shot while viewing Taiping positions through a telescope. He was borne unconscious by aides to *H. M. S. Hardy*, whose guns were supporting the ground attack. He died just before the following dawn, two months short of his thirty-first birthday.

When the Taipings had gained control of the lower Yangtze valley provinces of Jiangsu and Zhejiang, they sent in able administrators who reduced and simplified taxes and promoted silk and tea production. Exports through Shanghai, particularly of silk, rose dramatically.

How different the scene after the Taipings were routed! An English silk merchant who toured Jiangsu after the Qing troops and the "Ever Victorious Army" had gone through with fire and sword wrote to the Shanghai publication *Friend of China*:

> On to Changchow-fu, for 95 li, still the same howling desert, not a working soul to be seen. The depth and strength of the weeds now is prodigious. Alack, for my search for mulberry-trees! I could not see one. All are cut down, and if wood at all were seen, it was borne by hungry-looking people, propelled by soldiers who had impressed them into the wood-cutting line. It was for such a state of affairs as this, was it, that Gordon gave his talents? . . .
>
> Oh, the skulls again! From Changchow-fu to Tanyang the ground is literally white, like snow, with skulls and bones. The massacre of the unfortunate Taipings (inoffensive villagers, most likely) must have been awful. . . . I begin to think that my search for a mulberry-tree, in

what under the Taipings was a splendid silk-producing country, was useless, and I had better turn back.

Suzhou surrendered in December 1863, the Taipings and many inhabitants nevertheless being massacred there as elsewhere. A young British officer serving under Gordon related that

> the streets were inches deep with clothing, shops broken into and looted, many houses on fire, very many dead bodies of rebels, all ages and sexes, some of them half roasted, and numerous pigs feeding on them. Women and children running about the streets, screaming with terror, pursued by straggling bodies of Imperial Chinese troops maddened with lust and excitement, besmirched with blood, who were entering and looting the shops, cutting down with their sharp bill-hooked-shaped knife everyone who came their way irrespective of age and sex, and firing at random at locked doors and windows.[9]

Nanjing fell in July 1864. Hong Xiuquan, long ill, died a few days earlier. Li Xiucheng was captured outside the city soon after giving up his horse to Hong's son, and was shortly executed. Gordon and the Qing court had wanted Li brought to Peking [Beijing], and Gordon himself seems to have hoped that Li's life would be spared. Zeng Guofan and others, however, may have feared that an interrogation of Li in the capital would reveal how much they had enriched themselves in the looting of Nanjing. Zeng feared also, he wrote, "that there would be some risk of Li starving himself to death on the journey, or that a rescue might even be attempted, for this Li was extraordinarily popular with the common people."

A few months before his capture, Li wrote to some missionaries: "You foreigners are like the Manchus. You have no honor. You have deceived us."

Ward was eulogized by the Qing court and warmly praised by U.S. Commissioner Anson Burlingame in a letter to President Lincoln. An Imperial memorial directed that two temples be erected in his honor and one was actually built at Songjiang, site of his first victory and early headquarters. The inscription on the tablet over his grave there read: "A wonderful hero from beyond the seas has sprinkled China with his azure blood."

---

9. A. Egmont Hake, *Events of the Taeping Rebellion* (London: W. H. Allen 1891), 494.

Ward's riches—he was thought to be worth a quarter of a million American dollars when he was killed—quickly disappeared, looted by associates, but in 1902, after years of U.S. pressure, the Chinese government settled claims on behalf of Ward by agreeing to permit a payment of $200,000 to his sister, Elizabeth Ward, out of the Boxer Indemnity Fund. Of this, $10,000 was bequeathed to the Essex Institute in Salem where a room memorializes Ward.

Ward remained a macho figure in Shanghai's American community in the 1920s and 1930s. Periodic pilgrimages were made to the Songjiang temple. Detachments of American sailors were sent to fire volleys over his grave. The American Legion named its Shanghai post for him.

Viewing the living Ward from the Taiping side, Lindley (Lin-le) described him as the "whilom rowdie companion of ci-devant General Walker of Nicaragua memory, mercenary leader of a band of Anglo-Saxon freebooters in Manchoo pay. . . ." After Ward was killed, Lindley wrote that he was "brave and determined" and "sealed all his faults with his death, and left those who cherished his memory to regret that he had not fallen in a worthier cause."

In December 1864 the Lincoln administration reported in a message to Congress that the rebellion in China "has at last been suppressed" with "the cooperating good offices of this Government and of the Western commercial states." The United States looked forward to "the extension of our commerce" and "a more intimate intercourse with China."

A month later, speaking on a bill that would launch a mail steamship service between California and China, Congressman John Bassett Alley of Massachusetts said that the service would put New York twelve to fourteen days closer to Hongkong than London and then "We can direct and control in great degree the commerce of the world."

4. Bayard Taylor: Genteel Poetaster, China Baiter

Bayard Taylor (1825–1878) was a familiar name in the middle-class households of mid-nineteenth century America. Readers could hardly avoid him. He wrote or edited thirty-six volumes of accounts of his travels, literary criticism, essays, fiction, dramas, history and an effusion of poetry in the manner of Longfellow and Tennyson, besides many hundreds of newspaper and magazine articles and reviews.

And when he wasn't industriously writing he was often speaking. His lectures drew a crush of people and he commanded what was then the handsome sum of one hundred dollars or more for an appearance. He lived opulently on a Pennsylvania estate, his acquaintances included many of the truly talented of his generation, and toward the close of his life he was minister to Germany.

Taylor belonged to what was called "The Genteel Circle," of which, in the opinion of one critic, he was "Crown Prince." The refined versifiers with whom Taylor hobnobbed took as their models the English and New England romantics—Byron and Swinburne along with Tennyson and Longfellow. Sentimental and somewhat precious idealists, given to lofty rhetoric, remote from the earthiness of real life, Taylor and friends enjoyed during the middle decades of the century reputations beyond what their generally mediocre writings deserved. Walt Whitman, their great contemporary, had nothing but contempt for them. He called their writings "paste pot work" and asked, "Do you call these genteel little creatures American poets?"

Taylor died in 1878 and within a few years was nearly forgotten. He is barely mentioned in literary studies and none of his poems were anthologized. The critic Grant C. Knight commented that while the United States was "becoming a world power to the accompaniment of brazen imperialism and public and private rapacity . . . the genteel writers led us to tea-tables and walked us through rose gardens." Stephen Crane and others introduced a tougher poetry.

Taylor also figures unpleasantly in the history of the relations between China and the U.S. He was one of the first to argue that the inferiority and bestiality of the Chinese were so evident that they ought to be barred from our shores. He wrote this in his travel book on China,[10] which reviewers praised, and repeated it time after time on the lecture platform. A fine figure of a man, articulate, with aquiline features above a neatly trimmed beard, he brought to his racist pronouncements an appearance of respectability and literary renown.

A platform generality was "that every important triumph which man has achieved since his creation belongs to the Caucasian race." One of the particulars about the Chinese was that "their crooked eyes are typical of their crooked moral vision."

Taylor arrived in China with a letter of introduction to Humphrey Marshall, the U.S. commissioner or minister, and Marshall (later a

---

10. *A Visit to India, China, and Japan in the Year 1853* (New York and London: G. P. Putnam, 1855).

Confederate general) made him a member of the embassy and took him to Shanghai aboard the steam-frigate *Susquehanna*. He became well acquainted with two prominent missionaries serving Marshall as secretaries and interpreters, Dr. Peter Parker and S. Wells Williams, later the author of a two-volume work on China.

Williams, who had persuaded himself that God would bring good out of the Opium War, later concluded that instruction of the Chinese needed more than the Society for the Diffusion of the Gospel, saying, "I am afraid nothing short of the Society for the Diffusion of Cannon Balls will give them the useful knowledge they now require to realize their own helplessness."

Taylor arrived in the treaty port of Shanghai as the Taiping revolutionaries climaxed their sweep across south-central China by the capture of Nanjing and he accepted as true the most horrendous tales of Taiping atrocities. He delighted in the company of the foreign residents, "beyond dispute the most cheerful, social and agreeable community in China." He contrasted the large and handsome Palladian-style foreign residences along the waterfront or bund with the "disagreeable exhalations" and ugliness of the Chinese city and its inhabitants, promising to give his readers one account of the stench and no more.

These are some Taylorisms on the Chinese:
- The "stupid faces of the populace. . . . "
- The people have a sort of "listless curiosity. . . . " "The mental inertia of these people seems to be almost hopeless of improvement."
- Physically the Chinese are "totally wanting in that elegant symmetry" which marks Europeans.
- Chinese music is "dreadful discord."
- The Chinese "admire whatever is distorted or unnatural. . . "
- He quoted approvingly the Tennyson line "Better fifty years of Europe than a cycle of Cathay," and agreed with DeQuincy that to live among the Chinese is to go mad.

Taylor was welcomed aboard the steam-frigate *Mississippi* by Commodore Perry and went with him to the Ryukyus (Loochoo Islands then), the Bonins, and Japan. He was gratified to hear some Japanese samurai speak contemptuously of the Chinese deck hands.

On his return from the Perry expedition Taylor went to Guangzhou where he was splendidly entertained by the American merchants. He visited Peter Parker's hospital and was impressed, reporting that since its opening forty-nine thousand people had been admitted with generally positive results. But Taylor was "surfeited" with China and allowed himself to be taken only to several of the more important temples. His parting thrust was that China "was the very best country—to leave."

This is the summary view he set forth in his book, which he later paraphrased on the lecture platform: "It is my deliberate opinion that the Chinese are, morally, the most debased people on the face of the earth." He asserted that they were afflicted by "deeps on deeps of depravity, so shocking and horrible, that their character cannot even be hinted."

Taylor announced his "powerful aversion to the Chinese race," concluding that "their touch is pollution, and harsh as the opinion may seem, justice to our race demands that they could not be allowed to settle on our soil."

Taylor preached elegance and refinement and delighted in tales of heroism and love and sublime passions. He was distressed when his walks took him out of the rose gardens. But his racist declamations, in which he was a pioneer, contributed to the opinion that subjected Chinese in our country to persecution and abuse, to beatings and murder, and finally, as Taylor advocated, to exclusion.

5. Mark Twain's Chinese Education

Anson Burlingame, in Honolulu in 1866 on his way to resume his post of minister in Beijing, met the young Mark Twain, there on a newspaper assignment, and took a liking to him. He thought Samuel Clemens (Mark Twain's real name) a budding genius and earnestly invited him to visit him in China to get to know the country. Twain was tempted, but embarked instead on a trip to Europe and the Holy Land which provided the material for his first best-seller, *Innocents Abroad*. Literary projects, marriage, a continuing interest in Europe and his own publishing ventures seem to have crowded a trip to China out of his agenda during the late 1860s and early 1870s. He certainly kept a trip in mind, however, and in 1868 wrote to Burlingame with characteristic verve: *"Don't* neglect to refuse to keep a gorgeous secretaryship or a high interpretership for me in your geat embassy—for pilgrim as I am, I have not entirely exhausted Europe yet, and may want to converse with some of those

Kings again, by & bye."[11] Though he went abroad a number of times throughout his life, he never got to China. China and its people, however, were an important and positive influence on this giant of American literature.

Twain had a lot of bigotry in him in his early years. He grew up in the border town of Hannibal, Missouri, closer to the south than the north, and he shared its prejudices. His father and uncle owned slaves and he saw nothing wrong with that. The so-called "Know Nothing" movement, characterized by hatred of the foreign-born and Catholics, was then a national infection, and Twain was a sympathizer. Visiting New York at the age of eighteen, he wrote home that the immigrants, among them the inhabitants of Chinatown, were a "mass of human vermin." In Philadelphia, he wrote his brother, he found "abominable foreigners . . . who hate everything American."

Covering the trial of a Chinese for murder in Virginia City, Nevada, in 1863, Twain resorted to the common slurs of the time: "You see, these Chinamen are all alike, and they cannot identify each other. . . . They cannot tell each other apart. There is only one way to manage this thing with strict equity: hang the gentle Chinamen promiscuously until Justice is served."

But as Twain matured, he changed, not all at once and not without backsliding and a few enduring prejudices. In what may be called his middle phase, he clung to his feelings of superiority over the foreign-born and Blacks, but at the same time was upset by mistreatment of them. "I am not fond of Chinamen, but I am less fond of seeing them wronged and abused," he said.

Time and again he used his pointed pen to decry instances of such injustice. He recalled in his autobiography years later that one Sunday afternoon in San Francisco he saw "some hoodlums chasing and stoning a Chinaman who was heavily laden with the weekly wash of his Christian customers, and I noticed that a policeman was observing this performance with an amused interest—nothing more." He sent an account of the incident, written with "considerable warmth and holy indignation," to the *San Francisco Call*, but the editor refused to publish it.

Twain was accustomed to feather his arrows with humor, often sardonic, and in 1870 he penned his notable "Disgraceful Persecution

11. Twain to Burlingame, February 19, 1868, *Mark Twain's Letters*, vol. 2, Harriet Elinor Smith and Richard Bucci, eds. (Berkeley, Ca.: University of California Press, 1990), 186.

of a Boy." How could a "sunny-hearted" boy be punished for stoning Chinese when the great state of California imposed unlawful taxes on Chinese miners, often collecting twice, and when "so strong is the wild, free love of justice in the hearts of the people that whenever any secret or mysterious crime is committed, they say 'Let justice be done, though the heavens fall,' and go straightway and swing a Chinaman."

The lad had learned, Twain summed up, "that a Chinaman had no rights that any man was bound to respect; that he had no sorrows that any man was bound to pity; that neither his life nor his liberty was worth the purchase of a penny when a white man needed a scapegoat." So tripping along to Sunday school, the boy said to himself, "Ah, there goes a Chinaman: God will not love me if I do not stone him."

Mark Twain also used fictional Chinese characters to advance understanding of the Chinese. In a series in *Galaxy* magazine an immigrant named Ah Song Hi comes to America full of high hopes, but in San Francisco is beaten, robbed, arrested, and jailed for ten days—misadventures taken straight from reality, Twain tells his readers.

Twain's deep-seated concern for justice and his observations led him gradually to abandon his racist prejudices. Commenting on the so-called Burlingame Treaty with China in 1868, Twain wrote that "the idea of seeing a Chinaman a citizen of the United States would have been almost appalling to me a few years ago but I suppose I can live with it now." The Chinese were a hard-working, peaceable people and "remarkably quick and intelligent." Why then should they not be citizens? One of Twain's most popular books, *Roughing It*, published in 1872, has a chapter titled "The Gentle, Inoffensive Chinese." The first group of Chinese to come to study in America were settled in Hartford, Connecticut, where Mark Twain lived. When the program was threatened, Twain wrote to his friend President Ulysses S. Grant, a recent China visitor, and persuaded him to intercede.

Twain had an abiding admiration for Anson Burlingame and eulogized him when he died in 1870 at the age of forty-nine. "America lost a son and all the world a servant." In his autobiography, Twain wrote that Burlingame did not serve his country alone but China as well. "He held the balances even." Such sentiments helped Mark Twain to mistakenly conclude that the Burlingame Treaty would end at last the injustices inflicted upon the

Chinese. In fact, with the Exclusion Act barring Chinese immigration, things got worse; Twain denounced that affront to Chinese.

As Twain's thinking about Chinese became sensible, so did his attitude toward Blacks, then called Negroes. The idea of their becoming citizens "was startling and disagreeable to me, but I have become reconciled to it. . . . I am ready now for all comers." To assuage his feelings of guilt he later sent a Black youth through Yale University Law School.

In the latter decades of the century, the United States became a leading industrial power and joined Britain, France, Germany, and Russia in a contentious scramble for possessions, markets, investment opportunities, and power. Mark Twain observed developments with mounting dismay. As early as 1868, in appraising the Burlingame Treaty, he commented critically on the territorial concessions the imperial powers were wresting from China:

> The foreigners residing upon these tracts create courts of justice, orga-nize police forces, and govern themselves by laws of their own. . . . Again, these foreign communities took it upon themselves to levy taxes upon Chinamen residing upon their so-called "concessions," and enforce their collection. Perhaps these Chinamen were just as well governed as they would have been anywhere in China . . . but the principle was wrong. The municipal councils which taxed these Chinamen were composed altogether of foreigners, so there was taxation without representation—a policy which we fought seven long years to overthrow.

Five years later, writing in the *New York Herald* in 1873, he was caustic about the impending annexation of the Hawaiian Islands: "We can furnish them with some Jay Goulds who will do away with old-time notions that stealing is not respectable. . . . We can make that bunch of sleepy islands the hottest corner on earth. . . . "

Naturally sympathetic with the Cuban people oppressed by their Spanish rulers, Twain at first was all for the Spanish-American War of 1898, but reversed himself when the war plainly became an imperialist venture. He was outraged by the American betrayal of Emilio Aguinaldo in the Philippines and was at his most scathing in *A Defense of General Funston* and other polemics. He signed the 1901 manifesto of the Anti-Imperialist League and its second declaration of February, 1902, and erupted in print, even writing thunderous new stanzas for *Battle Hymn of the Republic:*

> Mine eyes have seen the orgy of the launching of the Sword;
> He is searching out the hoardings where the strangers' wealth is
> stored;
> He has loosed his fateful lightning, and with woe and death has
> scored;
> His lust is marching on.

Mark Twain expressed his disrespect for the powers in comments like this one in *Tom Sawyer Abroad:* "I asked Tom if countries always apologized when they had done wrong, and he says: 'Yes, the little ones does.' "

The Boxer Movement brought north China to turmoil, and Twain, unswayed by the fact that American troops joined in the international intervention in 1900 to suppress the uprising, was one of a very few distinguished Americans to side with the Boxers. "My sympathies are with the Chinese," he wrote to Joseph Twichell in 1900. "They have been villainously dealt with by the sceptered thieves of Europe, and I hope they will drive all foreigners out and keep them out for good. I only wish it; of course I don't really expect it."

But he added prophetically that in the end "China will go free and save herself."

Addressing the Lotus Club that same year, Twain argued:

> Why shouldn't all the foreign powers withdraw from China and leave her free to attend to her own business? . . . As far as America is concerned, we don't allow the Chinese to come here, and we should be doing the graceful thing to allow China to decide whether she will allow us to go there. China never wanted any foreigners, and when it comes to a settlement of this immigrant business, I am with the Boxer every time. . . . The Boxer is a patriot; he is the only patriot China has, and I wish him success.

If *Huckleberry Finn* is Mark Twain's greatest work of fiction, "To the Person Sitting in Darkness" is the most powerful of his many indictments of imperialism. Written in heat, it brought him a storm of abuse. A friend he met on the street suggested he hang himself and save the public the trouble. But a good number of those who read the February 1901 issue of the *North American Review* were shaken and some became converts to the cause of anti-imperialism.

"Shall we? Shall we go on conferring our Civilization upon the peoples that sit in darkness," Twain asked, "or shall we give those poor things a rest?"

Taking note of the Russian killings of Chinese in Manchuria, Twain wrote:

> And perhaps [the Person Sitting in Darkness] is saying to himself: "It is yet *another* Civilized Power, with its banner of the Prince of Peace in one hand and its loot basket and its butcher knife in the other. Is there no salvation for us but to adopt Civilization and lift ourselves down to its level?"

The papers had run a dispatch from China reporting that the Rev. William Ament of the American Board of Foreign Missions had collected an indemnity of 300 taels for each of the one hundred Chinese Christians the board said had been killed by the Boxers— and imposed fines amounting to thirteen times the indemnity, this to be "used for the propagation of the Gospel."

"Glad tidings . . . ," Twain began. He complimented Reverend Ament for representing the American spirit, especially the spirit of the oldest Americans, the Pawnees, who held that it was better that ninety and nine innocent should suffer than that one guilty person escape. What matter if women and children had to starve to raise the blood money squeezed out of impoverished peasants, inasmuch as the proceeds were to be "used for the propagation of the Gospel"? The collection, and the words explaining it, were a "hideous blasphemy," Twain wrote. He broadened his target to embrace all missionary collusion with imperialism.

In his "The United States of Lyncherdom," Twain called on missionaries to come home and preach to the mobs lynching Blacks: "O kind missionary, O compassionate missionary, leave China, come home and convert these Christians."

Twain worked up a statistical argument from data cited by the *London Times* correspondent in Beijing, Dr. George Morrison

(Wangfujing, a major Beijing shopping street, was formerly Morrison Street).

With 1,511 of them out there converting two Chinamen apiece per annum against an uphill birth rate of 33,000 pagans per day, it will take upward of a million years to make the conversions balance the output and bring the Christianizing of the country in sight to the naked eye; therefore, if we can offer our missionaries as rich a field at home at lighter expense and quite as satisfactory in the matter of danger, why shouldn't they find it fair and right to come back and give us a trial? The Chinese are universally conceded to be excellent people, honest, honorable, industrious, trustworthy, kind-hearted, and all that—leave them alone, they are plenty good enough just as they are; and besides, almost every convert runs a risk of catching our civilization.

Mark Twain did what he could with his pen and from the lecture platform for China in a painful time, and China has repaid him in the only way that meant anything to him: It has put his great works in its language and many of its people are his readers. Lu Xun, China's greatest writer in the period that began with the May 4th Movement (1919), explained in his introduction to the Chinese translation of Mark Twain's *Eve's Diary* that Mark Twain "had become a humorist because he had to live. However, resentment and satire figure in his humor. This was because he was not willing to be servile."

6. Herbert Hoover and the Kaiping Mines Swindle

Herbert Hoover, later the thirty-first president of the United States, arrived with his wife Lou Henry Hoover in Beijing in March 1899 after a honeymoon voyage from San Francisco. Two important jobs awaited him. He was to serve the recently established Bureau of Mines of Zhili (now Hebei) Province as consulting engineer, and he was to be the representative of Bewick, Moreing and Company of London, an international mining firm.

It was an era in which, as Hoover biographer David Burner wrote, foreigners "stole from the Celestial Kingdom everything from temple bells to whole provinces,"[12] and hindsight suggests that Hoover had already been instructed by his London employers to attempt one of the grandest of grand larcenies: A British takeover of the Chinese Engineering and Mining Company, owner of the vast Kaiping coal fields near Tangshan, northeast of Tientsin [Tianjin]. While still aboard ship Hoover wrote that he expected "to conduct some negotiations of considerable character."

At twenty-five, Hoover was a graduate of the then newly founded Stanford University, where he had studied geology and mining. Bewick, Moreing and Company had hired him in 1897 and sent him to the gold fields of western Australia. His performance, which included a reduction of the miners' wages and a lengthening of hours, had impressed Charles Algernon Moreing and Hoover's other superiors. Moreing hunted tigers enthusiastically in Manchuria in 1898, but that was only diversion from his attentions to the Kaiping mines, a highly profitable enterprise despite corrupt management. He had held fruitful discussions with Zhang Yanmao, a mandarin of the first class with peacock feather who was both director-general of the mining company and commissioner of the Bureau of Mines. Moreing persuaded Zhang that infighting among the European bondholders could be checked, and hopes of enticing additional foreign investment served, by employment of a foreign engineer. He argued that an American would be most agreeable to all parties, saying that he had a suitable person in mind. Hoover was summoned to London and given his assignments, for which he was to receive salaries coming close to $20,000 a year. He was well on the way to becoming, if he was not already, what the San Francisco *Chronicle* admiringly called him in October 1901: "the highest-salaried young mining engineer in the world."

Hoover was rarely idle. With a quickly recruited staff of Australian and American engineers, he stepped up the work of modernizing Chinwangtao [Qinhuangdao], the ice-free port serving the Kaiping mines. He suggested changes in the Chinese mining law, calculated to make foreign investment more attractive, but the Chinese court had already turned away from Western-inspired reformism. And he saw a lot of northern China.

---

12. David Burner, *Herbert Hoover: A Public Life* (New York: Knopf, 1979), 35. In addition to Burner's biography and the other published works cited below, information on Hoover's China experience is drawn from material in the collection at the Hoover Institute at Stanford University; Alfred Williamson's informed article, "Herbert Hoover in China: How the Chinese Lost the Kailan Mines," in *China Today,* January 1935, and from the 1928 *Congressional Record:* Senate, 3664–3667, 7426, and House, 3825–3827.

Zhang Yanmao was convinced that Hoover—Hu Hua, he called him—had a nose for underground riches, especially gold, and he promoted him to chief engineer and sent him on a series of prospecting expeditions, northeast into Jehol (now part of Inner Mongolia) and west as far as the Gobi. Hoover saw mostly ancient mines worked to the water level, and remained forever after convinced that, apart from coal, China was poorly endowed with subterranean resources, and was therefore barred from substantial industrial development.

Hoover did locate a treasure, but it was in Burma. Among the ancient documents he had read to him was an account of a fabulously rich silver mine off the road to Mandalay. Several years later Hoover invested in it and made a fortune.

But Hoover did not take his eyes off the main chance. In June 1899, less than three months after his arrival, he boldly proposed that the Chinese Engineering and Mining Company be absorbed into a new company to be organized by Moreing. But he came on too fast, and conversations with Zhang Yanmao and his German adviser and agent, Gustav Detring, made little progress.

The Boxer uprising in the summer of 1900 ended Hoover's wanderings. Tianjin's international settlement, where the Hoovers had a large blue-brick house on Racecourse Road staffed by what Hoover called "the necessary multitude of servants," was besieged like the Legation Quarter in Beijing. For a perilous month Hoover was occupied with the construction of barricades, fire fighting, and seeing to the needs of the several thousand Chinese, Christians, and hangers-on of foreigners who took refuge in the settlement—a foretaste of the relief work that was to establish his reputation in World War I.

But the uprising, a warped and manipulated response to imperialist encroachment, which Hoover saw as "one of the blind emotional movements not unusual among the Asiatic masses," proved the key to the realization of Moreing's highest hopes. Or as biographer George H. Nash put it, "From the anarchy and torment of the Boxer Rebellion arose a shimmering opportunity and the most controversial episode of Hoover's engineering career."[13]

Russian troops occupied Qinhuangdao and the Kaiping mines; ships belonging to the Chinese Engineering and Mining Company were seized by the Germans and Americans, and Japanese took over the company's Tianjin offices. And Zhang Yanmao was in custody, charged with being a spy and facing possible execution. Under duress,

13. *The Life of Herbert Hoover: The Engineer, 1874–1914* (New York: W. W. Norton, 1983), 124.

Zhang gave power of attorney to Detring, a retired customs commissioner who had turned to promotion ("a scalawag," some called him), and he and Hoover strenuously sought to persuade Zhang that the mines were in danger of permanent seizure and that only a link with the British lion could save them. On July 30, 1900, Detring deeded the whole of the Chinese Engineering and Mining Company in trust to Hoover, who had insisted on the personal conveyance. Zhang was then absent in Shanghai; he later indignantly denied having agreed to the action. As worked out by Detring and Hoover, a new British company would be formed; the shareholders of the Chinese company would receive a minority interest in it in exchange for surrendering the company's properties and other assets.

Hoover and his wife hastened to Shanghai aboard the SS *Tsintau* registered as Mr. and Mrs. Clark (his middle name). There on August 11, the day after his twenty-sixth birthday, he sent an exultant cable to Moreing and registered his trusteeship at the British Consulate on the Bund. On August 14 he took ship for London and there laid his prize at the feet of Moreing, setting off a flurry of activity. A landing party from HMS *Aurora* occupied Qinhuangdao and hoisted the Union Jack; later an army unit was stationed there. The *London Globe* and *Westminister Gazette* launched a vigorous campaign for a British takeover of Qinhuangdao and the coal fields, which were depicted as the key to military control of north China; the editors were later paid off with shares. On October 12 Moreing, who was a member of Parliament, was received by Lord Salisbury, the foreign secretary, who promised diplomatic support.

On December 21, 1900, the Chinese Engineering and Mining Company was registered as the Chinese Engineering and Mining Company Ltd., the new owner being the Oriental Syndicate, consisting of Belgian, French, Austrian, and Italian, as well as British interests, to which Moreing had turned for capital investment. Hoover's trusteeship deed was shaky ground for such a takeover, and Hoover was sent back to China with instructions to strengthen the underpinnings—to obtain a clear transfer. He went rewarded with nearly 8,000 shares in the syndicate.

Hoover reached Tianjin during the first week of January, 1901, where he was joined by the Chevalier Edmond de Wouters, named to represent the Belgian holdings. Hoover with some difficulty won Detring's agreement to the changes, but Zhang Yanmao, with whom Detring all along had been less than candid, adamantly refused to sign the new documents. There followed four stormy days during which Hoover and associates mixed blandishments and threats.

Hoover raged at Zhang—his excitement became "dangerous," the British consul in Tianjin, C. W. Campbell, said later—and he threatened to go to the foreign ministers in the Legation Quarter and seek the intervention of the powers. Indeed, Hoover and de Wouters divided up the task of calling on the ministers, and Campbell, perhaps decisively, threatened Zhang with British action. British troops indeed occupied Qinhuangdao and the coal fields upon the withdrawal of the Russians.

Hoover's rough treatment of Zhang, who remained his implacable enemy, was in accord with a view he had expressed in a *New York Times* interview in November: "Diplomacy with an Asiatic is of no use. If you are going to do business with him you must begin your talk with a gun in your hand, and let him know that you will use it."

Zhang gave in and on February 19 signed two documents. The key one was a transfer of title which not only legitimized the takeover but enlarged the definition of the properties acquired to include the entire Kaiping basin, to which the old Chinese company had had very restricted rights. In Hoover's estimate, the company's jurisdiction was quintupled.

The second document, called the Memorandum of Agreement, recorded the blandishments. Periodically, Zhang or Detring had been promised that a Chinese board would continue in authority, but the key London-written sections of the transfer had been silent about it. The memorandum provided that the affairs of the new company were to be conducted by a London board and a Chinese board, and the latter was to manage the China operation. Zhang was to continue as director-general. The business of the company was to be conducted "in such a spirit as to make Chinese and Foreign interests harmonize on a fair basis of equality. . . ." Hoover signed along with Zhang, Detring, and de Wouters.

Hoover immediately requested that he be appointed acting general manager of the mines, but the Belgian influence was such that he had to accept de Wouters as co-manager. Given an infusion of new capital, they set about reorganizing the company and bringing it under practical foreign control. Hoover was the active administrator, and during the half-year he held the managerial post the combination of rationalization measures, new equipment, and extremely favorable market opportunities launched what was to be a long period of large profits. On June 25, 1901 Hoover reported a first-quarter profit of £41,000. The average annual profit until another reorganization in 1912 was about $850,000.

Once Zhang Yanmao had signed the transfer of title, Moreing in London—"a ruthless old villain" in the judgment of one of his leading mine managers—and Hoover and de Wouters in Tianjin began to go back on their commitments to him and his associates. In London, Moreing joined the Oriental Syndicate in executing a share bonus plan for raising capital which gave the insiders what David Burner called "indelicately large profits"—about $1,875,000 according to one report. The holders of shares in the old company were given 375,000 shares in the new one, as pledged, but, in violation of promises by Hoover and others, they were non-voting shares.

In China, Hoover and de Wouters, joined later by Emile Francqui, an agent of King Leopold, paid scant heed to the concessions to Zhang in the Memorandum of Agreement. They were soon on a collision course with Zhang, his agent Detring and the Chinese board, which was given no authority and often just ignored. Zhang and Detring believed, or wished to believe, that the Chinese Engineering and Mining Company Ltd. was a joint Anglo-Chinese enterprise; Hoover and the growing foreign staff saw London and Brussels as in command.

Methodically, Hoover acted to eliminate "ghosts" from the payroll and reduce the Chinese staff generally. He found that the title transfers had not included the port facilities at Qinhuangdao, the railroad serving them, and certain other properties. He seized them by "main force," as he wrote Moreing, March 12. Three days earlier he had written Moreing that he was giving his mine manager "complete control" free of "any interference from the Chinese board," which he likened to a comic opera. In July de Wouters informed the London board that "Mr. Hoover and myself are doing what we want, informing the Chinese board of those things it may know without danger and going squarely to the front without it when necessary." Later Hoover wrote a successor general manager of the Kaiping mines that he should simply ignore the Memorandum of Agreement.

Hoover and his wife left China for good in the fall of 1901, glad to go. He remained a director of the Chinese Engineering and Mining Company Ltd. until the major reorganization of 1912. Moreing had resigned as director four years earlier.

In an article in the *Mining Journal*, October 30, 1902, which was several times reprinted, Hoover offered this judgment of Chinese labor: "The simply appalling and universal dishonesty of the working classes, the racial slowness and the low average intelligence, gives them an efficiency far below the workmen of England and America. . . . For crude labor, such as surface excavation, [the Chinese worker] has no equal, but as we proceed up the scale of skill he falls further behind. . . ." He also ascribed to the Chinese an inability to use machines efficiently and an "innate lack of administrative ability," and he noted what he called the "mulishness of the native miner in his refusal to accept instruction."

But his main argument was that a handsome profit could be obtained from coal mines worked by men paid a pittance. "In two years these mines, with the management now installed, will prove the economic value of the cheapest labor in the world. . . ."

Writing his memoirs some years later, Hoover had not changed his view of the Chinese but more tactfully chose to accentuate the positive. The 10 percent of literate Chinese "are highly intelligent," he declared. He said he admired the Chinese for their "patience in the face of hardship" and their "fidelity to family ties," but described them as lacking a "mechanical instinct," though capable of imitating anything "if given enough time." He had grave doubts that either industrialization or democracy were in China's future.

Hoover left China with a substantial fortune. He was earning $33,000 a year as acting general manager. In addition to 8,000 shares in the Oriental Syndicate, he was given 7,500 free shares in the reorganized Chinese Engineering and Mining Company Ltd., and when the Oriental Syndicate was dissolved in 1902, his shares in it were converted to 12,200 shares in the company, with a par value of $60,000. He estimated to his brother Theodore that his assets totaled about $250,000; a *New York Sun* correspondent who was his house guest in Tianjin thought he was worth double that. Mrs. Hoover took with her a rich collection of Ming and Kangxi (Qing) porcelain, one piece of which came to be worth a reputed $100,000. By the time he left China Hoover had been made one of the four partners in Bewick, Moreing and Company, assuring him of a large income. He remained a partner until 1908, by which time he had major capital resources.

Hoover was not to escape from his depredations completely unscathed, however. The victims of imperialist pilferings in China generally had no recourse, but in the case of the Kaiping mines swindle, there existed the February 19 Memorandum of Agreement, the evidence of the bonus share rakeoff, and the letters written by Hoover, de Wouters and Moreing. Cheated and humiliated, shareholders in the former company held protest meetings in Tianjin, Shanghai and Hongkong. Charges and countercharges were aired in the Chinese and English-language press in China, and in the London press. Zhang Yanmao was sent to London to press complaints against Bewick, Moreing and Company in Chancery Court. He was a powerful man, standing over six feet (he is supposed to have scaled the Great Wall with the Emperor Guangxu strapped to his back) and, resplendent in the rich attire of a mandarin, a pearl the size of a bird's egg on his hat, he added to the drama of the international court case.

Bewick, Moreing and Company, the defendants, had long claimed that Hoover and de Wouters had not acted as their agents in signing the February 19 memorandum, which they said had "not been intended to be an agreement" and which, in any case, was "executed without the consent of the Company." But Justice Matthew Ingle Joyce, presiding, early held the view that if the memorandum were invalid, so must be the other document signed that day, the title transfer. The defense reversed itself and agreed that the memorandum was binding, offering quibbling interpretations of its meaning and claiming that difficult circumstances had made its full execution impossible. Hoover, who lived in London (he kept a residence there until 1919), was the first principal witness. He too testified to the validity of the memorandum and persisted in claiming he had all along done his best to implement it.

The trial lasted sixteen days in January and February, 1905, generating a 634-page transcript. Illustrious attorneys were engaged by both parties—among them a future Lord Chief Justice and a Lord Chancellor. The proceedings were reported in detail in the press, particularly in the *London Times* and *Financial Times;* Edward VII followed them with avid interest.

Justice Joyce found for Zhang Yanmao, ruling that the memorandum was legally binding and that its terms had been violated by Bewick, Moreing and Company. He directed the firm to pay the plaintiff's court costs and declared that if the terms of the memorandum were not honored within a reasonable time, "this Court ought to do what it can to restore to the Plaintiff's the mines and properties. . . ." He said also that while the 1901 refinancing operation was not an issue before him, the evidence indicated that the Chinese shareholders were probably defrauded.

But Zhang's victory was very limited. Justice Joyce denied claims for damages, and the underlying reality was that the Chancery Court had no way of enforcing its decisions in China. Nor did the Court of Appeals, which substantially upheld Justice Joyce's decision. China took another route in seeking satisfaction. Viceroy Yuan Shikai organized a rival company, the Lanchow Company, and gave it major access to north China coal reserves. However, the 1912 reorganization established British hegemony and the Lanchow Company was brought into the Kailan Mining Administration along with the

Chinese Engineering and Mining Company Ltd. Zhang Yanmao received a payoff of $750,000. The Kailan Mining Administration remained British and profitable until after the Japanese invasion of 1937.

In a pre-trial affidavit in November, 1904, in which he opposed the calling of certain former associates as witnesses, Hoover said that "this action . . . involved the most serious allegations against myself personally." He was rightly concerned. Justice Joyce found persuasive evidence that Hoover had obtained the memorandum and title transfer by threats and misrepresentations, and he noted Hoover's admission that he had forcefully seized title deeds. His verdict contradicted Hoover's assertion that he had faithfully sought to execute the memorandum. The trial, in the words of David Burner, "gave Hoover for a time a somewhat unfavorable reputation in the City, the financial center of London."

In 1920, having gained an international reputation through relief work, and thinking of public office, Hoover began an extraordinary and costly effort to blur and falsify the record of the trial. He vainly sought statements exonerating him from Justice Joyce and a surviving prosecutor, and in 1921 instructed his London solicitor to "spare no expense or effort" to purchase all existing copies of the trial transcript. Burner's biography indicates that Hoover thought he had succeeded, but in fact his agents were unable to obtain the copy in the Bodleian Library at Oxford. In the early 1930s the publisher of a critical book about Hoover observed in a foreword that, trying to check on certain accusations, "At many sources we came only to find that someone had been there before us, going over the hard-beaten track of Mr. Hoover's past, and taking up, buying up, and otherwise obliterating important records."[14]

In his memoirs, Hoover permitted himself the fabrication that he had staunchly upheld the memorandum and indeed had left China because Emile Francqui insisted on violating it. But in the main he defended himself through others, engaging Arthur Train, a prominent New York attorney, to represent him on his China past as early as 1920.

According to George H. Nash, testimonials "were a favorite device of Hoover's as he strove to refute criticisms of his conduct in China. Although drafted in a form that suggested spontaneity, most of them—perhaps all—were solicited and, in some cases at least, prob-

---

14. John Hamill, *The Strange Career of Mr. Hoover Under Two Flags* (New York: William Faro, 1931), 5. The publisher commented that much Hoover material had disappeared even from the New York Public Library.

ably ghost-written or approved by Hoover himself." Nash observed that Hoover personally edited Arthur Train's whitewash, *The Strange Attacks on Herbert Hoover,* and went to "extraordinary lengths" to obtain adulatory rhetoric from Tang Shaoyi, a former premier of China.[15]

Hoover had reason to congratulate himself on his efforts. Although his connection with the Kaiping mines swindle and his role in the trial were repeatedly aired during his campaign for the presidency in 1928 and again in the 1930s, scores of articles and statements succeeded to a considerable extent not only in countering criticisms of him but in portraying him as the champion of Zhang Yanmao and the rights of the Chinese. Train wrote that at the trial, "Mr. Hoover was an important, if not the only important witness, and largely by virtue of his testimony the Chinese were able to establish their contentions."

But the reality was expressed at the time of the swindle by Britain's charge d'affaires in Beijing, Arthur Townley. With the help of a Yankee, he said, an Anglo-Belgian gang had "fleeced" the Chinese, and Moreing and associates "had made a pretty pile at their expense."

7. Ezra Pound's Chinese Translucencies

> The blossoms of the apricot
>   flow from the east to the west
> And I have tried to keep them from falling
> CANTO XIII

Ezra Pound was a convert to Confucianism and otherwise a reactionary eccentric, but a true poet and doer of some commendable literary deeds, among them admirable renderings of Chinese poems into English. Pound made many linguistic mistakes and took bold liberties for creative reasons and to avoid the kind of line that requires a footnote. The results are less than translations—and more, too. They are poems themselves. T. S. Eliot called them "translucencies."

Pound's hookup with China (he never actually got there) began early in his long career. In the British Museum he happened upon James Legge's translation of Confucius, and not being able to afford

---

15. *The Life of Herbert Hoover,* 656–59.

the book copied off passages to serve reflection. Later he or his wife bought a cheap Shanghai edition.

Over the years Pound absorbed a great deal of eighteenth-century Europe's idealization of China's empire and culture. His increasingly jaundiced view of his own times made congenial a system of thought that pointed back to a better past. He said once that Voltaire did just right to end his History of Louis XIV with a chapter on China. He took as his own motto that which a Chinese emperor was said to have engraved on his bath-tub: "Make it new . . . day by day make it new." And he put Confucianism, the Chinese landscape, snippets of Chinese poems, and even ideograms into twelve of the *Cantos,* (XIII, XLIX and LII–LXI),[16] his master work, a learned, patchily superb effort to sum up human experience and cultures.

The ideograms declared the existence of a great, very different language with a capacity to convey compactly shadings of meaning. But more than that they were a manifesto of Pound's developed poetic method. The spare syntax of the Chinese language—the minimal connecting words between words with real meaning—excited him and moved him to emulation in his own language. In the *Cantos,* James Laughlin has observed, "Words, phrases, whole sentences become 'ideograms' that are placed together without the usual connectives. These disjuncts, treated like collage in painting, work on one another to show relationships that enlarge the total meaning of the passage." China is in not just twelve of the *Cantos,* but throughout the total of 117.

In *Canto XLIX* Pound juxtaposes landscape scenes and a succinct description of countryside labors—four lines of four ideograms each—and compares the abuses of the state to the three-bodied monster, Geryon, slain by Hercules. Some lines:

> Wild geese swoop to the sand-bar,
> Clouds gather about the hole of the window
> Broad water; geese line out with the autumn
> Rooks clatter over the fishermen's lanthorns,
> A light moves on the north sky line;
> where the young boys prod stones for shrimp. . . .
>
> Sun up; work
> sundown; to rest
> dig well and drink of the water

---

16. *Cantos of Ezra Pound* (New York: New Directions, 1970).

dig field; eat of the grain
Imperial power is? and to us what is it?
The fourth; the dimension of stillness.
And the power over wild beasts.

But before the *Cantos* came *Cathay*.[17] In 1913 the widow of Ernest Fenollosa picked Pound, whose poems she had read in Harriet Monroe's *Poetry* magazine, to be her husband's literary executor. Fenollosa, of Portuguese extraction, was a Harvard graduate from Salem who went to Tokyo in 1878 as a teacher of rhetoric. There he undertook a study of Japanese art and literature at a time when they were being slighted by Japanese modernizers. He was eventually appointed Imperial Commissioner of Art and divided his later years between Japan and the Boston Museum of Fine Arts, which houses the Fenollosa-Weld Oriental Art Collection. He died in 1908 and lies buried near Lake Biwa. Among Fenollosa's papers (now in the Yale University Library) Pound found notebooks filled with transcriptions and translations of Tang poetry and some of the odes from the *Shi Jing* (Book of Songs), rendered literally with the aid of Japanese scholars. He turned eighteen of them into poems and collected them in *Cathay*, a two-shilling pamphlet published in Venice in 1915.

Fresh images and rhythms and astringent touches at a time when English poetry needed a fresh start brought praise from many quarters which has continued through the years. T. S. Eliot called Pound "the inventor of Chinese poetry for our time," and Carl Sandburg, suggesting that Pound was probably "the world's champion poet," said that reading *Cathay* made one realize "the closeness of the Chinese soul as a next-door human neighbor." Owning *Cathay*, "you need no porcelains," Robert Fitzgerald wrote in 1941. Michael Reek, one of the few to have examined Fenollosa's notebooks, concluded that "Pound worked a miracle in turning Fenollosa's sprawling lines into coruscant and durable poetry, without sacrificing their sense." An indirect form of praise was a good deal of poetic Chinoiserie by Amy Lowell, who railed at Pound, and others.

Ford Maddox Ford called the *Cathay* poems "things of supreme beauty" at the time of publication and a decade later was even more effusive. *Cathay* is "the most beautiful volume of poems in the world," he wrote, citing these lines from "The Bridge at Ten-Shin" by Li Bai (Li Po):

---

17. Poems quoted from *Cathay* appear in Pound's *Personae* (New York: New Directions, 1926).

March has come to the bridge head
Peach boughs and apricot boughs hang over a thousand gates,
At morning there are flowers to cut the heart,
And evening drives them on the eastward-flowing waters,
Petals are on the gone waters and on the going,
   and on the back-swirling eddies,
But today's men are not the men of the old days,
Though they hang in the same way over the
   bridge rail. . . .

Nearly six decades after publication of *Cathay*, John Gayley, an English critic and translator of Chinese poetry, wrote that it is "still, arguably, the best English poetry inspired by Chinese originals to date. . . . "

Cathay was an immediate success also because of its subject material and timing. World War I was turning from nationalist exhilaration into carnage and the themes of many of Pound's selections from Fenollosa—partings, long separations, perilous travel, frontier soldiering—were appropriate. The sculptor Henri Gaudier-Brzeska wrote from the Marne shortly before he was killed that he kept a copy of *Cathay* (it weighed two ounces) in his pocket and read it aloud to keep up the spirits of the men in his unit. "The poems depict our situation in a wonderful way," he wrote Pound. Standing in trench mud, men listened to Li Bai's eighth century *Lament of the Frontier Guard*, which includes these lines:

By the North gate, the wind blows full of sand,
Lonely from the beginning of time until now!
Trees fall, and the grass goes yellow with autumn
I climb the towers and towers to watch the barbarous
Desolate castle, the sky, the wide desert
There is no wall left to this village.
Bones white with a thousand frosts.

A writer could no more avoid Pound's influence than a traveler could walk untouched through a blizzard, Ernest Hemingway wrote. Pound had blue-penciled *In Our Time* and helped to get it published. Some of the *Cathay* poems foretell the later poems of Eliot (who dedicated *The Waste Land* to Pound), MacLeish (especially

"Conquistador") and many others, and a succession of "Ands" points to Hemingway—these lines from *The Exile's Return*, for example:

> And what with the broken wheels and so on,
> I won't say it wasn't hard going
> Over roads twisted like sheep's guts.
> And I was still going, late in the year,
> in the cutting wind from the North,
> And thinking how little you cared for the cost,
> and you caring enough to pay for it.
> And what a reception:
> Red jade cups, food well set on a blue jewelled table,
> And I was drunk, and had no thought of returning.

Pound knew no Chinese whatsoever when he put together *Cathay*, but he took up the study of it with the help of Morrison's dictionary. In later years he translated various writings of Confucius and Mencius into English and Italian—using them also as raw material for the *Cantos*, in which he sought to sum up the Chinese social experience as he understood it.

Pound, a cultural internationalist, was especially drawn to China for two reasons. He admired the Confucian governance of the long imperial era, and his love of China's poetry deepened the more he studied the ideograms. Although, influenced by Fenollosa, he at first exaggerated their pictorial aspect, they strengthened his imagist bent. China, like Greece, could inspire a Western renaissance, Pound thought. He was delighted when *Cathay* was translated into modern Greek. And his fascination was noted mockingly by James Joyce, who in *Anna Livia Plurabelle* concocted the words "taishantyland" and "maundarin."

In adversity after World War II, in which he was a Rome radio propagandist, Pound clung to China. His battered copy of Legge was one of the two books he had with him while he was confined by the U.S. Army in a cage made of airstrip landing mats, later in a tent, near Pisa. The second book was a pocket anthology of poetry he found in the latrine. He had been grappling with a translation of Mencius when the soldiers came for him. Confined, writing *Cantos* with a pencil stub, he called the mountain he looked out on Taishan, one of China's five sacred mountains.

And later, in St. Elizabeth's Hospital for the Insane in Washington, D.C., he turned to translating the 305 odes of the *Book of Songs*, a collection of ballads, folk songs, narrative verse, and temple hymns, originally set to music, that date from the eleventh to sixth centuries B.C. He went about it by reading other translations, probably Arthur Waley's, pondering the original characters, and reaching for re-creative words, devices, and cadences. Pound had within him an organ with many pedals, and while some of his renderings did not come off, many did, and a scattering come close to being reincarnations.

A comparison of Waley's generally praised versions of the odes[18] with Pound's suggests the differences between translations and translucencies—the differences, in Gayley's view, between "tame infelicities" and the "quirky but inspired vision of one of our greatest modern poets." Waley translated Ode 20, about a woman looking for a man, this way:

> Plop fall the plums, but there are still seven
> Let those gentlemen that would court me
> Come while it is still lucky!
>
> Plop fall the plums; there are still three.
> Let any gentlemen that would court me
> Come before it is too late!
>
> Plop fall the plums, in shallow baskets we lay them.
> Any gentleman who would court me
> Had better speak while there is time.

And this is what Pound wrought of it:

> Oh soldier, or captain
> Seven plums on the high bough,
> plum time now,
> seven left here, "Ripe," I cry.
>
> "No plums now," I cry, I die.
> On this bough
> Be no plums now.

Ode 124 is about a woman who lost her husband in a seventh century B.C. war. This is Waley's version:

---

18. *Book of Songs: The Ancient Chinese Classic of Poetry* (New York: Grove Press, 1987).

The cloth-plant grew until it covered the
    thorn bush;
The bindweed spread over the wilds.
My lovely one is here no more.
With whom? No, I sit alone.

The cloth-plant grew till it covered the
    brambles;
The bindweed spread across the borders
    of the field.
My lovely one is here no more.
With whom? No, I lie down alone.
The horn pillow so beautiful,
The worked coverlet so bright!
My lovely one is here no more.
With whom? No, alone I watch till dawn.

Summer days, winter nights—
Year after year of them must pass
Till I go to him where he dwells.
Winter nights, summer nights—
Year after year of them must pass
Till I go to his home.

Quoting Pound's rendering, William Cookson concludes that "A
Chaucerian clarity, robustness and humor pervades the anthology.
With the possible exception of *Cathay*, these are Pound's finest
translations." This is what Pound did with Ode 124:

Creeper grows over thorn,
bracken wilds over waste, he is gone.
Gone and I am alone.

Creeper overgrow thorn,
bracken spreads over the grave, he is gone.
Gone, I am alone.

The horn pillow is white like rice,
the silk shroud gleams as if with tatters of fire.
In the sunrise, I am alone.

A summer's day,
winter's night, a hundred years
and we come to one house together.

Winter's day, summer's night,
each night as winter night,
each day long as of summer,
but at last to the one same house.

Ode 242 is about a tower or castle, a holy place, built by a Zhou dynasty ruler near what is now Xi'an. This is Pound's creation:

Great drums and gongs
hung on spiked frames
sounding the perfect rule and rote
about the king's calm crescent moat.

Tone unto tone, of drum and gong.

About the king's calm crescent moat
the blind musicians beat the lizard skin
as the tune weaves out and in.

Pound's imaginative rendition of a segment of Ode 189 reminds us that the treatment of females as inferior has a long history:

Bears be for boys; snakes, girls.
boys shall have beds, hold sceptres for their toys,
creep on red leather,
bellow when they would cry
in embroidered coats
ere come to Empery.
Small girls shall sleep on floor and play with tiles,
wear simple clothes and do no act amiss,
cook, brew and seemly speak,
conducing so the family's quietness.

In 1958 Cookson wrote to Pound that it would be difficult to gather a body of poetry in any language that for wisdom and beauty would stand against his translations from the *Book of Songs*. When they met, Pound told him that the work of translation had saved him from madness in St. Elizabeth's Hospital.

But Pound's reactionary ideas and plain wrongheadedness warped and limited his poetic reach. They crippled the *Cantos* and kept him from discovering that China was more than Confucian elitism—from taking to heart the lamentations and social protests in the *Book of Songs*, from grasping the second line of these two by Li Bai's great friend Du Fu:

> At the vermillion gates the smell of meat and wine,
> On the road the bones of those frozen to death.

But this new period of China accessibility is an invitation to those who have Pound's poetic skills, or something approximate, and who see China as it is—a complexity but a testament to populist creativity. Some forty thousand poems are extant from the Tang dynasty alone, and many thousands more have been inspired by the century of revolution—treasures awaiting poetic transformation.

8. Frank Meyer, Plant Hunter

American flora of all regions has been enormously enriched by trees and plants from China, and one of those who did the great work of transmittal was Frank N. Meyer. Sent by the U.S. Department of Agriculture, he made four expeditions to China and bordering areas over a thirteen-year period. He walked, climbed, and rode donkey-back thousands of miles and himself packed hundreds of bundles of cuttings and roots and thousands of bales of seeds, resulting in some 2,500 plant introductions. Much of what he sent he never saw grown to maturity; he drowned in the Yangtze on June 1, 1918.

In the words of Meyer's biographer, Isabel Shipley Cunningham,

> his contribution changed the landscape and improved the economy of the United States. Today Americans eat foods and enjoy the shrubs he found in Asia; from the Dakotas to Texas his elms serve as windbreaks on formerly treeless prairies; and, perhaps most important of all, plant breeders are still using the genes that his introductions added to

America's crop germplasm in order to produce better grains, fruits, vegetables, and ornamentals.[19]

Meyer was a Dutchman who migrated to the United States, worked in hothouses, nurseries, and botanical gardens in California, Missouri and Washington, D.C., and became a naturalized citizen. The wide range of his experience and his reputation as a tireless walker got him the job of agricultural explorer.

His first expedition began in 1905. For three years he explored in Hebei, Shandong and Shanxi provinces and the lower Yangtze valley. He began by following basket carriers of persimmons out of Beijing back to orchards in the valley of the Ming tombs and there gathered scions of the Tampopan variety of persimmon. It was grown successfully in the Carolinas.

The second expedition began in Siberia and the Caucasus, and continued into Xinjiang (Chinese Turkestan) and Mongolia. Despite backward transport, Meyer was able to get some live shipments of cuttings and seeds out of Xinjiang to their destination. He was the first foreign explorer to do so.

A much more productive expedition began in 1913. For another three-year period, Meyer searched a swath of territory from Shandong to Gansu and the border of Tibet. Before sailing for home he explored in Jiangsu and Zhejiang. One important find after another rewarded his arduous travel.

Meyer came to China for the last time in 1916. He collected seeds of the wild pear in Chengde, north of Beijing, and then came south to the Yangtze valley and worked there until his death in the river.

Meyer loved what he was doing. He searched indefatigably and was filled with joy when he made a discovery. A venerable juniper awed him. The sight of a handsome grove made him forget privation: "I felt good and at peace with the whole creation." He himself made sure the packing moss was neither too wet nor too dry and did much of the wrapping in oiled paper and cloth. He made the copper labels and sat up nights in wretched inns preparing meticulous records. Such records were the basis of his 1911 publication, *Chinese*

19. *Frank N. Meyer, Plant Hunter in Asia* (Ames, Iowa: Iowa State University Press, 1984), 5–6. I was first drawn to Meyer by two articles by David Fairchild, his supervisor at the Foreign Seed and Plant Introduction Service: "A Hunter of Plants," *National Geographic*, July 1919, and "An Agricultural Explorer in China," *Asia*, January 1921. I am grateful to the U.S. Department of Agriculture for supplying me with information and a rare photograph of Meyer in China.

Plant Names, in which names are listed in English, Latin, and Chinese.

Though Meyer's China experience was in the wild, he was enraptured by Chinese gardens. "In an old Chinese garden there is far more imagination, more mystery, and more detail than in any Western garden," he wrote from Changsha in 1917.

Meyer sent back the blight-resistant Chinese elm and Chinese chestnut at a time when these species were diseased and dying out in the United States. His contributions to the windbreaks of the Western plains included a hardy poplar and the Khotan ash as well as the elm. A hard wheat from Turkestan, a broad-leafed spinach that added hardiness and blight resistance to American varieties (its discovery was said to be worth the entire cost of the first expedition), a splendid hickory in Zhejiang that was the first found by a Westerner, a yellow rose that was soon growing in American gardens, the wild Ussurian pear, the Fei (Shandong) peach long fancied by the Imperial Palace in Beijing, dwarf lemons and a dwarf lilac, varieties of bamboo, a golden hibiscus, a columnar cedar, jujubes, a gooseberry now being studied in New Zealand, the bush almond—these are just some of Meyer's plant introductions. Cunningham lists ninety-eight important ones in an appendix to her biography.

When Meyer made his dramatic discovery of the Zhejiang hickory, he asked that it not be named for him. He believed that plant names should relate to places of origin or characteristics. Nevertheless, his name is attached to the dwarf lilac, a tall, mountain spruce, a wild cherry found in northern Korea, and an ornamental lemon.

When Meyer came upon a plant new to him, he looked hard at it, felt it all over, tasted it, and committed it to his excellent memory. He cried when bamboo seedlings, denied proper mulch upon arrival in the United States, died one after another.

Meyer shared with W. W. Rockhill, the American minister to China, a love for the white-barked pine, which is generally found only in botanical gardens in the U.S. Rockhill told him that he hoped that a white-barked pine would be planted on his grave, and it was grown from a seed sent by Meyer. Among Meyer's photos is one of a 1,500-year-old white-barked pine—"the noblest tree in the world" he called it. On another occasion he called these trees "beautiful and serene enough to worship."

Another of Meyer's favorites was the pistachio, and he photographed an ancient male specimen close to the sepulcher of Confucius. Surrounded by venerable pistachios and junipers, the memorial tablet "exhales a spirit of the gray, hoary past," he wrote.

Meyer thought about where his discoveries could grow in the United States and how useful they could be—either in themselves or as parentage of a new strain. Over the years he gained great respect for China's horticultural achievements and penned detailed descriptions of Chinese practices. His careful studies of soybean cultivation and of soy sauce preparation initiated their transfer to America.

The ecological abuses that afflict China today were common even then, and made a deep impression on Meyer. In Shanxi he was brought to a keen grasp of the link between deforestation and floods, and he came away from Chengde (Jehol) with the fear that a once-fertile area could turn into desert. He wrote that he had seen "with sad eyes the last vestiges of a once grand vegetation." The Chinese were guilty of[20]

> enormous crimes in destroying the balance of nature. Every wild tree or shrub is mercilessly cut down; every edible bird is trapped and eaten. Their mountains are barren wastes which let the rains rush off with great velocity, bearing with them arable soil and covering valleys with stony and sandy matter. Their climate gets drier year after year and famines result. Their birds are being exterminated; caterpillars of all descriptions destroy whole plantations of pine trees and catalpas and fruit orchards.

Meyer endured hardship for months on end, appreciating all the more his occasional stays with missionaries—"little oases," he called their homes. In filthy inns the choice was often between warmth and infestation. He knew thirst and the ecstasy of slaking it, hunger and the comfort of a mutton soup. In Gansu he narrowly escaped being shot as a smuggler of opium. Many times he had difficulty explaining what he was about. How could it be that the rich country across the ocean needed more plants!

Meyer was cheated and affronted by some of the Chinese he encountered, but his general admiration for them was little affected. He wrote that "China is going to come to the front, for the people are a solid kind of men and they possess sterling virtues. In agriculture, they are experts."

Traveling without companions with whom he could converse, Meyer had time to meditate and brood, and during the third and fourth expeditions the war was on his mind. The waste of young lives and the

---

20. Cunningham, *Frank N. Meyer*, 75–76.

devastation of the land saddened him. "Has hell broken loose on earth?" he wrote from Xi'an in August 1914. "There seems to reign darkness over the Earth now, and this after nearly twenty centuries of Christian teaching." And in Lanzhou, having walked the hundreds of miles from Xi'an, he wrote, "When will mankind be ready to inaugurate the United States of the World and do away with armies, navies, etc.? Some centuries to come, people will know how horribly senseless we were." Returned to Beijing in February 1915, he sent worries with a shipment of herbarium specimens and photographs: "A dark cloud hangs over all humanity. . . . If only we are not at the threshold of another dark age."

For months Meyer exchanged no more than a few words with guides and bearers. He complained of loneliness in his letters, and in his last year of travel wrote:

> Of course this exploration work, with its continuous absence from people who can inspire one, gets pretty badly on one's nerves. One must be some sort of a reservoir that carries along all sorts of stores. Soldiers in the field have more dangers to face, but they at least get companionship. . . .[21]

His reservoir began to run dry. In Beijing he denounced secret diplomacy and munitions makers and feared that the U.S. would get into the war. He complained of sleepless nights and walked off fits of depression. In Shanghai a war film sickened him. Then, in the treaty port of Yichang, on the Yangtze Meyer received the news of America's entry into the war. He suffered a nervous breakdown— "nervous prostration," it was called then. He could neither eat nor sleep.

On the insides of three envelopes pasted together, Meyer set forth reasons for submitting his resignation. Some had to do with work difficulties, others with the state of China and the world:

> Not feeling as well as formerly—sleeplessness
> —less energy
> Mentally soon tired; not being able to do as much
> work as formerly.
> Paralyzing effect of this terrible everlasting war

---

21. Fairchild, "A Hunter of Plants."

Loneliness of life and very few congenial people
    to associate with
Travel with all this enormous amount of baggage
So much squalor and dirt in China
No garden to study the plants one has collected.[22]

Apparently recovered later, Meyer energetically collected pear and wild lemon seeds and herbs in Hubei and visited a bean curd factory. But the impoverished villages depressed him; he looked into the faces of underfed, diseased children and knew they would never grow into healthy adults. F. C. Reimer of the Southern Oregon Experiment Station, with whom he worked for some weeks, wrote later, "Few people ever realized the tremendous battle that was raging within his soul."

Shortly, warlord strife confined Meyer to Yichang. He busied himself helping missionaries and foreign traders to improve their gardens and was gratified that he was able, with a team of twenty-five laborers, to transplant large tea olives. In May he made his way down river to Hankou. He wrote to his family in Holland that he was weary, couldn't sleep because of the hot weather, had little appetite, and longed for a home and a garden. The war was on his mind. "Times are certainly sad and mad, and, from a scientific point of view, so utterly unnecessary."

On May 31 he boarded a Japanese river vessel, the *Feng Yang Maru*, Shanghai bound. As usual, he traveled Chinese first class rather than foreign first class. He disappeared over the side the following night some miles west of Wuhu.

He left a bequest to his associates in the Department of Agriculture and the money was used to award an annual medal in his name. One face of the medal shows the white-barked pine and the jujube. The inscription reads: "In the glorious luxuriance of the hundred plants he takes delight." Since 1983 the medal has been awarded by the Crop Science Society of America, an affiliate of the American Society of Agronomy, Madison, Wisconsin.

Meyer's recovered body was buried in the Bubbling Well Cemetery in Shanghai. The headstone has been taken away, presumably when the cemetery was made part of a park after the establishment of the People's Republic.

---

22. Cunningham, *Frank N. Meyer*, 225.

9. Joseph Stilwell, Road Builder

The famine of 1920–21 made evident that poor transportation, in particular lack of roads, limited relief efforts. An American Red Cross report[23] summed it up this way: "Whole provinces are dependent on rivers and pack animals for transportation. And whole counties are so far from rivers that pack animals consume almost all the food they carry in making a round trip."

A remedial project was made possible by an exceptionally successful appeal for relief funds in the United States. Responding to an appeal initiated by President Wilson and publicized by missionaries, Americans contributed over a million dollars, more than what was needed to finance the direct relief program. The most urgent transportation need was for an east-west road linking the relatively prosperous provinces of Hebei, Shandong, and Henan with Shaanxi in the northwest, and the Red Cross therefore agreed to spend the surplus on the construction of an eighty-two-mile road across Shanxi to Chungdu on the Yellow River.

Major Joseph Stilwell, thirty-eight, engaged in Chinese language study in Beijing, applied for and got the post of chief engineer, and the result was an experience that helped to shape his attitude toward Chinese society and the Chinese people.

His instructions, he wrote in his own account[24] of this experience, were simply "to push a road from Fenchowfu to the Yellow River, make it twenty-two feet wide, keep the grades under six percent and finish by August 1."

Working with him was "the usual rickety organization, part volunteer and part paid." Though his assistants were a motley group—"we were a rum lot"—they "made up in willingness and energy something of what was lacking in technical ability and experience."

The deadline was not met, but the road did get built, and the standards were largely adhered to, though the road narrowed somewhat in traversing solid rock stretches. For most of four months from April

---

23. *American Red Cross Famine Relief in China, 1920–21* ([New York]: Russell Sage Foundation, 1943). Stilwell apparently never understood that the Red Cross was not just a relief agency. It was, in its own words, "a creature of the government of the United States," and the mission was to build infrastructure, such as highways and irrigation sytems that would serve American investment projects.

24. This and the following of Stilwell's observations on construction are from his "Opening China for 'Gas Wagons,' "*Asia*, July 1924.

through July of 1921, Stilwell worked hard and endured considerable privation. He had to deal with scores of contractors, some of them slippery, and had to keep a sharp eye out for shoddy stone work—ill-fitted stones held in place by an excess of lime. Often he slept in the open to avoid the lice-ridden inns.

But the aggravations were relieved by the friendliness of most of the villagers, by joking banter with the overseers and laborers, and by occasional sport. A photo shows Stilwell in the middle of a new-built section of the road holding a golden pheasant, a revolver at his side.

At a lavish banquet given him by the military commanders and officials in Yungnanchow, he consumed "hundred percent alcohol" and a succession of "wonderfully cooked dishes . . . but stupefying by mere number." Stuffed, Stilwell labored through a brief speech with the help of a nervous Norwegian lady missionary. "But the awful moment finally ends, and hearty applause greets his unintelligible remarks. The Chinese are a polite race."

Construction included a great deal of stone work. Four hundred and fifty-eight culverts and thirty-eight bridges, one of five arches, had to be built. The work was done under contract, and Stilwell saw to it that the big contractor was systematically ignored in favor of the little man.

> He [the big contractor] could never understand why he was so slighted: he and his kind were men of influence and resources; they never spoke to a coolie except to drive him. . . . It is inexplicable to such gentry that work should be reserved for Li Mulin, in breeches well patched and a dirty shirt, instead of for them, dressed in silk as they are, and so refined and elegant that they cannot walk up six steps without puffing.

Stilwell was not above luring a chubby, silk-clad contractor into panting up and down hillsides in the belief that he was in pursuit of a contract. At the brow of a hill Stilwell finally told him, "We just came up to get the view!"

At first most of the peasants working on the road—about two thousand at one point—"were very hazy about" who was financing it. Some thought it was the government, more thought it was the missionaries, "but in the end probably nine-tenths of them realized that the American people, from a feeling of friendship with China, had given the money that was paying their wages."

Stilwell's performance enhanced his reputation. Soon he was invited by Feng Yuxiang, the so-called "Christian General" who was then the power in Shaanxi, to build a modern road linking the Yellow River with Xi'an. But Stilwell had hardly got going on this project when Feng's troops had to go east to come to the aid of Wu Peifu, and construction was halted. But Stilwell and Feng formed a lasting relationship of mutual respect.

Stilwell came away from his Red Cross employment with a feeling for the people, as against those who ruled and abused them, that would stay with him.

> They are a quiet, well-behaved lot, those Shanxi folk, still living a thousand years back. But they are endowed with keen perceptions and a sense of humor that is delightful to an American. When the engineer meets man after man who can see through a joke, even when it is on himself, and laugh as heartily as the bystanders, his heart warms to the whole race.

In later years Stilwell studied China's past and observed its present. He sent away to Orientalia, a New York bookshop, for a copy of *Ti-ping Tien-kwoh: The History of the Ti-ping Revolution*, by Linle (Augustus F. Lindley), a two-volume work by a Taiping partisan. He made friends with Americans sympathetic with revolutionary change in China—Agnes Smedley, Jack Belden, and Edgar Snow. He told Snow in the mid-1930s that he was impressed by the performance of the Chinese Reds against Chiang Kai-shek—"they're masters of guerrilla warfare."

In command in China during the anti-Japanese war, he brought to his judgment of Chiang Kai-shek—"The Peanut," he called him—and his coterie the populist perspective with which he had sized up the silk-garbed contractors. These excerpts from letters and undated notes[25] reveal his judgments and feelings.

Undated Note: "Chiang Kai-shek is confronted with an idea, and that defeats him. He is bewildered by the spread of Communist influence. He can't see that the mass of Chinese people welcome the Reds as being the only visible hope of relief from crushing taxation, the abuses of the Army and (the terror of) Dai Li's Gestapo. Under Chiang Kai-shek they now begin to see what they may expect.

---

25. Theodore H. White, ed. *The Stilwell Papers* (New York: W. Sloane Associates, 1948; Shocken, 1972; Harper & Row, 1978).

Greed, corruption, favoritism, more taxes, a ruined currency, terrible waste of life, callous disregard of all the rights of men."

Note, probably July 1944: "The cure for China's trouble is the elimination of Chiang Kai-shek. He hates the Reds and will not take any chances on giving them a toehold in the government. . . . "

September 21, 1944: Excerpts from verses sent to his wife, Winifred Stilwell, on the occasion of a momentary triumph:

> I've waited long for vengeance—
> At last I've had my chance.
> I've looked The Peanut in the eye
> And kicked him in the pants.
>
> The old harpoon was ready
> With aim and timing true,
> I sank it to the handle,
> And stung him through and through.
>
> The little bastard shivered,
> And lost the power of speech.
> His face turned green and quivered
> As he struggled not to screech.[26]

September 24 letter home: "Madame Sun (Soong Ching Ling) wants me to represent China at the Peace Conference. Says I would do more for China than the Chinese. That I have a reputation among the Chinese for standing up for them. The Burma campaign made them feel respectable again."

On October 19 President Roosevelt—"The Softie," Stilwell called him—came down on the side of Generalissimo Chiang and recalled Stilwell, who wrote to his wife: "The ax has fallen and I'll be on my way to see you in a few days. The politicians are in full command. . . . So now I am hanging up my shovel and bidding farewell to as merry a nest of gangsters as you'll meet in a long day's march."

More on October 20: "The Peanut offers me China's highest decoration. Told him to stick it up his ass. Saw Madame Sun Yat-sen. She cried and was generally broken up."

Stilwell was in command in Okinawa when the nuclear bombings of Hiroshima and Nagasaki helped end the war. Back home, he sent

---

26. White, *The Stilwell Papers*, 334.

his fur-lined overcoat to Zhu De and in 1946, the last year of his life, rendered one final service to the people of China. He spoke out with his customary vigor against U.S. intervention in the developing Chinese civil war

10. Gunboats on the Yangtze

The largest concentration of foreign warships on the Yangtze ever—over fifty—took place in 1926–27 as nationalist armies, organized by the united front of the Kuomintang and the Communist Party, drove north from Guangdong to take on the warlords and try to unify China. The armada was not neutral. Its purpose was to protect tangible foreign interests and foreign nationals and do whatever was possible to stave off the grave threat to imperialist hegemony.

By the end of 1926 nearly all of the U.S. Asiatic Fleet (later the Seventh Fleet) was stationed on the Yangtze or on the China coast. Shipboard complements of marines were augmented by reinforcements from Guam; the Fourth Marines had been based in Shanghai for some years. In January Admiral Clarence E. Williams, in command of the Asiatic Fleet, was ordered to China.

An early confrontation took place at Wanxian, a Yangtze port west of the gorges. But the shelling of the city was entirely a British action; the role of the American gunboat was limited to conveying the British wounded to Wuhan. The U.S. Navy, specifically its Yangtze Patrol, didn't bring its guns to bear until Nanjing.

Unlike Wuhan, Nanjing was free of foreign concessions and was less important commercially. Devastated by the Taiping Revolution (as late as 1910 you could hunt pheasant within the city walls), it had not been made a treaty port until 1899. But by 1927 it had a substantial American community of 430, mostly missionaries. Standard Oil had an installation on what foreigners called Socony Hill and the patrolling American gunboats had an intimate relationship with it. At its various installations along the Yangtze, Standard Oil set aside rooms for the rest and recreation of American seamen. Beijing Five Star beer was always on ice.

The American consul at Nanjing, John K. Davis, was hostile to the nationalists, as his habitual references to "the Kuomintang so-called government" suggested. He hoped and for some weeks believed that the Northern Expedition would end in defeat. But in March of 1927 the warlord defense collapsed and on the twenty-fourth, nationalist troops poured into the city.

An imposing array of foreign naval vessels was anchored in the roadstead. Japan, France, and Italy were represented, as well as the United States and Britain.

A plan to evacuate the foreigners had been worked out, but in the words of Admiral Kemp Tolley,[27] chronicler of the American navy's Yangtze experience, it assumed "that the opposition would be mobs of unorganized coolies who would turn tail . . . if somebody so much as dropped a light bulb. What turned up instead were hundreds of thousands of professional Cantonese troops, fresh from a victorious march of a thousand miles, heady with success."

At Shanghai and Shameen [Shamian], the concession at Guangzhou, foreign police and troops had fired murderously on Chinese demonstrators. Nanjing was a counterpoint to those inflammatory incidents. Southern soldiers, instilled to excess with anti-imperialist feelings, killed six foreigners and wounded and abused others. "We're Bolsheviks, we're proud of being Bolsheviks, and we are going to act like Bolsheviks," one foreigner said he was told.

Given direction by a naval shore party signaling from Socony Hill, the American destroyer *Noa* opened fire, quickly joined by the *Preston* and HMS *Emerald*, a cruiser. Altogether over a hundred rounds of four-inch and six-inch shells were fired on the city; the barrage enabled nearly complete evacuation of the foreigners. The loss of Chinese lives was considerable, but the count by officials anxious to placate the foreign powers was only six.

The initial reaction of the powers to the Nanjing affair was punitive demands. Admiral Williams proposed a harsh reprisal, including seizure of nationalist vessels, bombardment of forts and arsenals along the Yangtze, withholding of taxes due, and a blockade of the southern coast under nationalist control. The American minister, John V. A. MacMurray, was like-minded. But Secretary of State Frank B. Kellogg, supported by President Coolidge and by considerable missionary and press opinion, advocated a cautious and more sophisticated course. He was persuaded that Chinese nationalism could not be extirpated and had to be appeased—"If you can't lick'em, join'em." The dramatic turn at Shanghai in April validated his assessment.

27. *Yangtze Patrol: The U.S. Navy in China* (Annapolis, Md.: Naval Institute Press, 1976), 152.

Shanghai was the climax. Assembled there was imperial naval and military might. Forty-seven foreign warships were in the harbor and the flags of admirals flew over eight of them. The United States was represented by four cruisers, four destroyers, an oiler, a transport, a minesweeper and a gunboat; Britain by five cruisers, an aircraft carrier, a destroyer and two gunboats; Japan by six cruisers, seven destroyers and three gunboats; Italy by two cruisers, a sloop and a gunboat; France by two cruisers and a sloop; Spain and the Netherlands by one cruiser each; Portugal by a sloop.

Reinforcing the Shanghai volunteer corps of armed foreigners were 9,500 British and 1,500 American troops.

The American Chamber of Commerce in Shanghai called for armed intervention by a concert of powers and the *North China Herald* and other foreign-run newspapers talked tough. But then Chiang Kai-shek, whose occupation of Shanghai had been made easy by the militant trade unions, turned on his Communist allies, and his troops and local gangsters began a massacre of unionists, students, and all suspected Reds.

The assembly of foreign armed forces found that its work was being done for it. The newspapers that had portrayed Chiang as a Communist ogre began to sing his praises. Admiral Tolley observed that "all the former talk about relinquishment of concessions and 'extrality' (extraterritoriality) went pianissimo. The foreign taipans began to breathe more freely."

All those in the State Department, the British Foreign Office, and business offices who had argued that the so-called moderates in the Kuomintang could be played off against the radicals were shown to be right. Support for the Kuomintang began a long-lasting American policy that tried and failed to prevent the triumph of the revolution.

The Navy abandoned its menacing posture in favor of hospitality. In 1929 Admiral Yates Stirling, Jr., in command of the Yangtze Patrol, jovially entertained Chiang Kai-shek, T. V. Soong, Wang Jingwei and Sun Fo aboard the 560-ton *Luzon*, just off the ways.

The American and other foreign gunboats on the Yangtze were at their busiest in 1926–27. Their guns inflicted considerable damage at slight cost, and that led some foreigners to misread the evidence. After the clash at Nanjing a letter signed "Americano" to a Shanghai newspaper said: "The sooner the Chinese get the idea out of their heads that they could by any chance use force to drive the foreigners from China the better it will be for all concerned. If they want force, all they have to do is to keep on as they are now doing and they will get all they are looking for."[28]

A comment by the *China Weekly Review* on November 13, 1926 following the Wanxian shelling was more farsighted: Wanxian "shows that the present type of gunboat used in China is becoming obsolete. A little tin gunboat on a narrow river is no match in a fight with a Chinese army equipped with modern heavy artillery . . . the Chinese are shortly going to drive the gunboats off the river anyway."

The Japanese invasion of 1937 and the revolution it helped to generate put an end to the gunboat era.

The frigate *Susquehanna* ventured up the Yangtze in 1854, the first American warship to do so. It had a friendly exchange with the Taiping rebels at several ports, but friendship did not become a precedent. What became the regular Yangtze gunboat patrol was an instrument of American imperial policy, there to protect the string of Standard Oil installations and other such interests, and to support, and occasionally chastise, the succession of conservative or reactionary Chinese regimes with which the U.S. was more or less allied. The American river fleet of two to six gunboats worked closely with the British, who much of the time had a gunboat in each of the treaty ports.

For the American officers duty was made pleasant by the welcome extended to them at such port establishments as the Hankou Race and Recreation Club, which, in addition to the race track, had tennis courts, a golf course, a swimming pool, a famed bar, and a heavy schedule of parties. The sailors of course were barred from such clubs, like the Chinese, and for them drunken binges and whoring were common. "Most of my pay goes for liquor and women, and the rest I spend foolishly," one seaman explained.

Venereal disease was widespread. Sometimes a fourth of a crew would be infected.

In their last decades, the Yangtze gunboats hired Chinese as servants and for the hard work. According to Kemp Tolley, a gunboat sailor "enjoyed a breakfast of pancakes and eggs any style, per order, had his bunk made up and shoes shined by a Chinese 'boy,' and allowed the six Chinese boatmen carried on each gunboat to do all the dirty work aboard."

---

28. Tolley, *Yangtze Patrol*, 162.

The crew of the *Guam* (later captured by the Communists) had a good deal. A group of coolies scrubbed the sides of the vessel in exchange for garbage rights.

The end came on January 19, 1942 when the gunboat *Tutuila*, confined to Chongqing by the Japanese control of the lower river, was turned over to the Kuomintang navy.

Not all Americans saw as glorious the presence of the U.S. Navy on China's great river. Will Rogers, who at his best sounded like Mark Twain, commented that if American gunboats were to be allowed to ply the Yangtze to protect Standard Oil, Chinese gunboats ought to be welcome to patrol the Mississippi and look out for laundries in Memphis.

11. Agnes Smedley and Lu Xun: Friends in a Dark Time

Take up the pen;
　　　fall into the net of law.
Resist the times,
　　　offend popular sentiments.
Accumulated abuse
　　　dissolves the bones,
And so, one gives voice
　　　to the empty page.
　　　　　　　　　Lu Xun

Agnes Smedley came to China from Berlin late in 1928 via the Trans-Siberian Railroad—the journey a long hyphen between years of political and personal involvement with Indian revolutionaries and the Chinese experience that was the center of the rest of her life. Smedley served as a correspondent for the *Frankfurter Zeitung*, the leading liberal German newspaper, until shortly before Hitler came to power. From Manchuria she sent back an account of the Japanese penetration so condemning that the skeptical editors declined to publish it until Japan turned Manchuria into "Manchukuo"[29] in 1932. South of the Great Wall she stopped at Tianjin, Beijing and Nanjing, seeing, listening, and gaining insights into Chinese society—"This is the Mid-

---

29. A puppet regime set up by Japan in the northeastern part of China, consisting of Heilongjiang, Jilin and Liaoning provinces, formerly referred to as Manchuria.

Frank Meyer beside his cart while traveling in Xinjiang in 1911
(*U.S. Department of Agriculture photo*).

Greetings:
to the Chinese people

On this 37th anniversary of the Chinese Republic we Americans hail with great joy your inspiring achievements in the struggle for freedom and proudly reaffirm our friendship with you.

Your long and tortuous fight for national and social emancipation is approaching its final triumph over enemies who betrayed our common victory in the recent war.

Your victorious struggle for liberation has given new heart to the millions all over the world who strive for freedom. The age-old serfdom has been shattered. 170 million Chinese peasants now, for the first time, till their own debt-free land. You are building new industries which give promise of a life of plenty for all.

Your achievements are bringing to a close the bitter chapter of "cheap coolie labor" with which the profiteers of East and West undermine the living standards of workers throughout the world.

We Americans have not forgotten that our nation was born out of revolution. Nor have we forgotten that we, like you today, once had to fight a civil war to preserve our national unity. We stand firm with you against those who provide and use American dollars and guns to hinder your advance.

To you, professional men and women, who prefer persecution, imprisonment or exile to treason, our salute!

To you, heroic students, professors and intellectuals, who, resisting the establishment of thought control, face death without fear, our salute!

To you, magnificent workers and peasants, vast majority of the Chinese people fighting for a new and better life, our salute!

As a token of our solidarity, we have each contributed to a fund which will be used to help awaken the American people to an appreciation of the great part your valiant fight is playing in our struggle for freedom and peace. We pledge intensified efforts here at home against reaction, and look forward, with you, to the day when all the free peoples of the world will live together in friendship and peace.

Communist victory in the 1946–49 civil war and the establishment of the People's Republic was nearing when the Committee for a Democratic Far Eastern Policy, New York-based, sent these greetings to the people of China.

General Joseph Stilwell, whose dismissal by President Roosevelt in October 1944 began the downward slide of US-China relations.

General Joseph Stilwell and Soong Ching Ling held each other in high regard.

Agnes Smedley in Yanan in 1937. Her many interviews with Zhu De led to her biography of him, *The Great Road: The Life and Times of Chu Teh.*

Above from left, Hugh Deane, Graham Peck, and Jack Belden. *Below from left,* Chen Jiakang, aide to Zhou Enlai, later ambassador to Egypt; Li Gongpu, a progressive intellectual, a leader of the Democratic League, assassinated by Kuomintang agents on July 11, 1946; Mao Dun, playwright and novelist, close colleague of Lu Xun; Anna Wang, wife of Wang Bingnan, liaison between the Chinese Communist Party and foreign journalists; Israel Epstein, now editor-in-chief emeritus of *China Today*; and Zhang Hanfu, an editor of *Xinhua Ribao* (New China Daily), later a vice-minister of foreign affairs. This photo is in the Red Crag Village museum, Chongqing.

Dr. Ma Haide (George Hatem) and Koji Ariyoshi were Yanan friends.

Koji Ariyoshi and Mao in Yanan during Dixie Mission days.

Seated in front of a poster-sized photo of a good friend, the recently deceased Evans Carlson, Agnes Smedley listens to a eulogy of him. She then went to the rostrum to add her warm remembrances of the marine officer who was won over to the cause of the Chinese revolution. The occasion was a memorial meeting in New York arranged by the Committee for a Democratic Far Eastern Policy, of which Carlson was chairman.

Left to right: Hugh Deane, Jack Belden, and Israel Epstein, Press Hostel, Chongqing, 1941.

The great singer and actor Paul Robeson signs a scroll calling for recognition of the newborn People's Republic of China. To right is progressive congressman Vito Marcantonio, New York.

PAUL ROBESON

CHINA AID
CONCERT

Atlantic City Convention Hall

Atlantic City, N. J.

Sunday Evening, August 18, 1940

PAUL ROBESON, Internationally known concert artist and other outstanding musicians will perform. All proceeds to aid the Chinese people.

Tickets Reserved at
CHINA AID COUNCIL
Philadelphia Chapter

1336 Walnut St.   Phila. Pa.

Robeson gave concerts and did an album of Chinese songs to aid China's resistance to Japan.

Soong Ching Ling acknowledged receipt of $300 donated to the China Defense League by American friends.

Edgar Snow and Helen Foster
Snow (Nym Wales) in Peking in
the mid–1930s.

Edgar Snow, left, and Rewi Alley, at right, dining with Mao Zedong.

Rewi Alley and Zhou Enlai at a sports event during the Cultural Revolution.

Zhou Enlai and Deng Yingchao felicitate Anna Louise Strong on her birthday.

Hugh Deane with Ye Junjian (Chun-chan Yeh), renowned novelist and translator, and Ye's wife. *(Photo by Gordon Deane.)*

Dr. Ma Haide with grandson Ma Jun and granddaughter Ma Lan at home.

John S. Service at the Chicago
convention of the US-China
Peoples Friendship Association,
1975.

Max and Grace Granich, editors of *Voice of China* (Shanghai) and *China Today* (New York), with children during their 1971 visit.

Howard Adams and granddaughter, Jilin.

dle Ages," she told her interpreter. She arrived in Shanghai in the spring of 1929.

This was an agonizing period in the life of that city for those with a social conscience. Two years earlier Chiang Kai-shek had smashed the trade unions in a great slaughter, in the supportive presence of an armada of Western warships. The terror had become particularized. The Kuomintang police, often with the covert help of the police in the International and French Settlements, were hunting down intellectuals, writers and artists critical of the regime. Early in her China experience Smedley wrote to her friend Robert Morss Lovett that "not only workers and peasants captured in battle were killed like animals in the streets, but intellectuals of every kind in the cities were dragged from the universities, or from their beds at night, tortured and beheaded."

On December 25, 1929 Lu Xun, already established as China's foremost writer, noted in his diary that he had received a note from Agnes Smedley seeking an interview. Two days later two teachers brought her to his house. They met again on January 21, 1930 and on this occasion Smedley presented Lu with the German edition of her largely autobiographical novel *Daughter of Earth,* which she had written, she said, "in a desperate effort to reorient my life." The volume, admiringly inscribed, is now in the Lu Xun Museum in Shanghai.

Lu Xun helped to find a translator for *Daughter of Earth.* Through Smedley, Lu Xun got to know the graphic works of Kaethe Kollwitz. Their collaboration flourished. The diary entry of December 25, 1929 was the first of twenty-four about Smedley.

When Lu Xun's fiftieth birthday was celebrated at a Dutch Indonesian restaurant in the French Settlement on September 17, 1930, Smedley made the arrangement with the restaurateur and served as lookout herself while the guests arrived. Invitations had been sent by word of mouth, but there could be no assurance that informers had not got wind of the gathering that was to include many who lived in hiding.

Smedley took a famous photo of Lu Xun seated in a rattan chair in the garden outside the restaurant and has complemented it with a memorable word portrait of him at the celebration:

He was short and frail, and wore a cream-colored silk gown and soft Chinese shoes. He was bareheaded and his close-cropped hair stood up like a brush. In structure his face was like that of an average

Chinese, yet it remains in my memory as the most eloquent face I have ever seen. A kind of intelligence and awareness stemmed from it. He spoke no English but considerable German, and in that language we conversed. His manner, his speech, and his every gesture radiated the indefinable harmony and charm of a perfectly integrated personality. I suddenly felt as awkward and ungracious as a clod.[30]

The guests were a motley group of writers, poets, translators, dramatists, actors, and artists. Some were radicals, some liberals, several were members of the scholar gentry. What they had in common was a sense of Lu Xun's preeminence and a respect for his writings and his courage.

Born Zhou Shuren in Shaoxing, Zhejiang Province in 1881 into a family of penniless scholars, Lu Xun acquired an advanced education in government schools in Nanjing and studied medicine in Japan. But he forsook the practice of medicine for the literature of criticism and protest, becoming one of the leaders of the cultural renaissance identified with the May Fourth Movement of 1919. He contributed to *New Youth*, the magazine which pioneered the use of the vernacular language, and in the 1920s turned out a stream of stories and essays of the highest order. *The True Story of Ah Q*, published in 1921, quickly made him nationally known, and its translation into English, German, French, Japanese, Russian and other languages gained him an international reputation. Romain Rolland wept when he read it. Critics compared Lu Xun with Maxim Gorki. Smedley, thinking of the essays Lu Xun was then writing, considered him a Voltaire.

Like his German contemporary Bertolt Brecht, Lu Xun frequently had to change his address because of politics. He spent years in Beijing, employed at the Ministry of Education and lecturing at three universities, but had to leave precipitately when a warrant for his arrest charging him with organizing student unions and preaching revolt was issued. He spent some time in Amoy [Xiamen], taught at Zhongshan University in Guangzhou, and fled into hiding in Shanghai after Chiang Kai-shek turned on the left in 1927.

---

30. *Battle Hymn of China*,(New York: Alfred A. Knopf, 1943; New York: Da Capo Press, 1975, and as *China Correspondent* London: Methuen, 1984), 78. Smedley's account of her relations with Lu Xun was vivid, insightful and heartfelt but her recollection of dates was faulty. She forgot her early meetings with Lu Xun and gave the wrong dates for the execution of six writers and Lu Xun's "Written in Deep Night." The errors were first brought to my attention by Ge Baoquan and Gladys Yang.

The fierce political struggle in China moved Lu Xun from the role of bystander-critic to one of profound and painful engagement. Yet his emotional involvement did not impair his commitment to artistry. He disdained rhetorical posturing. He wrote and rewrote, polished and polished again, searching for the telling phrase, for an allusion people would grasp, always having to be mindful of censorship. The "perfectly integrated personality" that Smedley sensed was complemented by an integration of insights with craftsmanship.

Lu Xun told Smedley that he hoped to write a historical novel based on his life, but that the times did not permit. He had to use his pen as a political dagger. In Smedley's view,

> Of all Chinese writers, he seemed the most intricately linked with Chinese history, literature and culture. It was almost impossible to translate into English some of his political criticisms because, unable to attack reaction openly, his writings were a mosaic of allusions to personalities, events, and ideas of the darkest periods of China's past. Through these political criticisms ran rich streams of both Chinese and Western culture, couched in a style as fine as an etching.[31]

Lu Xun had helpful encounters with several Americans. He was interviewed two or three times by Edgar Snow in 1931, and Snow, encouraged by him, translated some of the best of contemporary short stories, including seven by Lu Xun; the collection, *Living China*, was published in New York in 1936. Smedley introduced Lu Xun to Harold Isaacs, editor of *China Forum*, a Shanghai publication, and he also translated some of Lu Xun's stories, which were included in a later collection, *Straw Sandals*. *Voice of China*, a successor publication to *China Forum*, edited by Max and Grace Granich, featured several contributions by Lu Xun, including the powerful essay, "Written in Deep Night." The November 1, 1936 issue, which appeared shortly after Lu Xun's death, included an obituary, eulogistic statements and photos under the title "Immortal Is Lu Xun."

But Smedley was the American closest to Lu Xun. From 1930 on their lives were intertwined. Widely introduced by Lu Xun, Smedley met all kinds of people, and from her typewriter came a stream of articles and her book, *Chinese Destinies* (1933). With the novelist Mao Dun, Lu and Smedley worked to keep alive the League of Left-wing Writers, formed in March 1930, and, with the help of a small

---

31. Smedley, *Battle Hymn of China*, 82.

network of others, repeatedly took to the outside world news of the outrages committed by the Kuomintang regime as it hunted down dissident voices.

They had some success in rousing distant consciences. When six young writers, among them leading members of the League of Left-wing Writers, were executed on February 7, 1931, Lu Xun's fierce denunciation was translated by Mao Dun and Smedley, and smuggled out. Worldwide protests followed. Sinclair Lewis, Upton Sinclair, Theodore Dreiser, and John Dewey were among more than a hundred Americans who sent a condemning statement to the Chinese Minister in Washington.

In 1932 Soong Ching Ling and a small group of intellectuals formed the League of Human Rights as a counter to Kuomintang repression. Assassinations and arrests decimated its leadership, and after a painful year it ceased to exist. A famous photo taken in Soong Ching Ling's garden at the time of George Bernard Shaw's visit to Shanghai in 1933 includes some of those who did what they could in behalf of Chinese civil liberties. With Shaw and Soong Ching Ling are Agnes Smedley, Lu Xun, Cai Yuanpei (head of Academia Sinica), Harold Isaacs, and Lin Yu-tang. Smedley remembered:

> Often Mao Dun and I would meet on some street corner and, after a careful scrutiny of the street on which Lu Xun lived, enter his house and spend an evening with him. We would order dinner from a restaurant and spend hours in conversation. None of us was a Communist, but we all considered it an honor to aid and support men who were fighting and dying for the liberation of the poor.[32]

Ruth Weiss, later on the staff of *China Pictorial*, was one of those enlisted by Smedley to help distribute progressive literature and to attend and report on meetings and demonstrations. "Agnes lived in an apartment house with many entrances," Weiss recalled, "and the first thing one had to learn in visiting her was to remember which entrance one had come in by, in order to be sure to leave by another." To her Smedley's place was "like a way station on the Chinese freedom fighters' underground railroad."[33]

In Berlin Smedley had worked with Margaret Sanger and others to promote birth control and that remained one of her causes in

---

32. Smedley, *Battle Hymn of China*, 81.
33. Remembering Agnes Smedley in Shanghai," *China and Us* 3, no. 2 (March–April 1974). *China and Us* was the publication of the New York chapter of the US-China Peoples Friendship Association.

China. With a small grant from Sanger, she, Maxwell S. Stewart, and several others opened a birth control clinic in Beijing.

According to Agnes Smedley's principal biographers, Janice and Stephen MacKinnon, 1935–36 was an especially fruitful period of the Lu Xun-Smedley collaboration.

> Together they smuggled writers and artists out of Shanghai who were targets of Chiang Kai-shek's brownshirts. They edited and published a book of Kaethe Kollwitz's prints with funds raised by Smedley. This book was reprinted in 1956 and remains today the most important Chinese work on the subject. Lu Xun continued to introduce Smedley to promising young writers like the couple from Manchuria, Xiao Jun and Xiao Hong, and of course both continued to work closely with the League of Left-wing Writers.[34]

The work of Kollwitz had an enormous impact on the rapidly developing medium of woodcuts and also gave Chinese a better sense of foreign realities. Lu Xun commented in "Written in Deep Night":

> Chinese who have not had an opportunity to travel abroad often have the idea that all white people are either preachers of the ideas of Jesus, or well-dressed, well-fed managers of business firms given to the habit of kicking people about when out of humor. But the works of Kaethe Kollwitz show that the "injured and insulted"—our national friends—exist in very many other places on the earth and have among them artists who mourn, protest and struggle on their behalf.

In 1935 both Lu Xun and Smedley contributed substantial articles to the New York publication, *China Today*. Lu Xun's "Monsters in the Chinese Literary World," (February 1935) bitingly mocked writers who had accommodated to Kuomintang terror and censorship. "The suppression of literature cannot last long," Lu concluded. "We are on the eve of another bloody struggle."

---

34. The MacKinnon's well-researched and informative article, "Lu Xun and Agnes Smedley," appeared in *Chinese Literature*, October 1980. Smedley's photo taken at Lu Xun's birthday party accompanies the article. Janice and Stephen MacKinnon's excellent biography, *Agnes Smedley—The Life and Times of an American Radical*, was published by the University of California Press in 1988.

Smedley's article ("China Betrayed," May 1935) was a general condemnation of the Kuomintang regime. In Shanghai, she wrote:

> There is not a week but the foreign and Chinese police unite in hunting down men and women. There are constant raids, arrests, and killings. And the most barbarous methods of torture are applied to political prisoners. There are no trials of any kind—there is only torture, slow strangulation, or beheadings and shootings.

When Lu Xun learned that the Long March to the Northwest had been completed in the fall of 1935, he sent a round-about telegram of congratulations to the Red Army through Smedley. Some months later Feng Xuefeng, a leading member of the League of Left-wing Writers and one of the few writers to make the Long March, returned to Shanghai on the instructions of the Party and met several times with Smedley and Lu Xun. Smedley's news story based on their talks was the first informed account of the Long March to reach the outside world.

The Communist Party's revived United Front strategy in 1936 led to controversy over work in the literary field. Lu Xun was convinced that the new Party policies were overly soft and compromising—in effect that they were long on unity and short on struggle. He argued for the slogan, "Mass literature of the national revolutionary war." Smedley agreed with him.

Lu Xun lived and worked in two kinds of pain—sorrow over the disappearance of his pupils and friends one after another, arrested by authorities who dared not touch him but went after his lesser known associates, and physical pain. He was dying of tuberculosis. Smedley linked the two: the loss of his friends "acted like corrosive poison on Lu Xun's body and mind, and he began to weaken."

A doctor told him he had to have prolonged rest in a dry climate, but he paid no heed. Smedley had gone to the Soviet Union in 1933 for treatment and rest and there had completed her second book, *China's Red Army Marches*. She urged Lu Xun to go there also, and Gorki invited him to come for a year as his guest. But Lu Xun would not go. "Everyone cannot run away," he said. "Someone must stand and fight."

Lu Xun died on October 17, 1936. Despite all difficulties and constraints, some five thousand mourners attended the funeral, including many who had to emerge from hiding places. Smedley, in Xi'an, was the one foreigner named to the funeral committee. She wrote:[35]

The death of Lu Xun came to me not only as a personal sorrow but as a national tragedy. He had not lived aimlessly, nor had he given himself over to the search for wealth, power, or position. Of all Chinese intellectuals, he had wielded the greatest influence over educated youth. He embodied the common good, and the disease which killed him was fostered by sorrow and struggle.

A library, and later an art academy, were named for Lu Xun in Yan'an. Agnes Smedley became keeper of the seals of the foreign-language section of the library, to which she donated all the books she had collected in China.

12. China Crisis, American Journals

In 1931–32 Japan transformed Manchuria into "Manchukuo" and soon was moving south to gulp further bites of China, on its way to creating what it came to call the Greater East Asia Co-Prosperity Sphere. Generalissimo Chiang's regime in Nanjing remonstrated on occasion but did not seriously resist. Its army, advised and in part equipped by the Germans, was engaged in "bandit annihilation," a succession of campaigns to crush the Communists. In 1934 it finally succeeded in dislodging the Red Army from Jiangxi in the Southeast, forcing it to undertake the historic Long March to the Northwest.

But the nationalist feelings of more and more Chinese were offended by the Kuomintang's choice of adversaries. Student demonstrations in Beijing in the autumn of 1935, culminating on December 9, had an electrifying effect. A broad-based National Salvation Movement developed rapidly. University and middle school students were joined by workers, some struggling in underground unions, patriotic intellectuals, writers and artists and all sorts of people. Local groups were linked in a Federation of National Salvation Associations and officials and generals were bombarded with declarations, manifestos and circular telegrams.

Among those stirred were exiled troops from the Northeast (Manchuria) who had been sent to fight against the Communists in

---

35. Smedley, *Battle Hymn of China*, 137.

Shaanxi. The climax came in December 1936 when a conspiracy of officers and men under Zhang Xueliang, in command of the Northeast troops, and Yang Hucheng of the Seventeenth Route Army, seized the person of the Generalissimo at a hot springs near Xi'an and forced him to agree—temporarily, it turned out—to call off his effort to extirpate the Communists and to agree to a united front against the Japanese aggressors. This became known as the Xi'an Incident.

Two American initiated publications—the *Voice of China* in Shanghai and *Democracy* in Beijing (Peiping then)—did what they could to promote democracy and the national salvation cause, and that was considerable. While not entirely free from the attentions of the Kuomintang censors, they did enjoy some measure of immunity by virtue of their American sponsorship. And the *Voice of China* enjoyed the protection of the International Settlement in Shanghai.

Volume 1, Number 1 pledged to give voice to students and others in the national salvation struggle who were demanding that "the government and people unite to save the nation from the aggressors." A photo of a huge rally on International Women's Day in Shanghai was on the cover. Contents featured an article on the student movement by Agnes Smedley (the first of three contributions); she signed it R. Knailes—for "Rusty Nails." In the issue also were a short story by Ba Jin titled "Dog," and a poem honoring Captain Robert Short, an American airman who had volunteered his services to the Chinese defenders of Shanghai in 1932 and been killed. "Warm was your love/ Dissolving the barrier of nations," the poem said in part.

Number 2, dated April 1, ran Lu Xun's "A Little Incident," a second article by Smedley, and a warm message from He Xiangning, an associate of Soong Ching Ling in the opposition to Chiang Kai-shek. "The *Voice of China* is a sharp weapon for the liberation of the oppressed nation," she wrote.

Succeeding issues reported in detail on the gathering movement, the Xi'an Incident and its aftermath, and the first months of the Japanese invasion begun in July 1937. Soong Ching Ling wrote an appeal for true implementation of Sun Yat-sen's Three Principles and signed her name to National Salvation statements. Lu Xun and Guo Moruo, poet, essayist and archeologist, were interviewed, and stories by Lu Xun, Mao Dun, Xia Yan and other leading writers were published. Messages of support from the American Student Union, the Chinese Hand Laundry Alliance in New York, and leading American intellectuals were given prominence. Those in the U.S. who signed a telegram of protest following the arrest of seven leaders of the Federation of National Salvation Associations included Albert

Einstein, John Dewey, Norman Thomas, Paul Douglas (later Senator) and Maxwell S. Stewart, an editor of *The Nation*. A regular feature adding to the historical value of *Voice of China* was a section consisting of the texts of the various declarations and telegrams of national salvation groups.

Most writers were Chinese. A few were foreigners, among them anti-militarist Japanese. An article by Edgar Snow assessed the outlook for national unity after the Xi'an affair. Israel Epstein and Rewi Alley were frequent contributors, but signed with Chinese pseudonyms. Ruth Weiss helped with the business end and published under the name Lucy Vey. Originally *Voice of China* was entirely English but a Chinese language section was added later.

Published at 749 Bubbling Well Road in the International Settlement, *Voice of China* was out of reach of the Kuomintang police, but ran into endless difficulties in getting the magazine through the mails. Circulation grew rapidly from the initial 2,000 copies nevertheless, soon climbing to 5,000 and then to 7,500. Two Chinese dollars bought a year's subscription.

One of the liberalizing effects of the Xi'an turnover was that several months later *Voice of China* was registered in Nanjing as a legitimate publication. Max Granich remembered:

> The British found us obnoxious. The Chinese shops on their own initiative mailed bundles to overseas compatriots and we learned of their arrival in Sarawak, Singapore and other spots when the *North China Daily News* in Shanghai published a note of their suppression by the local authorities.
>
> But another and more heartening interest in the magazine was told to us by the Japanese writer who translated Lu Xun into Japanese. Every issue of *Voice of China* was translated into Japanese by him and the script passed along the Manchurian Railroad by the workers, up and down the line.[36]

The last issue appeared on November 1, 1937. The next issue was ready for the press when Japanese raided the print shop and destroyed the type.

Returning to New York, the Graniches took over the editorship of *China Today*, a monthly published by the American Friends of the

---

36. *China and Us* 3, no. 5 (New York) (September–October, 1974), 16.

Chinese People. They continued to bring the China story to interested Americans through the 1940s.

Max and Grace Granich were in the first group of Americans invited to China following the "pingpong opening." In a gesture of thanks, Zhou Enlai had them seated beside him at the welcoming banquet in the Great Hall of the People.

In its issue of May 15, 1937, *Voice of China* welcomed a new publication—*Democracy* (with a small "d" on the logo), published in Beijing.

> The fresh effort made by *Democracy* to shed light on problems so often concealed by the conditions of censorship in China will undoubtedly be hailed by all sincere students of contemporary China. It has assumed an important task. The editors of *Voice of China* greet it and wish it well in its venture.

Democracy was born through the efforts of two Americans. J. Spencer Kennard, a Baptist missionary and socialist who was expelled from Japan for anti-militarist publications, came up with the money—part of a thousand dollar grant from the American Friends Service Committee. Helen Foster Snow (Nym Wales) took on most of the work of turning the idea into printed pages.

An impressive editorial group was assembled, largely from Yenching (Yanjing) University. In it were Hubert S. Liang, under whom Edgar Snow taught journalism at Yanjing in 1934–35; Randolph Sailer, head of the Psychology Department and a popular teacher; Chang Tung-sung, professor of philosophy at Yanjing; Harry Price, instructor of economics there and assistant dean of the Public Affairs Department; Ida Pruitt, head of the Social Service Department of the Peking Union Medical Hospital; James Bertram, a Rhodes Scholar from New Zealand who was writing a book on the Xi'an Incident; and finally a young Englishman, John Leaning, who had been secretary to Hugh Dalton, Labor Party member of parliament. Helen Snow was getting ready for the trip to Yan'an that resulted in her book *Inside Red China* and persuaded Leaning to take her place as managing editor. She recalled:[37]

---

37. This and the two following Helen Snow recollections are from "Rememembering *Democracy*—a Lightning Flash of a Magazine," *China and Us* 3, no. 5 (New York) (September–October, 1974). Helen Snow later included a chapter on *Democracy* in her book *My China Years: A Memoir* (New York: William Morrow, 1984).

I remember very well the night we made up the dummy [a model of how a paper will be laid out, used as a guide for typographers]. Neither John nor I had ever done that before, and that night Ed had to go to the hospital for a kidney stone operation (a result of his trip to the Communist Northwest). Besides the technical difficulties, there were differences among us and the problems seemed so intolerable that I wept copiously into the paste as we sat on the floor at No. 13 Kuei Chia Chang putting the dummy together. And then I remember a silent rickshaw ride to a dark and sinister "hutung" (lane) to take the dummy to the printer, where no one spoke a word of English. And then on to Peking Union Hospital to see Ed.

After weeks of work the first issue appeared on May 15, 1937. The design was handsome and the contents included an article on Mao by Edgar Snow, which provided many intellectuals with their first reliable information on the Communist leader and his views; an appraisal of Japanese policy by Liang under the title "Japanese Diplomacy—Dr. Jekyll and Mr. Hyde"; an article on the outlook for democracy in China by J. Leighton Stuart, then president of Yanjing, later American ambassador. James Bertram wrote on Xi'an, Ida Pruitt contributed a sketch based on her experiences at the hospital, and Helen Snow wrote the policy article on *Democracy's* objectives.

Snow's article on Mao was to have been illustrated by a photo of him but the authorities barred the use of it. The omission was explained to readers in a box in the space assigned to the photo.

Censorship problems continued. The Kuomintang's Department of Publicity accused the editors of giving prominence to "materials favorable to the Communist Party and the United Front." The magazine was banned from bookshops in Nanjing.

Only five issues appeared, the last on July 8, the day after the armed clash at Marco Polo Bridge [Lugouqiao] which began the Japanese invasion. Among the contributors to the five issues were Zhou Enlai, reporting on the People's Congress; Edgar Snow on Lu Xun; Ran Sailer on "Christians and Communists." Translations of many articles appeared in Chinese periodicals.

Most of the letters to the editor were complimentary, though some urged that cheaper paper be used so that the price of thirty cents a copy could be reduced.

Helen Snow wrote later:

Only those living in China during those dark desperate days could imagine what a lightning flash this magazine was. None were more astonished than the Japanese. They said: "Mrs. Snow is being paid by President Roosevelt." I was told Roosevelt had made his "quarantine the aggressors" speech the year before, and the Japanese more than anything feared the awakening of Americans to action.

Many copies of the magazine were bought by the Japanese and sent back to Tokyo. Helen Snow and others who had helped the students throughout the December protests and founded *Democracy*, later moved on to launch the Chinese Industrial Cooperatives (Indusco) in Shanghai in 1938, being joined by Rewi Alley and the British consul, John Alexander. Revival of *Democracy* was discussed at the first meeting in Shanghai; a plan to do so in Chengdu was never realized. What was left of the money given Kennard by the Friends Service Committee helped to finance the *Chengdu News Bulletin*, edited at various times by Kennard, Ruth Weiss and me.

Reflecting in 1974, Helen Snow wrote:

> I think back to those old days in China and realize an era was drawing to a close. Most of the people I knew are dead or in the eighties or late seventies. Those old China hands on the left were exceptional people. The Americans among them represented the best of our country, and they were aware of their responsibility to show it in China.

13. When Americans Learned Gung Ho

The revival of the Chinese Industrial Cooperatives in the 1980s ought also to revive memories of the years when they were a cause abroad as well as in the China resisting the Japanese invasion. Indusco, as the movement immediately came to be called, was of international parentage, and soon fired imaginations and gained organized support in the West and among overseas Chinese communities everywhere at a time over-supplied with worthy causes. The American effort, which I know best, is a chapter of warm friendship in the sweet and sour history of U.S.-China relations.

That effort is also being revived. Indusco II is getting some essential help from the American cooperative movement, and the New York Chapter of the US - China Peoples Friendship Association has launched a campaign to raise money for it. Helen Foster Snow and others active in the earlier Indusco are again doing what they can to help.

The movement that gave Gung Ho (Work Together) to the American language was born in Shanghai's International Settlement in 1938, the second year of the anti-Japanese war, the result of a creative collaboration of foreign friends of China and progressive, patriotic Chinese.

Edgar Snow and his wife Helen (Nym Wales), Americans, were among the founders who devoted themselves to publicizing and raising funds for the cause. The New Zealander Rewi Alley (engaged in the revival before his death in December 1987 at the age of ninety) became not only technical adviser but moving spirit and constantly traveling coordinator. Sir Archibald Clark-Kerr, the British ambassador, was an early convert whose influence was critically important in the beginning. Bishop Ronald Hall of Hongkong became chairman of the supporting International Committee, and American missionaries Dr. Lewis Smythe and Charles Riggs and British cooperator J. B. Tayler established an Indusco support center in Chengdu.

On the Chinese side were such veteran cooperators as Lu Guangmian, now vice-chairman of the revived Indusco, and a number of engineers who had received technical training at the Ford plant in Detroit or elsewhere through a program initiated by an American missionary, Joseph Bailie (Indusco named its training schools for him). The outstanding agrarian economist Dr. Chen Hansheng served Indusco in Hongkong and later in Guilin; the late Elsie Fairfax-Cholmeley was his assistant. Indusco enjoyed from birth the unflagging support of Soong Ching Ling, who herself chaired the Hong Kong Promotion Committee.

The essential concept that quickly took hold was that small-scale cooperative industry could in some measure substitute for the urban industries lost to the Japanese. It would give jobs to some of the refugees, many of them skilled, fleeing west, and it would be a democratic experience. Helen Snow, in a plea recalled by Alley, put it this way:

> Now look here Rewi, what China wants today is industry everywhere. It must have it. To get it spread wide enough it will have to be a movement. . . . Industry can work through cooperatives. . . . I tell you Rewi, you say you like China, you ought to drop this job of making Shanghai a better place for the Japanese to exploit [Alley was

then Chief Factory Inspector] and get out and do something that will be useful at this time. The Chinese are made for cooperation.[38]

The Indusco plan was accepted and initially supported by the Nationalist Government, then in Wuhan. Rewi Alley got there in July and two months later the first cooperative was launched. By October 1939, when I interviewed Director K. P. Liu and Rewi Alley in Chongqing, 1,298 cooperatives were producing a wide variety of much-needed consumer goods and blankets and other things for the military. Clusters of cooperatives were opening primary schools and clinics.

That the Chinese Industrial Cooperatives got off to a good start and persevered thereafter was the result of the ingenuity, resourcefulness, determination, and selflessness of many people, some experienced in cooperation but most new to it. They organized and by hard work kept alive the thin line of cooperatives that stretched from Inner Mongolia to Guangxi. But important financial and material help was soon coming from abroad.

To take charge of the U.S. effort Helen Snow called on a Beijing friend, Ida Pruitt, for years a social worker at the PUMC Hospital and author of such notable books as *Daughter of Han*. Pruitt had a long conversation with Rewi Alley and that decided her. Before long she was in New York directing Indusco Inc., American Committee in Aid of Chinese Industrial Cooperatives, with offices on Fourth Avenue (now Park Avenue South).

Opening doors and pocketbooks for her was a long list of sponsors which included Eleanor Roosevelt and many other distinguished Americans. The industrial cooperatives seemed to be "the best foundation on which to build a better standard of living for the people," the president's wife wrote. She devoted part of her column, *My Day*, to Indusco.

In its first fifteen months of effort, Indusco Inc. sent $146,364.20 to the cooperatives, a very substantial sum at a time when $200 would start a cotton-weaving cooperative, $500 a machine-making cooperative, and $625 would support a Bailie training class for one year.

A committee headed by Walter Rautensrauch, dean of Columbia University's School of Engineering, working with Indusco Inc.'s technical director, David Leacock, prepared blueprints and instructions for the manufacture of gasogenes (gas producers fueled by wood, char-

---

38. Rewi Alley, *Two Years of Indusco* (Hongkong: Hong Kong Promotion Committee, 1940).

coal, or anthracite), sponge iron, and improved simple looms. Norman Applezweig, Indusco Inc.'s chemical consultant, prepared instructions for making penicillin, which were transmitted by the Office of War Information in Washington. Data on dyestuffs, coal tar distillation, adhesives, varnishes and stains, and cleaners and alloys were also sent, and China-bound travelers took in their luggage such scarce items as vernier calipers, chemical balances, steel rules, and thickness gauges.

Ida Pruitt personally saw that a consignment of American machinery got to its destination in the interior, riding in the truck every jolting mile and holding her breath at every ferry.

The reports from the five regional headquarters and long letters from Alley to Pruitt, now in a collection at Columbia University, specify the aid needed and are appreciative when it is received. Rewi Alley wrote that David Leacock would be happy to know that his technical articles were being published in translation by the Loyang branch. Alley was especially thankful for help in coke and iron work processes and grateful also for reports on castor oil, indigo, jute and ramie. "Indusco Inc., as the USA committee styles itself, is a force to be counted on," he wrote to a friend in Calcutta.

To tell the Indusco story the New York office set up committees in major cities which held fund-raising events, scheduled speakers (among them Josephine Brown, Talitha Gerlach, and Pruitt), showed a film *(A Nation Rebuilds)*, organized exhibits of Indusco products and photos, and published pamphlets, leaflets, and a monthly bulletin. Americans who wanted to know more were referred to Helen Foster Snow's book, *China Builds for Democracy*, published in Hongkong and New York.

"Gung Ho" was made much of in the publicity. Its triangular logo appeared on the letterhead and all publications. But what introduced it into the language was its adoption by a battalion of Marines. Colonel, later General Evans Carlson, had worked with Rewi Alley for the Chinese Industrial Cooperatives a year before Pearl Harbor and he used the Gung Ho idea—which became extended to mean enthusiastic—in training his renowned unit, which won important island victories in the Pacific war. The accounts of the origin of Gung Ho in the press and later in a film (Randolph Scott was Carlson) made many more people aware of China's industrial cooperative movement.

Class 8-A of Public School 91 in Brooklyn reported to the New York office of Indusco that it had adopted Gung Ho as its slogan and had written letters to boys at the Bailie School in Shuangshipu. The

Commodore Stockton School in San Francisco performed a radio play *Gung Ho*. "If the world practices this spirit of Gung Ho, we will have the better world for which we are striving," a character said.

Letters and visitors from China increasingly told of difficulties and setbacks along with some hard-won successes. The goal had been to organize thirty thousand cooperatives and Rewi Alley had thought that the minimum for a viable network was ten thousand. But that plateau was never even approached. In effect, two Induscos developed. In the areas under the Nationalist regime, removed to Chongqing, the cooperatives were subjected to all sorts of bureaucratic and police harassments—just one of the reflections of official fears of popular movements. Inflation and a flood of goods from Japanese-controlled areas, the result of deliberate Chongqing policy, added enormously to Indusco's problems.[39]

But to the north, in the Shaanxi-Gansu-Ningxia Border Region and areas liberated by the Eighth Route Army, there was a thriving Indusco. Reporting to Washington on the economy in these areas in August 1944, U.S. diplomat John S. Service wrote from Yan'an that "Societies organized under the Chinese Industrial Cooperatives increased in three years from less than thirty to 343." He noted that the local government provided capital without exacting interest.

Indusco was beginning to flourish in the New Fourth Army liberated areas in Anhui but was among the victims of the attack on the New Fourth by Nationalist troops in January 1941.

New York Indusco, and indeed the entire International Committee, brought progressive Western opinion to bear on the plight of the cooperatives in the Nationalist areas, and the succession of statements and remonstrances did somewhat alleviate the pressure.

The New York committee also worked hard, with help from many influential Americans, to get a portion of an American loan to China of $500 million earmarked for Indusco, but while President Roosevelt expressed himself as sympathetic, he concluded that he had to avoid any semblance of interfering in China's internal affairs. He sent this message to the committee through Lauchlin Currie, his administrative assistant:

> While the allocation of the sums authorized by the act of February 7, 1942, is, of course, a matter entirely within the province of the Government of China, the President desires me to assure you of his

---

39. For an early account of the difficulties in the Kuomintang area, see Hugh Deane, "The Travails of China's Cooperatives," *China Today*, October 1941.

continued interest in the efforts of the Chinese Industrial Cooperatives to contribute to the development of industrial production in China.[40]

The New York committee increasingly had its own internal problems—a reflection of the polarizing politics of China. Indusco Inc. was part of an umbrella organization, United China Relief, for purposes of fund raising and fund allocations, and United China Relief was ever more obviously dominated by powerful corporate friends of the regime of Generalissimo Chiang. About a half-dozen Chongqing officials were actually members of its board. The New York committee had to battle for a fair share of revenues and for its right to decide how its share should be spent. Communist baiting, which reached its peak in the heyday of McCarthyism, fueled the controversy. In the U.S., as in China itself, those associated with Indusco were accused of being Red and the faint-hearted of those serving on its board of directors found excuses to resign.

In 1952, three years after Liberation, Indusco was abolished in China—a mistake, hindsight suggests. The New York committee had ceased activity somewhat earlier, by which time it had raised $3.5 million for the industrial cooperatives and inspired and nourished American feelings of friendship for the people of China.

Some of those feelings survived the long chill of U.S.-China relations and went into the creation of the US-China Peoples Friendship Association. And some in the leadership of the New York committee became leaders in the USCPFA. Polly Babcock, now Polly Babcock Feustal, who organized Indusco's Manila committee and later served as a director of the New York committee, became an organizer of the Palm Beach chapter. Richard Pastor, labor secretary of Indusco Inc., is a member of the New York chapter; he and I co-edited *China and Us*, the chapter's publication. Ida Pruitt herself was a founding member of the Philadelphia Chapter and a constant help to it until her death in 1985 at the age of ninety-six. She and Indusco were honored by the chapter at a memorable banquet rich in Gung Ho reminiscence.

---

40. This message was sent to Indusco, Inc., American Committee in Aid of Chinese Industrial Cooperatives, Dr. J. Henry Carpenter, Chairman, probably in March 1942. The committee's papers are in the Columbia University archives. On March 19 a group of twenty prominent Americans cabled Chiang Kai-shek expressing the hope that $50 million from the $500 million American loan would be allocated to the industrial cooperatives, but the reality of course was the plundering of the loan for the further personal enrichment of the Soong family; the cooperatives got nothing. The signers of the vain cable included such prominent individuals as Pearl Buck, John Dewey, Gifford Pinchot, Carl Crow, Arthur N. Holcomb of Harvard, Nathaniel Peffer, and of course Dr. Carpenter.

14. Serving Counterrevolution: Mary Miles And SACO

Happy Valley is an old name for an area of mountainside and valley a dozen miles up the Jialing River from Chongqing—Chungking we called it in the years when it served as China's wartime capital. But the name became an irony in the 1940s when Dai Li, head of China's equivalent of the Gestapo, turned an area four miles wide and six miles deep into an 800-building complex that included barracks, a parade ground, an armory, rifle and pistol ranges, classrooms, police dog kennels, pigeon cotes, radio communications, a prison, and interrogation, torture and execution facilities. The compound, girt with watch towers and, later, electrified fence, served two organizations—Dai's "Bureau of Investigation and Statistics," which operated a net of secret police, assassin specialists, armed units, twenty concentration camps and twenty prisons, and its ally, the "Sino-American Cooperation Organization" (SACO, pronounced "socko").

The end was blood and fire. On November 27, 1949, the eve of the arrival of the People's Liberation Army, police trained and armed by SACO executed the inmates of the two prisons, which were burned along with the SACO files.

The central section of the old SACO compound has now become the U.S. and Chiang Kai-shek Criminal Activities Exhibition. Daily groups of cadres and students, units of the PLA, family groups, and a sprinkling of abashed Americans and other foreign tourists are guided through a museum and then taken to the two prisons, which have been reconstructed, the torture chamber, and the acid pool.

The American face that looks out at you from a grainy photo as you start the museum tour belongs to Commander (later Captain, Commodore, and Admiral) Milton E. Miles, USN. "Mary Miles," everyone called him, without smiling. Mary Miles Minter was a silent screen heart throb of the 1920s, when Miles was at Annapolis. His fellow midshipmen gave him the nickname Mary and it stayed with him, though Edgar Snow tactfully changed it to Merry in his *Journey to the Beginning*.

Miles did two tours of duty in China waters and got an advanced degree in engineering which helped to win him the post of head of Naval Group China and deputy to Dai Li in SACO. He was the perfect choice from the point of view of the Kuomintang regime. He knew the workings of technical equipment, and was a virulent anti-Communist and a sucker for flattery. His credulity was such that his notion of Chinese realities was an almost perfect reversal. As the Chinese Communists were converting peasant support into military and political power, Miles declared that "the peasants hate the Communists because they take away their land." As the Eighth Route and New Fourth Armies armed themselves with captured Japanese and later American weapons, Miles reported that they fought with Russian weapons sent to them from Mongolia. He thought that the Japanese and the Reds had formed an alliance; Dai Li, who in fact had dealings with the puppets and probably with the Japanese themselves, told him so. To his last years, when he was writing his book, *A Different Kind of War*,[41] he believed that naive and traitorous Americans had "sold China down the river."

Joint U.S. Navy-Dai Li activities began in 1942, the outcome of conversations between a Dai agent posted to the Chinese embassy in Washington and several naval officers, among them Miles. SACO, based on a broader agreement and including the Office of Strategic Services (OSS), was established in the spring of 1943. Dai and Chiang Kai-shek (who personally signed the agreement, as did Roosevelt) saw SACO as a separate source of U.S. supplies, as a foil to "Vinegar" Joe Stilwell, as a device for keeping a stranglehold on U.S. intelligence in China, and, most importantly, as a way of getting specialized training and equipment for Dai's secret police and counterinsurgency forces. The Navy wanted weather reports for the benefit of the Pacific Fleet (weather moves east out of Mongolia) and data on coastal shipping and possible landing sites. It had a China tradition—gunboats patrolling the Yangtze, the port calls of the Seventh Fleet, and Marines in Shanghai and Beijing—and it looked ahead to a major postwar role.

For half a year Miles was nominal head of the OSS in China, as well as of Naval Group China, but the OSS found itself in a straitjacket. Dai feared it as too independent and suspected rightly that it wanted links with the Reds. Wild Bill Donovan himself came to Chongqing, exchanged savage threats with Dai Li at a banquet and removed the OSS contingent from Miles' command. The OSS was part of the Fourteenth Air Force intelligence, sent five agents to Yan'an as part of the Dixie Mission and ran two deep cover operations (Starr and Clam) that Dai knew nothing about. But, in general, it was lim-

---

41. (New York: Doubleday, 1967). Miles joined Ambassador Patrick Hurley and General Wedemeyer in testifying before the Joint Chiefs of Staff in March 1945. They said the Communists were weak and that "Rebellion in China could be put down by comparatively small assistance to Chiang's central government." Michael Schaller, *The U.S. Crusade in China, 1938–45* (New York: Columbia University Press, 1979), 216.

ited to a secondary role in the China theater. It had strong reason to believe that some of its Chinese agents were being killed by Dai's.

Having taken in the photos memorializing SACO's birth, we move on. More photos and artifacts depict the Happy Valley compound and tell the SACO story. Some 2,500 Americans, most of them Navy, did tours of duty with SACO during the three years it functioned, serving in Happy Valley, in the fourteen SACO branches, with Dai Li's Loyal Patriotic Army and other counterinsurgency units, or as coastal watchers.

On display are familiar helmets, small arms, radio and weather reporting equipment, odds and ends of military Americana collected by the PLA from the Happy Valley debris.

SACO did some useful work, though many of the claims for it were inventions, like the military pronouncements of the Kuomintang regime generally. Its weather reports, gathered at some fifty stations, and those obtained independently by Fourteenth Air Force intelligence, ended a Japanese advantage and helped the fleets on the offensive in the Pacific. Sightings of coastal shippings fetched bombers and resulted in substantial Japanese losses.

But SACO's major role was counterinsurgency. It was providing expertise and equipment to a secret police engaged in a perpetual hunt for Reds and other dissidents; it was training and arming forces being prepared for use in the expected civil war, forces which even then were attacking small Communist guerrilla bands. Altogether SACO trained and/or equipped forty to fifty thousand of Dai Li's troops.

Unit Nine in Happy Valley did the police training. It consisted of former FBI and Secret Service agents, "Narcs" from Treasury, and veterans of the Bomb Squad of the New York City Police and the New York State Police—"two dozen hand-picked specialists in mayhem and protection," Miles called them. Carefully selected Dai Li agents were instructed in the latest techniques and devices serving bullet analysis, surveillance, interrogation and information evaluation. And when General Albert Wedemeyer,[42] Stilwell's successor, insisted that U.S. personnel not take part in the assassination of Communists, Dai Li told him not to worry: "Americans would not be asked to do that. Their job was to train the Chinese to do it."

U.S. equipment provided included shackles, lie detectors, and truth serum. Miles says in *A Different Kind of War* that Unit Nine

---

42. Schaller, *The U.S. Crusade in China*, 243.

was Dai's pet project and that no expense was spared by him in making the instructors comfortable and content.

U.S. policy at the time was to stay clear of the Kuomintang-Communist conflict. Until the war ended—when intervention in behalf of Chiang Kai-shek became the policy—the U.S. had to consider the potential usefulness of the Eighth Route and New Fourth Armies and it had to keep in mind that downed American pilots were being rescued by them. The increasingly evident weakness of the Chiang regime had convinced some shapers of policy, not yet found disloyal, that the Communists had to be allowed some political future. In any case, the possibility of Soviet intervention had to be taken into account. SACO was an affront to this policy. Stilwell despised it and sought to terminate it, and even his more pro-Chiang successor, Wedemeyer, moved to control it and belatedly succeeded. Even General Chennault of the Fourteenth Air Force had to temper his anti-Communist zeal as long as Communist guerrillas were rescuing his flyers.

Miles and SACO were soon part of the cabal to force Stilwell's recall, which succeeded in 1944, and later cooperated with Ambassador Pat Hurley in backstabbing American diplomats critical of the Chiang regime and in sending slanted appraisals of the China scene to Washington. Miles enabled Hurley to bypass regular channels by giving him access to SACO's own radio communications with Washington, the consequence being that Dai Li and Chiang were instantly privy to internal U.S. bickering.

More photos, many of them blurred, more artifacts and blown up extracts of key documents bring us to a depiction of SACO in the last stages of the war and the first months of what proved to be a fragile peace.

Chiang and his generals were fond of saying that the Japanese were just a skin disease, while the Communists were a disease of the heart.[43] So Dai Li built up his own armed forces, saw to it they were used sparingly against the Japanese, and stockpiled supplies from the U.S., meanwhile engaging in large-scale smuggling in cooperation with Shanghai gangsters and Chinese puppet regime officials. U.S.

---

43. OSS agent Oliver J. Caldwell believes that Dai Li may have betrayed Twentieth Air Force information to the Japanese, causing heavy plane losses. Caldwell also charges that Dai Li placed obstacles in the way of operations in the Japanese-held areas, though he had seven million troops and secret society members under his command. "Wonders were to be performed. Time passed and wonders failed to materialize." *A Secret War: Americans in China, 1944–45* (Carbondale, Ill.: Southern Illinois University Press, 1972), 55, 90.

Army intelligence believed that Dai, or high-ups in his organization, were selling intelligence to the Japanese themselves.

Japan's surrender in August 1945 activated Dai Li and SACO. The Loyal Patriotic Army and other counterinsurgency forces raced to occupy Shanghai and other cities and towns in the lower Yangtze basin and also in Fujian Province to the south, helped by deals with the top puppet, Zhou Fohai (successor to Wang Jingwei), and the Shanghai Mafia (Miles and the head of it became "fast friends"). In direct violation of a Wedemeyer order, Miles sent SACO units into areas where armed clashes with the Communists could hardly be avoided, cabling these provocative instructions on August 12: "General Dai Li has ordered Commando Army, Loyal Patriotic Army and other miscellaneous forces under his command to proceed to major cities in occupational zones to establish order for Central Government. . . . SACO Americans will proceed with their authorized Chinese unit commanders. Carry with you complete radio equipment and go fully armed. Keep this secret from your outside friends. Send all possible arms and ammunition to the Loyal Patriotic Army as soon as possible. . . . Continue logistic support. . . . " In a follow-up, Miles told recipients to "burn this after swearing your units to secrecy."[44]

The succession of crises, increasing criticism, fatigue, and excessive use of drugs shattered Miles' mental health. He saw betrayal and Communists everywhere, even in Wedemeyer's headquarters; he raved that he would "blow the lid off." Navy medical staff constrained him and hustled him back to Washington. Recovered, he pressed for a Navy decoration for Dai Li, but the State Department and the Army blocked it. In March of 1946 Dai was killed in a plane crash, possibly caused by a bomb explosion. Miles was officially forbidden to attend the services, but with high-up Navy help was able to go in civilian clothes.

By April 1946 SACO was reduced to a handful of Navy personnel, soon homeward bound. By then it had provided Dai Li's Bureau of Investigation and Statistics with $17 million worth of supplies, about half arms.

We turn a corner and see instruments of torture—bamboo slivers for driving under fingernails, a flexible steel whip said to be U.S.-made, a nail-studded club used in what was called the Mourning Torture. The club made tiny wounds which were bound tightly with white cloth, which was ripped off when the blood congealed. White is the

---

44. Miles, *A Different Kind of War*, 520; Schaller, *The U.S. Crusade in China*, 247. The versions differ. Miles omits "keep this secret from your outside friends."

color of mourning in China; the look of the victims when wrapped in the cloth gave the torture its name. Dai's interrogators were said to boast that they could make a skeleton open its mouth.

The main prison was in the northernmost of the three valleys in the SACO compound, and when the wind was right, the Americans could hear the screams. OSS agent Oliver Caldwell recalled that one summer night he could not sleep because of the heat. A light breeze carried over the hill from the prison, hour after hour, the screams of a woman.

> The next night I was exhausted and thought I could sleep in spite of the heat. But again the soft breeze bore terrifying subhuman screams. There was no escaping the reality represented by these sounds. One could only swear to tell the story of the Valley and Dai Li where it would do some good. But it did no good. Report after report was sent to Washington and ignored. . . . [45]

Miles sat beside Dai Li at the trials of sorts that preceded executions; some of those found guilty were buried alive. (Dai Li never had anyone executed without proper authorization, Miles asserted in his book.) At some interrogations, according to surviving inmates, Americans operated lie detectors or administered truth serum.

Looking down at us from the museum wall is a gallery of the known prisoners, men and women, almost all young, some of the men wearing ties for the photographer, the women with tidy hair. Leading members of the Communist underground in the Kuomintang-ruled areas. Teachers, writers and artists disenchanted with the Chiang regime. Xu Jianye, leading organizer of workers. Jiang Zhuyan, a woman given the bamboo torture. Tang Huangyan, journalist, one of the few who survived. With some of the photos are poems, songs, or extracts from letters they wrote. Li Lailai, my interpreter, quickly identifies each with the fictional names given them in *Red Crag*, a popular novel of the bloody end of Happy Valley by two survivors.[46]

Also on the wall are diary extracts, capsule entries: February 10— My teeth were smashed; May 10—the hunger strike. These were

45. Caldwell, *A Secret War*, 77.
46. *Red Crag*, by Luo Guangbin and Yang Yiyang, was published in English in 1978 by Foreign Languages Press in Beijing. A film, *Immortality in the Burning Flames*, and a play and an opera relate the SACO-Happy Valley story.

killed by Yuan . . . ; August 21—Forbidden to read newspapers; September 5—I was taken to the special rooms. . . .

We come to the evidence of the end. A photo of the pit where ninety-four bodies were found, still handcuffed. I learn later that the handcuffs were made in Springfield, Massachusetts, my home town.

We see the shoes of executed children . . . the stained coat of General Yang Hucheng, who was stabbed to death in the fall of 1949. Yang and the Young Marshal, Zhang Xueliang, organized the kidnapping of Chiang Kai-shek at Xi'an in December 1936. They spared his life, but he did not spare Yang, nor even the members of his family.

A hurried attempt by the Chongqing Communist underground and local guerrillas to rescue the prisoners did not come off, but smuggled messages informed them of the advances of the People's Liberation Army. They celebrated by shaping red stars out of toothbrush handles and making a huge red flag out of bed clothes. A radio description of the new flag, unfurled October 1, was smuggled to them and they got it about right, though one yellow star was bigger than the others.

Approaching the exit, we see the red stars and the flag, a photo of weeping women identifying bodies, a photo of the prison commandant at his public trial. And finally a page from the confession of a captured U.S. Army officer, one of those who had worked with Dai Li's successors during the civil war. He was released in 1956.

From the museum we walk to the two prisons.

The most prominent prisoners were kept in the twenty-room Bai House, converted from a mansion named for the Tang dynasty poet, Bai Chu-yi (Bai Juyi). Yang Hucheng and family were held here, as was General Huang Xiansheng, a Kuomintang member who had commanded an anti-Japanese force in the Northeast (Manchuria). We paused at the small bridge where Huang was shot and killed by his guards. During the final weeks before Chongqing was captured by the Reds' Second Field Army, the Bai House prisoners were handcuffed and taken away in batches, usually after the 4 p.m. meal. They were told they were being transferred to another prison but were taken to a pit and cut down by submachine fire.

The main interrogation/torture chamber was a cave directly behind Bai House, and the acid pool where individual prisoners were fatally immersed was close by.

The larger of the prisons, built on what had been a coal mine, consisted of seventeen rectangular cells, fifteen for men and two for women, facing an exercise yard and a high wall. On the wall, appeals to the inmates to repent and confess were scrawled: "Your youth will pass, never to return. Think of where you are and how much time you have. . . . "

Some of the prisoners were executed singly or in twos or threes, but the approach of the Peoples' Liberation Army was swifter than expected and so a mass killing was carried out on the eve of its arrival. One of the fourteen survivors, Fu Boyong, a teacher at a girls' school at the time of his arrest, gave me a blow by blow account of what happened as we stood in the courtyard:

It was the night of November twenty-seventh. The second floor prisoners were brought down to first floor cells. I was in Cell Number 8 but was moved to Cell Number 7 along with my cell mates. The women were collected in Cell Number 8.

Officials and guards were coming and going. Agents we knew came and said they had to leave but others would take care of us.

Two trucks drove up. Soon we saw the light of a huge fire. SACO files were being burned, I learned later. The air thickened with smoke.

We grew apprehensive and fearful and asked what was happening. Soldiers were taking over the work of the prison guards, they told us.

The commandant arrived, and soon after soldiers with submachine guns took posts in front of the cell doors. A whistle blew. The soldiers thrust their guns through the square windows in the cell doors and fired.

We sang the *Internationale*. Some shouted slogans and cursed Chiang Kai-shek.

The firing lasted about twenty minutes, ending when the singing and screaming died away. Then the whistle blew again. The soldiers went around back and fired through the rear windows for some minutes.

The commandant shouted cease fire. Agents came into the cells and shot prisoners in the head.

I was in a corner and the submachine fire only wounded me in the leg. The shot at my head missed and I lay quiet.

They thought we were all dead but more than thirty were still alive. We got through the cell doors and burst into the courtyard. Some nineteen were killed there but fourteen of us got through a break in the wall that was undergoing repairs. Prisoners had been making the repairs but worked slow.

I scrambled up the mountain and got safely to the house of a friend and stayed there until the PLA marched into the city.

When Fu Boyong began his recital, he was speaking only to my two companions and myself. A crowd gathered. I remember the face of a boy of about ten or eleven which for the moment had lost the look of childhood.

The prison was burned after the killings but has been painstakingly reconstructed from the foundations. At the door to each cell are the names of those confined there, to the best of the recollection of survivors. As many names as possible are with photos. Inside on the walls are poems and songs:

> Flaming irons sear our breasts,
> Sharp bamboo splinters pierce each finger.
> Icy water floods our nostrils,
> Electric currents rack our bodies . . .
> In the evil flames of hell
> Man is tempered
> Until his will
> Becomes hard and bright as gold . . .

A couplet celebrating the New Year of 1949:

> Only months we've been in this cave,
> While outside millennia have passed.

And a renowned poem by Yeh Ting (Ye Ting), commander of the New Fourth Army, treacherously attacked by the Kuomintang during the Anti-Japanese War, seemed to respond to the appeal for confessions on the courtyard wall:

> Locked fast, the way out for men,
> Wide open, the escape hole for dogs. . . .

As death and fire came to Happy Valley, Miles was assuming command of a cruiser group. One of the succession of posts he held until his retirement in 1958 was naval attache in Chile, and in that post he rendered one more service to counterrevolution: he started a dossier on a promising young socialist politician, Salvador Allende.

The People's Republic turned SACO headquarters into a prison—tactfully called a training center—for captured high-ranking Kuomintang officers and officials. Among them were Xu Yuanji, one of those responsible for the November 27 massacre and for the torture of many prisoners, and Shen Zui, who had ordered the arrest and torture of many Communists and dissidents in Chongqing. One of Dai Li's principal aides, Shen had planned in detail the assassination or crippling of Soong Ching Ling in a contrived Shanghai auto accident but the project was abandoned at the last minute.

Xu, Shen, and others thought they would be executed, but were treated leniently and gradually brought to feelings of remorse. In a book published in English as well as Chinese, Shen has much to reveal about Dai Li, SACO and the murders of Communist prisoners.[47] He is now a member of the National Committee of the Chinese People's Political Consultative Conference, the highest advisory political body

15. Guerrillas Rescue a B-29 Bomber Crew

In August of 1944 a B-29, returning from a bombing mission over Japan, had engine trouble and caught fire and crashed some 150 miles north of Shanghai. It shattered four trees and a windmill, crossed a river and came to a halt in a rice field.

The crew had taken to parachutes. This account of how they were rescued and made much of is based on five articles published in the north Jiangsu area controlled by the Communist-led New Fourth Army. Chu Yin, Su Ming, Pei Hua and members of the staff of the North Jiangsu Branch Office were the reporters.

In a village only two miles from Japanese-occupied Hutao, peasants heading for home with their hoes on the rainy evening of August 20 cried out: "Clouds are falling from the sky and there are people in them."

A religious old woman, nervous, murmured prayers to Buddha. People shut themselves in their houses.

At dawn two red faces were discovered in a haystack. The red faces crept out and said things no one could understand. They waved small banners with the Chinese and American flags entwined. "Dear Chinese friends, we are Americans who came to China to fight against the Japanese," the banners said.

---

47. Shen Zui, *A KMT War Criminal in New China* (Changsha and Beijing, 1986).

People immediately knew that these were indeed Americans and invited them into their homes. The religious woman said, "These are members of the American New Fourth Army!"

Invited to sit down the Americans shook their heads. An elderly man cleaned the bench with a cloth but they still stood up. The old woman swept the whole area with a broom. "The New Fourth Army likes to be clean," she explained.

But the pair of Americans were looking east and the villagers understood that they were fearful of capture by the Japanese. Guards were then posted in the direction of Hutao.

A five-year-old touched the Americans' glittering things but was pulled away by the grown-ups.

A little later ten peasants, their clothes soaked through and muddy, escorted the Americans to the protection of peasant militia in a nearby village. A bed was prepared for them and they seemed to relax.

One American took red 100-yuan bills and handed them to the man who led the escort party, but he shook his head with a smile and turned to go. The American tried in vain to give him two silver pieces and then put a gold piece in his pocket. "Comrade, that would disgrace me," the man said, and handed back the coin.

Guards arrived escorting two other Americans who had dropped close by, one beside a small creek, the other in a rice paddy.

A woman brought boiled water in a teapot and invited the four to drink but they shook their heads. A youth thought they were afraid to drink and stood up and drank a mouthful. From then on the Americans dared to eat and drink whatever was offered them.

A unit of the New Fourth Army came, lined up, and saluted the Americans. People gathered from all over and the guests were served cakes, eggs, and tea.

An elderly woman set a good example, bringing out from under her bed twenty eggs she had saved for her daughter, who was pregnant. "Please tell our American friends I'm poor and the eggs are too few," she said.

A welcoming meeting was held after the Americans were fed, and they sang and laughed and praised their hosts by making a gesture with the thumb.

On the fifth day, the crew commander, Lieutenant Colonel William Savoie was brought to headquarters and reunited with four others: O'Brien, Stelmach, Lutz and Brundage.

Savoie had had a narrow escape. He had dropped into a puppet-controlled village and some of the peasants urged that he be turned over to the Japanese. But a young man stood up and protested: "He is helping us to fight the Japanese. With whom does our future lie? Let me guide him to the north and safety." The majority supported him and the others fell silent.

The youth hid Savoie in his own home and when Savoie would not eat the rough food offered him, went into Hutao itself and bought cakes for him. The next day he took Savoie to the New Fourth Army and handed over one by one the bills, silver dollars, ring and weapons belonging to him. A long look of gratitude and friendship was the young man's reward.

The arrival of two university students who knew some English made real communication possible. Savoie, who had a long face and short blond hair and blue eyes, said he was twenty-eight, came from Chicago, and had been on four bombing missions over Japan and one over Anshan in Liaoning.

He couldn't use chopsticks, though eager to learn. A spoon was found for him. He especially liked eggs. He carried with him a ground-up tea that could be quickly served in boiled water and had a strong taste. In the morning young and old gathered around him, he was happy and played with the children. He had a boy and a girl himself, he said. He sang American songs. Meanwhile, the New Fourth Army and peasant militia fought to keep the downed plane out of Japanese hands. While descending over Hutao the plane had dropped gasoline like raindrops and the Japanese knew it had crashed in the vicinity. A force of about seventy, plus forty puppet soldiers, headed for the plane. But it took the entire night to get close to the plane; apparently their respect for the New Fourth made them move cautiously.

Fighting started about 9 a.m. several hundred yards from the plane. The enemy came on in four columns, firing mortars and automatic weapons, and the Sixth Company could not prevent it from fording the river. But the Chinese were helped by a heavy downpour and then by the arrival of a large force of gong-beating peasant militiamen shouting: "Beat the Japanese devils! Save the Americans!"

A second militia force appeared to the north and the Japanese, surrounded, withdrew. The plane was saved at a cost of three wounded.

On August 26 a welcoming assembly was attended by about three thousand people. Each of the five Americans was presented with a Japanese sword. An exchange of speeches was followed by dances and skits performed by the Eighth Brigade Drama Association.

"We had heard about the New Fourth Army but thought it was a small force that fought only in the dark," Colonel Savoie said two days later as the group prepared to begin its trip west to its unit. "We have now seen that the New Fourth is a very strong, formally organized army controlling vast areas and able to fight also in the daylight."

Lieutenant Lutz said: "We have eaten too much. Your food has been delicious. We have different dishes every day and the banquet given us by the chief of staff consisted of fifteen courses. You yourselves, however, lead hard lives."

Captain O'Brien added: "I know what you have developed here. Everything necessary has been done. You have united troops and people, commanders and soldiers. You have a great potential and I hope your forces will be combined with the American forces."

Sergeant Ernest Brundage sang, danced and made jokes hour after hour as if he were at home. "The next time I fly over here, I will lean out and call your names," he said, and made a gesture of calling with his hands.

The contrast between two photos, one taken shortly after the rescue and one taken in New Fourth uniforms on their departure, bear out assurances that they were well nourished and cared for. Their smiles are wider.

Thirty-five years later, in 1979, Savoie and Brundage returned to China in a group of American veterans of the China theater and had an emotional reunion with members of the New Fourth Army who had rescued them. "All of us were staggered and touched by the amount of research that had been done to bring together so many participants in the rescue and to celebrate it so impressively," commented Gilbert Wasserman, a former B-29 bombardier who led the tour.

A Postscript   Guerillas and villagers got a brutal thank-you from the U.S. Marines who joined Kuomintang, Japanese, and puppet troops in trying to wrest control of north China from the Communists in 1945. Theodore H. White and Annalee Jacoby reported in *Thunder out of China* that "by a bitter irony the very area where the situation was most tense—around Peking [Beijing] and Tientsin [Tianjin]—was one in which Communist partisans had risked their lives time and again to rescue American flyers from the Japanese; crews of B-29s bailing out on their return from bombing Japan had been smuggled to safety by villagers who were now held to be enemies. In this area

Communists now sniped at marine trains; marines shelled a village in retaliation."

16. Remembering Koji Ariyoshi:
An American GI in Yan'an

In the spring of 1985 I visited Yan'an with a group of veteran American journalists who had worked in China. Once the center and symbol of a great cause and struggle, it had reverted to a prefectural seat. The state had poured in large sums to lift it out of the poverty that persisted through the first decades after Liberation, and the minds of most of those we interviewed were on the more hopeful present. Still, Mao's cave dwellings (he moved twice) and other historical sites are kept tidy for the dwindled flow of visitors, and reminders of the American presence abound.

We reflected at the stone table and seats where Mao gave the famous interview to Anna Louise Strong in which he likened reactionaries to paper tigers. We entered the Dixie Mission cave residences that now serve an outstanding middle school as dormitories, and chatted with students full of aspirations.

Edgar Snow and Ma Haide (George Hatem) were just the first Americans to make the pilgrimage to the Northwest. Photos on the walls of the caves and in the Memorial Museum of the Revolution recall the Americans who recorded their hopes and sympathies in enduring books—Agnes Smedley in her Red Army uniform, Strong with Zhou Enlai, and photos by, as well as of, Snow. The photo of the Canadian Dr. Norman Bethune, whose medical service in north China and death there is known to all Chinese school children, was on the wall of Mao's cave. And coming upon a group photo I found myself looking into the eyes of Koji Ariyoshi.

In a highly publicized trial in 1952–53, Koji Ariyoshi, editor of the *Honolulu Record*, and six other Hawaiians were convicted of conspiring to overthrow the government of the United States by force and violence, in violation of the Smith Act. ("We're trying you for what's in your head," the prosecutor snapped at him once.) In June of 1953 Ariyoshi was sentenced to five years in prison, but appeal proceedings won a reversal after dragging on for five years.

FBI agents arrested Ariyoshi on August 28, 1951. That evening, out on bail, he went to the *Record* office and found, as he wrote years later to a friend, that the staff "thought we were done for." If the staff believed that, what were the plantation workers and other readers of the weekly newspaper thinking? He pounded out a long article, "Meaning of the Arrests," which "stiffened the backs of the people."

That article was followed by another, "My Thoughts: For Which I Stand Indicted," which turned into a series of fifty-nine under that title. A sustained act of resistance to McCarthyism, the series linked the crackdown on Communists and other dissidents to the domestic assault on unions and other popular organizations and to the world-wide U.S. offensive against revolutions and national movements. He went into the specifics of his own experiences and thinking to show how he had come to his conclusions.

And, as a powerful counterpoint to a U.S. scene marked by considerable pessimism and retreat, he told the China story. He told what he himself had seen there, and he related that to an overall account of how the Chinese people had stood up to their oppressors and begun the transformation of an ancient society. Of the fifty-nine articles, thirty-two deal wholly or in part with China. They are a treasure of U.S.-China peoples' friendship.

In Article XXVII of the *My Thoughts* series, Ariyoshi described how profoundly moved he was by his first view, a view from the air, of China. His feelings then presaged many moving experiences to come. The *My Thoughts* articles tell how, step by step, a Nisei (second generation Japanese-American) worker turned GI gave his heart and mind to the Chinese revolution.

China had long been in Ariyoshi's consciousness. At the University of Hawaii he had pleaded China's case against Japan to Nisei students and others. He helped to raise money for Chinese students fleeing westward from the Japanese invaders, and wrote an article for the student newspaper about a university in caves, in Yan'an. But Ariyoshi was touched by China for deeper reasons, because of what he had gone through, because of what he was.

Ariyoshi was born in Kona in 1914. He was the son of an indentured sugar plantation worker who became a small cotton farmer—one of the victims of Japanese feudalism who had knocked at Hawaii's golden door and found waiting a life of toil so hard that strong men gulped soy sauce to induce a fever that would give them a day of rest. And he was the son of a small woman with callused, grass-stained hands who ended every day prostrate with exhaustion.

He learned early about struggle. About the two hundred Japanese sugar workers who in 1890 threw down their tools and marched eighteen hours on Honolulu to obtain redress of grievances and who, rebuffed, came on again. About the sugar strikes of 1909 and 1920. And when he was in jail, his mother reminded relatives that the great leaders of those strikes, Yasutaro Soga, Fred Makino, and others, had been there before him.

As a child, Ariyoshi picked coffee berries. As a teenager, he scrambled for any sort of job, handicapped by the Depression and his Japanese extraction. "Because I have worked all my life with my hands, even while a student, my loyalty has always been with the downtrodden, the workers and the farmers," he wrote in Article I of *My Thoughts*. He pulped coffee, clerked store, was a bricklayer's helper, did WPA (Work Projects Administration) road work, drove trucks, worked in a pineapple cannery. Finally he caught on as a longshoreman, working the docks in Honolulu and later in San Francisco, becoming a militant member of the International Longshoremen's and Warehousemen's Union led by Harry Bridges.

Ariyoshi was an inquisitive man, a thirsty reader. He scoured libraries that seemed to be overflowing with the works of Zane Grey for books of substance. He found Theodore Dreiser's *An American Tragedy* and, moved, read it again and yet again. Years later he was deeply pleased to discover that his son Roger was a serious reader. Returning home late at night after long hours of work he would "find my son waiting for me. He wanted to discuss Plato, Socrates, Voltaire, Marx and Lenin, and Mao Zedong. We would have a dialogue until two or three in the morning and you can imagine the feeling of satisfaction I obtained from such an opportunity."

In 1937 work on the docks brought Ariyoshi to the University of Hawaii, and conscientious study won him a scholarship at the University of Georgia, where he took a course in journalism. In Georgia he was busy with more than book learning. He had applied to go to the University of Georgia because of a stimulating talk with author Erskine Caldwell, and with the help of Caldwell's parents, Mr. and Mrs. Ira C. Caldwell, he found for himself that Tobacco Road was not fiction, as some of his fellow students claimed, but a harsh reality. And later in India, Ceylon, and China he learned the broader truth, observed by Mrs. Caldwell, that "Tobacco Road is not just in Georgia. It's a belt running around the world." His experiences with Black people gave him a lasting fellow feeling for those who rode the back of the bus.

Ariyoshi was working on the San Francisco docks when the Japanese struck at Pearl Harbor. He was one of the 110,000 persons of Japanese ancestry—many of them citizens like him—who were placed in detention camps.[48] The watch towers and barbed wire of Manzanar were for him, as for many prisoners before and since, a school—teaching him, among other things, that rights don't depend on what the law says, but on the organized strength of understanding people. Scores of thousands, including his wife Taeko, were in the camps until 1945. His daughter Linda was born there. The gate opened for him first because of the need of Idaho beet farmers for people to do stoop labor, and stayed open because of the army's need for Japanese-speaking personnel. Manzanar lived in Ariyoshi's consciousness. Six months before he died he wrote an account of it in the form of a letter to his granddaughter Wendi. He wanted those who came after to know of this bitter time.

Ariyoshi volunteered for the army in December 1943 and was assigned to the China-Burma-India Theater after training in intelligence in Minnesota. His China tour ended in July 1946 and he shipped out of Shanghai for home.

China engrossed him from the time he flew over the Himalayas—The Hump—to Kunming, capital of Yunnan Province and a U.S. military center. "Only a few times have I been moved so deeply by the sight of land as I was when I saw China for the first time from the sky," he wrote in a *My Thoughts* article.[49] He saw scarred land, cultivated to the hilltops, showing every mark of human toil. From the sky he saw "so much beauty on the face of the good earth," but when he hiked around the countryside afoot, he saw "a picture of poverty and struggling humanity." In the villages he looked into the faces of peasants who handed over 50 to 60 percent of their crops to landlords for rent, and in Kunming he saw both "pompous, porky and smooth-skinned landlords drinking and dining and wasting food" and on narrow, cobble-stoned streets "GIs hurrying away as emaciated, sore-covered beggars in tattered rags ran after them." He remembered the Battle Cry of Kunming, "Joe, no papa, no mama, no first sergeant." He remembered the "You say how much" of the prostitutes.

In the fog-shrouded wartime capital of Chongqing, Ariyoshi undertook his first assignment—to investigate efforts to change the thinking of Japanese war prisoners. He found that some captives had indeed been won over and formed into propaganda teams at the front lines but he was dismayed to learn also that the Chiang Kai-shek

---

48. In August 1988 the U.S. government agreed to pay more than $1 billion, or about $20,000 each, to the surviving Japanese-Americans who were held in World War II detention camps after the Pearl Harbor incident in 1941.
49. The following quotations are also from *My Thoughts*.

regime had discerned a threat in the prisoner program and placed such limitations on it that by 1944 it had been reduced to a show window used to impress visiting journalists and diplomats.

But a more effective program of prisoner conversion was going on in the vast areas of north China liberated by the Communist-led Eighth Route Army, and late in October 1944, Ariyoshi was sent to Yan'an by the China director of the U.S. Office of War Information (OWI) to see for himself. He was to stay a month, long enough to prepare a report, but the month stretched into nineteen with the thirty-member U.S. military observer group that had been sent to Yan'an the previous July—called Dixie Mission because it was located in "rebel" territory. When he left he was the senior member in length of service, and he had been promoted from a T4, a technical sergeant, to a second lieutenant. But the main change was inside him. He came away a staunch partisan of the Chinese revolution.

The transport that took Ariyoshi north to Yan'an crossed over the wall of soldiers that separated Chiang Kai-shek's China from the new China in hard birth. Chiang and his officialdom saw the Communist areas as a more serious adversary than the Japanese, and assigned a half-million of their best troops to blockade Yan'an. Supplies, even medical supplies, were not allowed through. Students and others trying to get through were imprisoned; many were tortured to make them abjure sympathy with a resistance to the Japanese that was also beginning to change Chinese society. The U.S. was then somewhat unhappy over Chiang's divisive policy. It viewed the Eighth Route and New Fourth Armies in north and central China as necessary ingredients of the effort to bring Japan down. It wanted weather reports from north China and the cooperation of guerrillas in rescuing downed American pilots, and it looked ahead to possible joint military operations along the China coast. General Joseph Stilwell, before Chiang forced his recall, and American officers and diplomats even after that, urged Chiang to preserve China's unity. In the spring and summer of 1944 sustained U.S. pressure brought about a visit to Yan'an by American and other foreign correspondents, and the establishment of Dixie Mission.

Yan'an was in a north-south valley with a thin stream and a pagoda on a hill. Ariyoshi wrote:

> The land looked old and tired, bare after the autumn harvest. Everything looked ancient, peaceful and desolate. A few buildings were in sight. A fairly large Western-style church nestled close against a hillside. It was the most impressive edifice. But more

striking than anything were the caves, hundreds and hundreds of them pockmarking hillsides and cliffs, tier upon tier, up from the valley floor.

The Americans were warmly welcomed. Ariyoshi saw that the women were dressed like the men. Their hair was hidden by deep caps and they wore no rouge or lipstick; chapped lips were painted with honey.

> I saw a kindly face, broad and seamed, half-smiling at me. A warm, firm hand gripped mine. The man before me was like a peasant, extremely simple in appearance, clad in a faded, brown woolen-tweed uniform. He was stocky and heavy. This was the legendary Chu Teh (Zhu De), commander-in-chief of the Communist-led forces.

In his first weeks in Yan'an, Ariyoshi found out, first by talking to Americans and then learning for himself, that the area, called the Shaan-Gan-Ning (Shaanxi-Gansu-Ningxia) Border Region, was truly a unique segment of China. No beggars, no prostitutes, no hands stretched out for bribes. Life was austere, but all ate and were clothed. The first steps were being taken to ease the age-old burden of the peasants and to give the people a say in the making of decisions. A spirit of caring and selflessness prevailed. Some of the Americans called the area "Shangri-La." "If you describe things the way they are in reports, they'll think you are making propaganda, so be very careful," a captain cautioned Ariyoshi.

Earlier an American member of a transport crew made persistent passes at a young woman at a dance given to honor the visitors. The next day General Ye Jianying, chief of staff, indignantly protested to Colonel David Barrett, the U.S. commander. Forget anything you may have heard about Communist "free love," he said. Yan'an was not Chongqing. Though the Americans were denied pleasures of the flesh available to them elsewhere, entertainment was provided them by the Chinese. Every Saturday night they crossed the Yan River and went to a dance at army headquarters.

Ariyoshi plunged into his work of investigating the prisoner program. He spent days in cold caves talking to the responsible cadres, most of them Japanese exiles, and listening to the halting efforts of prisoners to express new thoughts about themselves, Japan, and the war. In the evenings he typed with numbed fingers reports destined for distant, and presumably skeptical, superiors.

In 1944, after painful beginnings, the Yan'an program made real progress, partially solving the problem of obtaining live prisoners from guerrillas enraged over the smashing of their villages, and the even more difficult problem of getting any positive response from the prisoners. The first captives lay on their bunks day and night, in a state of profound depression, refusing even to wash their faces, their thoughts on suicide. But gradually their ideas of *bushido* (a Japanese feudal code of behavior stressing self-sacrifice) and the shame they felt at having been taken prisoner by a people they had been taught to look down on yielded to outstretched hands and weeks of discussion. A Japanese People's Emancipation League was formed. Teams of former prisoners went to the front-line guerrilla areas and addressed Japanese units over loudspeakers, sometimes with good results. Ariyoshi remembered interviewing five soldiers induced to desert Blockhouse 50 in northern Hebei.

As Ariyoshi's stay extended beyond the originally scheduled thirty days, his assignments broadened. He debriefed rescued pilots and other U.S. military personnel who had visited guerrilla areas and he interviewed Japanese and Korean refugees and deserters for intelligence purposes.[50] Much of his time was given to the U.S. propaganda effort in north China conducted by the OWI with the cooperation of the Communist authorities.

In 1944, and early 1945, when relations between the U.S. and Yan'an were good, U.S. films, film strips, and photo collections were shown through the liberated areas. A Chinese army unit did the showing, using an old gasoline generator and a projector and amplifier taken from village to village on an ox cart and a mule. In the Yan'an area Ariyoshi himself showed U.S. documentary films on an OWI projector. Films on the TVA, farm mechanization, and factory production were well received but one titled "Farmer Henry Brown," about a successful Black farmer, stirred skeptical comment.

The period of good relations was marked by cooperative work in such areas as weather reporting and intelligence gathering and by mutual learning—the Chinese learned that not all the Americans were womanizers who drank too much, and many of the Americans adapted themselves to and came to like the simple, purposeful society about them. The Chinese and the Americans entered into an unending dialogue on a wide variety of subjects. The Communist liaison officers (one of them was Huang Hua, earlier Edgar Snow's inter-

---

50. Five of Ariyoshi's intelligence reports are in *The Amerasia Papers: A Clue to the Catastrophe of China*, vol. 2 (Washington: U.S. Government Printing Office, 1970).

preter, later Foreign Minister) and other cadres and students asked many questions about politics and economics in the United States.

Largely ignorant of Marxism ("Was this guy Karl Marx the first Russian dictator?" a perplexed officer asked once), some Americans concluded that since what they observed was good, Chinese Communists couldn't really be Communists. This led to discussions in the mess hall, which was named Whittlesey Hall by the Communists in honor of a member of the Dixie Mission who lost his life in the area. Ariyoshi enjoyed listening to the comments and adding his own.

One American in Yan'an, not a member of Dixie Mission, had studied Marxism-Leninism and could discuss informatively Chinese Communist perspectives and Mao's thinking. He was Dr. George Hatem, who had arrived in the Communist northwest with Edgar Snow in 1936 and was there for good. Becoming a Chinese citizen and adopting the name Ma Haide, he was beginning a life of service to Chinese medicine and the health of the people. Dr. Ma ate many of his meals in the American mess hall, usually arriving with his friend Huang Hua, and took part in the lively conversations there and in the frequent evening bull sessions. Ariyoshi learned a great deal from him and years later wrote, "China has no greater friend among Americans than Ma Haide."

Ariyoshi saw the turn in U.S. policy. From one of hesitant movement toward cooperation with the Communist forces in north and central China, it changed into a counterrevolutionary effort in support of the Chiang regime. Overtures to the Communists were replaced by barely concealed hostility. As long as Japan appeared to be a formidable adversary, as long as the U.S. military analysis envisaged massive ground operations, a strong case could be made for joint arrangements with the forces fighting against Japan extending, intermittently, from Inner Mongolia to Hainan Island. Stilwell was for cooperation, as were John S. Service and most of his State Department colleagues in China. But as the tide of war turned and the perimeter of Japanese-held territories shrank, the anti-Communist ideologues and friends of Chiang in top U.S. circles became assertive. The recall of Stilwell in October 1944 was the first of a series of successes for them. The incineration of flesh at Hiroshima and Nagasaki and the collapse of Japan fixed the American commitment to sustain the Chiang regime.

A self-promoting, eccentric, and finally negative role in the making of U.S. policy was played by Patrick J. Hurley, an oil millionaire from Oklahoma, whom President Roosevelt sent to China as his envoy in the fall of 1944, following the recall of Stilwell and the resignation of Ambassador Clarence E. Gauss. Hurley initially set himself as the builder of Chinese unity, as a peace-minded mediator between the Communists and the Kuomintang, but his objective, like that covertly pursued later by the Marshall Mission later, was an agreement embodying Communist subservience to the Kuomintang. The false promise of Hurley's arrival in Yan'an was replete with dramatic contrasts, of which Ariyoshi was a sharp observer:

Like a seasoned ham actor, Hurley played up to the cameras. He gripped the visor of his cap with a sweep of his hand, swung the cap over his head and vigorously waved it in short spiral motions as he pierced the north China stillness with a blood-curdling whooping "Yahoo" of the Choctaw Indians.

The changes in U.S. policy wrought changes in the Dixie Mission—changes which both caused Ariyoshi mental anguish and gave him vastly expanded duties and opportunities for observation.

In February of 1945 John S. Service, the chief political officer of the Yan'an mission, and his Foreign Service colleagues attached to the U.S. Embassy in Chongqing urged, in a carefully prepared policy recommendation, that the U.S. desist from giving exclusive support to the Chiang regime, the growing weakness of which was obvious, and thus make possible a flexible American policy in a future certain to be marked by Chinese civil strife. The advice of this group of experienced China diplomats was rejected by the State Department ("Spanish moss hung from its chandeliers," Service had observed earlier) and the White House. In the spring Hurley forced Service's recall. Service left Yan'an on April 1, removing from this incubator of China's future the author of a perceptive series of reports on it which presented a far more accurate and sympathetic view of the Communists than the U.S. government was willing to accept. Service's reading of the situation was prophetic, and if the government had respected his views and acted on them, more constructive relations with China might have begun long before the "opening" in the 1970s.

Removed also was the officer in charge, Colonel Barrett, who higher-ups falsely thought was becoming a Communist sympathizer. (Barrett was later military attache in Taipei.) Barrett's successor was instructed by General Albert C. Wedemeyer, Stilwell's successor, to minimize American cooperation with the Communists.

As members of the mission were recalled and replaced, relations with the Communists deteriorated quickly. Many of the remaining officers took to baiting the Communist liaison officers and other cadres, engaging them in constant argument and giving voice to their hostility. Differences in rank among the Americans had been minimized in deference to Communist practice, but now protocol was restored. In the mess hall, separate tables were set up for the officers and GIs. Morale declined and the consumption of the potent Tiger Bone wine increased. One officer was acknowledged to hold the lead in breaking emptied earthen Tiger Bone bottles against the walls of his cave.

With the departure of Service, Ariyoshi came to be recognized as the member of the mission with the most comprehensive knowledge of the Communist areas, and he was called on repeatedly to brief his superiors in Yan'an, as well as the principal U.S. military and diplomatic representatives in China. He twice gave long verbal reports to General Wedemeyer in Chongqing, repeating one to Ambassador Hurley. He was sent to Shanghai to brief four air force captains, and he was questioned extensively by General George C. Marshall early in 1946 as Marshall began his futile counterrevolutionary mediation effort.

For Ariyoshi, the onrush of events in 1945–46—the retreat and then the collapse of Japan, the Kuomintang-Communist confrontation, and the increasingly open U.S. policy of intervention in support of Chiang—meant a flurry of assignments and much travel, though Yan'an remained his base. Wherever he went, he looked closely and listened hard, putting questions to people of all sorts, and this diverse experience strengthened his feelings of partisanship for the forces of revolution and his dismay over the direction of U.S. policy.

During a stay in Chongqing he had a memorable conversation with Soong Ching Ling (who had broken with her sisters, the wives of Chiang Kai-shek and H. H. Kung, when the Kuomintang turned reactionary in 1927), but who had taken up residence in the wartime capital in the interests of national unity. Visiting her in her home, which was kept under close surveillance by Chiang's secret police, Ariyoshi was plied with questions about the flow of medical supplies to the guerrilla areas (the China Defense League, founded by Soong Ching Ling, was trying to get supplies through) and about the livelihood of the peasants. But Ariyoshi was surprised and moved by her knowledge of the plight of Nisei in the U.S. and her concern for them. "She said it was remarkable that my people were coming through the evacuation experience with dignity and new strength."

Ariyoshi admired Soong Ching Ling for her steadfast political courage to the end of his days. That she reciprocated his esteem was revealed dramatically at the time of his Smith Act trial in 1952–53 when she sent him her mother's wedding dress in the expectation that it could raise money for his defense.

In Yan'an, immediately after Japan's capitulation, Ariyoshi saw the impressive beginning of another long march—the departure of many thousands of people eastward to take up new assignments in areas taken over from the Japanese. While they went on foot, U.S. ships and planes were transporting Kuomintang troops to key points occupied by the Japanese in what was plainly an effort to beat the Communist troops and cadres to them. "You will see that the tortoise will win the race," cadres in Yan'an assured him.

On the first of two visits to Zhangjiakou (Kalgan), gate city to Inner Mongolia, Ariyoshi saw people newly conscious of their united strength elect members of the city council. Illiterates—80 to 85 percent of the people—took part, voting by dropping beans in jars placed behind the backs of lined up candidates. A merchant, puffing on his long pipe, casually remarked to Ariyoshi and a companion: "It seems now the toilers have their chance. Up to now, they have had nothing to do with the government."

As Ariyoshi was seeing something of a new China in birth, he was keeping a sharp eye on his fellow Americans and thinking constantly of American policy. He cringed to hear GIs call Chinese "Slopeys" and in various ways demonstrate prejudice and ignorance. But he found, too, in Yan'an and elsewhere, proof that Americans and Chinese could be friends. He was pained to see tentative friendships withered by the veering of U.S. policy, but he was heartened by incidents showing that some Americans did not go with the tide. He recorded the story of Edward Rohrbough, an OWI editor in Fujian, in the southeast, who staged a one-man, one-week sitdown strike in a prison in a vain effort to save the life of Yang Chao, an OWI employee who was arrested and tortured by the Kuomintang police.

Ariyoshi interviewed an American pilot who had been rescued by north China guerrillas. People in many villages sheltered the pilot and helped him evade the Japanese until he got across the Yellow River to safety in Yan'an. By the time of the interview, the U.S. was already siding with Chiang Kai-shek in the spreading civil war. The pilot told Ariyoshi he didn't want to fly any more in view of that. "If we helped the Chinese peasants to get a better deal, there would be no war, there would be peace," he said.

Later Ariyoshi saw for himself the effect of U.S. support of Chiang. With a radio team he rode on horseback south of Yan'an to investigate repeated Communist charges that U.S. arms were being used against their forces by Kuomintang troops. He found evidence of

Kuomintang use of bazookas and other weapons and read this boast written on village walls: "The Red Army cannot last long; we have American guns." He wrote:

> I visited villages Chiang's soldiers had occupied and looted. Whatever they could not haul away on stolen oxcarts and pack animals they rendered useless. They had destroyed the furniture, large iron kettles and quilts. They had mixed corn, wheat and millet with manure to render the grain inedible. Deep-water wells of this mountainous region were filled with earth and precious ropes for drawing water were stolen or cut to pieces. Pigs and chickens had been slaughtered and their entrails stuffed in table or dresser drawers. [51]

Upon his return to Yan'an, Zhu De, Zhou Enlai, and Chen Yi, then commander of the New Fourth Army, questioned Ariyoshi closely and asked him to report his findings to U.S. headquarters in Chongqing. Zhu De said, "We want to ask your government to take all lend-lease equipment from China, for every bit of it will be used by Chiang Kaishek to kill Chinese people."

In September 1945 Ariyoshi was sent to Chongqing to report to General Wedemeyer, whose top aides were freely predicting that Chiang's thirty-nine U.S.-trained divisions would mop up the Communist forces in three months.

> I discussed Yan'an's guerrilla warfare, which did not require extensive supply trains. The guerrillas lived off the land and fought with popular support.
>
> I also said the guerrillas would slash communication lines. They would force the Nationalists to contend with their military tactics. And while politics was the Yan'an force's cutting edge, graft and corruption would weaken the Nationalists. Eventually, heavy American equipment would become an encumbrance to the Nationalists. U.S.-supplied arms would pass into the hands of the Yan'an forces. The struggle would drag on into a bitter war of attrition. Chiang could never crush the guerrillas in three months. His corrupt regime would eventually crumble.[52]

---

51. Hugh Deane, *Remembering Koji Ariyoshi: An American GI in Yenan* (New York: US-China Peoples Friendship Association, 1978), 29.
52. Deane, *Remembering Koji Ariyoshi*, 30–31. A report Ariyoshi forwarded to Washington on November 27, 1945 elaborating his views is summarized in Herbert Feis's *The China Tangle* (New York: Atheneum, 1966).

Ariyoshi went on to disagree with Wedemeyer's statement that the Communist Party was split wide open, giving an account of the Party congress held in the spring which had worked out a comprehensive program reflecting Mao's thinking. Wedemeyer's face turned cloudy and his manner brusque, but he directed Ariyoshi to repeat his assessment to Ambassador Hurley, who wholly dismissed it. Shaking his finger in Ariyoshi's face, Hurley scolded, "Young man, you have been fooled by Communist propaganda." He said it twice.

Three months later, in November, Ariyoshi reported to Wedemeyer again. The weaknesses of the Chiang regime were already becoming evident, and he found the general more willing to accept a critical estimate of Chiang and his civil war capabilities. But an aide asked, what if the U.S. were to commit its full force to Chiang's side?

Ariyoshi pointed to the chorus of protests in the U.S. and doubted that white soldiers could do better than the Japanese. But the "generals felt the GIs could crush Yan'an's forces in short order. I reminded them that in September they told me that Chiang's forces could do that in three months."

A month later Ariyoshi was in Shanghai in connection with the arrival of General Marshall. His immediate assignment was to investigate an incident that had marred the beginning of the general's mission. Several thousand students had marched to the airport to greet Marshall and ask him to work for peace in China. Ariyoshi discovered that they were sidetracked, beaten, and their leaders jailed by Chiang's police. The police substituted a welcoming group with no peace slogans. But Ariyoshi was impressed by the continuing student protests against the civil war and by a January demonstration of some 100,000 workers that, he wrote, "made the U.S. military brass hats gnash their teeth in helplessness."

Shortly before taking ship for home in July 1946, Ariyoshi visited the guerrillas in the Jiangsu-Anhui Border Region, and his conviction that the Chinese revolution was beyond the reach of U.S. intervention was reinforced.

On a plane to Shanghai, Ariyoshi, as he had when he had flown into China, looked down on the countryside, but this time he saw more than beauty and the mark of human toil. He saw people in motion. Below him the Kuomintang and Communist armies faced each other, maneuvering for advantage. He knew one was the instrument of the peasants pressing for change and would prevail.

Settling in New York with his wife and young daughter in 1946, Ariyoshi became active in the Committee for a Democratic Far Eastern Policy, headed by Evans Carlson until his death, and after that by Maud Russell. A predecessor of the US-China Peoples Friendship Association, the committee was formed to oppose U.S. intervention in China's civil war and in revolutions and nationalist movements elsewhere in Asia. Ariyoshi helped prepare and hand out leaflets and organize meetings, and he contributed to the committee's publication, *Far East Spotlight*, which named him a consultant. And he put a great deal of time into writing a book on his Yan'an experience. Reynal & Hitchcock accepted it and paid him an advance but canceled publication after the onset of McCarthyism.

In 1948 Ariyoshi with his family returned to Hawaii and founded the *Honolulu Record*, a weekly newspaper addressed to working people. It came out on schedule even during Ariyoshi's trial; he gave up a night's sleep a week to help make this possible. But in a time of Red-baiting and repression the burden of the *Record* became insupportable, and it ceased publication after a life of ten years. Ariyoshi opened a flower shop—"the Red florist," the local newspapers called him.

For years Ariyoshi was isolated. But the social struggles and anti-war movement of the 1960s changed that. He lectured in the University of Hawaii's Ethnic Studies Program, and resumed research and writing. Governor John A. Burns appointed him to the Hawaii Foundation for History and the Humanities and he served as its president.

The "ping-pong opening" that culminated in Nixon's China visit of February 1972 brought immediate changes in Ariyoshi's life. He became a sought-after authority on China. In 1971 Soong Ching Ling saw to it that he was among the first to be invited to the People's Republic, and in this first of four visits (one with a film crew from Hawaii Public Television) he found the China of reality even more impressive than the picture of China he had formed in his thoughts. The *Honolulu Star Bulletin* published many of his articles, and schools and organizations that had shunned him now invited him to speak.

Ariyoshi was a principal initiator of the Hawaii-China Peoples Friendship Association (later the US-China Peoples Friendship Association of Honolulu), and served as its president from the beginning. He was chief editor of the association's *China Newsletter*. He played a leading role in the formation of the national US-China

Peoples Friendship Association and served on its national board until his death.

He took pride in being one who labored with his hands and in being able to add flower to flower and create beauty. In a note to a distant friend on a Christmas Day, he wrote: "If you were here, I'd make up a beautiful Christmas basket for you and your family. I am good with flowers, though not at much else. . . ."

Addressing a Buddhist audience in Honolulu, he said, "I have seen change and sought change in society, and by choice taken up unpopular causes. There were times in my life when I could have taken a different route. Had I done so, I could never have achieved inner satisfaction."

Ariyoshi did not go gently into the good night. He fought against the fading of the light by taking on work, writing, lecturing, attending USCPFA meetings. Just weeks before his final hospitalization, he was a vigorous participant in the USCPFA convention in Philadelphia, though at nights he lay in pain, grateful if he was able to doze. He fought to live.

In April 1976, six months before Ariyoshi's death, the Hawaii House of Representatives unanimously adopted a resolution honoring him. It cited his fight for the rights of interned Japanese at Manzanar, his resistance to McCarthyism, his founding of the USCPFA of Honolulu, and his long commitment to social change.

When he worked on the docks in the green of his years, Ariyoshi was a member of one of the star teams—teams of especially strong, agile and alert men capable of handling the trickiest and heaviest loads. He left the docks for other things, but he never left the star team.

17. Captain George S. Wuchinich: An OSS Encounter with the Chinese Reds

OSS (Office of Strategic Services) officers attached to the Dixie Mission in Yan'an in 1944–45 had a belittling attitude toward the Eighth Route Army troops they saw about them. Koji Ariyoshi listened to them brag that a heavily armed OSS demolition team could take on a company, even a battalion, of Communist guerrillas. But after an armed OSS intelligence-gathering team was captured without a shot and brought to Yan'an, they did not press the point.

The OSS team of four left Xi'an late in July 1945 with orders to probe the north China areas where the Japanese were being challenged by the Eighth Route Army. In command was an experienced officer, Captain George S. Wuchinich, who had been awarded the Distinguished Service Cross for a hazardous mission with Tito's partisans in northern Yugoslavia. (The local Nazi radio claimed he was an imposter, a Jew wearing the clothes of a downed American flyer, and several times reported his death.) The others in the team were Arthur Hensley, radio operator, and Peter Gallagher and Fred Wing, interpreters.

The Yugoslav mission had been called Alum I; the north China mission was called Alum II.

The team started off with a command car and a truck heavily laden with supplies, but soon had to abandon them and shift to carts and ponies. By the time they crossed the Yellow River into Shanxi, the atom bomb had demolished Hiroshima and Nagasaki and an urgent order from OSS headquarters directed the team to move north as far and as fast as possible. The Russians had entered the war and OSS wanted close-up intelligence.

At the Shanxi border they were met by a contingent headed by a general sent by Yan Xishan, the provincial warlord, and the general became their guide. In a village with an ancient temple tower they found themselves uncomfortably close to an exchange of fire between, they learned later, Communist militia and a unit of Yan's army. Wuchinich suspected the general had set them up.

But the guerrillas, youths with white towels wrapped around their heads, prevailed, and the OSS team was soon their captives. But the reception was friendly. The Americans and the guerrillas shook hands and peasants gathered around clapped and offered watermelons. The combined party proceeded north, slipping between Japanese-held points, a journey thus described by Wuchinich:

> North China was then a treeless, sandy canyon country. No forests existed, paths or cart trails were worn so deep by centuries of travel that the soft loess soil formed cliffs a hundred feet or more high on either side of their narrow passages.
>
> Our arrival at a village was an event of some cheer to the people, who gathered to hear the latest news from the militiamen. Cheng (in command) paid for flour in Communist currency, soldier cooks asked for permission to borrow pots or jars and others foraged for twigs or sticks for a fire. On a flat stone the flour was kneaded into dough with water; the cook pinched off balls of dough and threw

them into the pot to make steamed bread. This with greens and peppers also thrown into the pot made our meal, three times a day.[53]

Peasants and militia had a familiar closeness with each other and at night would sit discussing many things. Some of the militiamen carried pamphlets and books which they read aloud. Often while reading they would scratch with a twig on the sandy soil to delineate characters they were learning.

On the third night the party reached the Eighth Sub-region of the Eighth Route Army, the headquarters of the Thirty-ninth Brigade. There Yan Xishan's general and aides were separated from the Americans and confined. In a cave lit by candles the OSS team met Jia Suiyang, the commander, and two of his aides. Jia was reserved and suspicious. He asked what they were doing in north China and observed they had no permit to be there from Yan'an.

The next morning the Americans were searched from head to foot and their sleeping bags pinched inch by inch. Their arms were taken away. Jia invited them to lunch and was cordial, but said he could reasonably wonder if the team was there to spy out Communist troop dispositions for the Kuomintang or Yan Xishan. He said the team could either go to Yan'an or be taken to a point held by Yan. The choice was Yan'an.

Yan'an was a 600-mile trek away by an indirect route. Wuchinich was a close observer and was increasingly impressed by what he saw. Often he was reminded of his experiences with Tito's partisans. "The farther we went, the more comfortable life appeared and the more stability we saw," he wrote later. "Soldiers and villagers worked in the fields. There were no beggars or loafers about. Homespun cloth covered all the people."

One morning Wuchinich heard soldiers discuss the relative merits of Roosevelt and Truman as they prepared the morning meal. He thought to himself that not many American GIs could compare Chiang Kai-shek and Mao.

"The soldiers we marched with were dedicated," Wuchinich wrote. "Some had served ten to fifteen years in the army, coming from all parts of China. They spoke not of provincial concerns, but for the whole of China. They talked of the government that would rule their country after the war was over—one for which they were already working out a social, economic and political system."

---

53. "An OSS Team Meets the Eighth Route Army," *China and Us* 3, no. 5 (New York) (September–October 1974). This article is condensed from a chapter in an unpublished manuscript titled *Made in America—Spy to Subversive*.

Asked by Wuchinich why he was a Communist, a soldier replied with a paraphrase of a well-known quotation from Mao: "If you live and die for the good of the people, your death will be as weighty as Tai Mountain, but if you live for yourself alone, your death will weigh no more than a swan's feather."

Sergeant Gallagher then quoted his favorite German proverb: "Mensch werden ist eine Kunst (To become human is an art)."

The marchers went north and west to near the border of Suiyuan in Inner Mongolia and then turned south toward Yan'an. "Life here was completely free of enemy interruption," Wuchinich recalled. "Towns had banks where Communist money was legal tender. I saw clinics and dispensaries where peasants were cared for and women were taught not to have their children in the gao-liang field and not to cut the umbilical cord with a piece of broken and dirty tile. There were libraries where the readers were mostly soldiers. Posters, cartoon magazines and wall newspapers abounded. We met women soldiers at army posts, not as timid as the peasant women in our presence, but with a manner of equality with men."

Despite the length of their journey, the OSS team stayed in Yan'an only one week, and that long only because foul weather closed down the airfield. But during that week Wuchinich had memorable conversations with Dr. Ma Haide (George Hatem), Dr. Hans Mueller, and Koji Ariyoshi, and he and the others were taken on a tour of Government House, the International Peace Hospital founded by Dr. Norman Bethune, the medical school, and the printing plant in the Cave of the Ten Thousand Buddhas where seven presses turned out newspapers and pamphlets under the gaze of the Buddhas in wall niches.

Wuchinich was distressed by the lack of equipment and medicine at the hospital, a set of caves in a hill two miles from Yan'an. It was pitiful, he wrote later. "No sulfa whatsoever, hardly any rubber tubing, and only one microscope. The operating room was in the center of the grounds and made of brick. They had no electric light and less than 250 instruments to perform all types of operations. More than half of these instruments would have been discarded by any American hospital."[54]

General Ye Jianying, chief of staff of the Eighth Route Army, was the host at a banquet for the four Americans. Wuchinich remembered

---

54. From a press release of the Committee for a Democratic Far Eastern Policy, New York, March 29, 1946.

a convivial evening and many toasts in "Bai Gar," the strongest drink going.

Just before they flew out, Colonel Ivan Yeaton, then in command of the Dixie Mission, asked Wuchinich who he thought would win out in China, the Nationalists or the Communists. "Based on what I've seen, I think the Communists have the upper hand," he replied.

Back home in the U.S. and finally discharged from an army hospital after a grave illness, Wuchinich restated this opinion many times, in the same breath arguing that the U.S. should not intervene in China's internal struggle. He joined the Committee for a Democratic Far Eastern Policy, which distributed his account of his north China experience. He got a long letter published in the *Congressional Record* of February 14, 1946 which concluded:

> It is my opinion that our marines and other armed forces should be drawn out at once, and that any economic help we give China be based only on the understanding that a real broad political government be formed including all parties and all sections of the Chinese people.

In the Pennsylvania community in which he grew up he worked with progressive Slav groups. In 1948 he campaigned actively for Henry Wallace. All this made him a target for the McCarthy-McCarran Inquisition. In June 1953 he was summoned to appear before the McCarran Committee—the Senate Judiciary Committee's Subcommittee on Internal Security—and subjected to hostile grilling which included variations of the standard question: "Are you now or have you ever been a member of the Communist party?" Wuchinich told local reporters that he was not a Communist, but as a matter of principle took the fifth amendment to avoid the question before the committee.

Wuchinich was not a soft-voiced witness. He rasped back at Senator Jenner and Robert Morris, counsel, and was especially incensed when Jenner observed that Benedict Arnold had served in the armed forces. Years later a clip of Wuchinich's blunt retorts to the committee made a dramatic opening in the documentary film *Seeing Red*.

For Wuchinich and his family (he had a wife and three children) the aftermath was painful. The appearance of a bemedaled and defiant OSS officer before the committee got a big play on television and radio and made press headlines. Though a local Long Island newspaper was sympathetic, the news agency accounts were unfriendly and that in *Time* typically snide. Wuchinich was instantly fired by General Motors and doors to other employment closed on him. Alleviating his feelings were expressions of support from many friends and even strangers. He was especially heartened by a letter from Albert Einstein, then at Princeton, who wrote, "May I express my admiration for your devotion to the common cause of democratic rights . . . if you believe that I could in any way be of help to you, please do not hesitate to give me the opportunity."

18. The U.S. Aids Counterrevolution in China: a 1946 Appraisal

Editor's Note: The following section is an article that the author contributed to The Nation *(September 14, 1946) under the title, "Counter-Revolution in China."*

The civil war in China is essentially a counterrevolution. It is being waged because the reactionary factions of the Kuomintang, with which Chiang Kai-shek must be identified, understand that for them a real compromise with the Communists and liberals is out of the question, since a compromise would crack their political monopoly. Hence, like the emigres of 1792, like the South in 1861, like the czarist and Spanish officers in 1918 and 1936, these defenders of the status quo are playing the traditional trump card of war.

During the eight years of struggle against the Japanese, a shift in power took place in China which only armed force can reverse. In the vast social effort made possible by the war, the Communist-led agrarian movement spread from a score of counties in the northwest over a third of China: across north China to the coast, into Inner Mongolia and Manchuria, into parts of the rich provinces of central China. Agrarian reforms, democracy, and peasant unions—backed by peasant armies—have shifted the balance of political power in these areas from the landlords to the peasants. This new power is the greatest challenge to the semi-feudal status quo in the long, tortured history of the Chinese revolution.

Even in the areas policed by the Kuomintang, as the fascist-like assassinations and censorship testify, a substantial middle-class and intellectual opinion opposes the Kuomintang's cramping dictatorship. The Kuomintang has even felt obliged to move against the mild Chinese Association of Labor, which grew out of the "white" unions organized by the Kuomintang after the left-right split in 1927.

In China the Communists and liberals are in firm alliance, a unique phenomenon. The simplest explanation is that the Kuomintang has demonstrated repeatedly that it will not tolerate even a liberal opposition. The assassination of Li Gongpu, a leader of the Democratic League, and Professor Wen Yiduo, head of the School of Chinese Studies at the Southwest Associated University, and the recent arrests, beatings, and killings of scores of other well-known and unknown democrats have precedents extending back through the two decades of Kuomintang rule. Liberals understand that alone, without an army, they have no more future than did the Japanese liberals of the 1920s. The Communists, on the other hand, have given them freedom to work and a real share of the leadership in the rural governments of northern and central China.[55]

Underlying this reason for Communist-liberal cooperation is the fact that communism is not an immediate issue in China. This is so not just because the Communists are willing to make temporary concessions in order to win the support of liberals; it has a solid basis in the primitive, semi-feudal character of the Chinese economy. The peasants are obviously interested not in socialism but in more land and lower rents and taxes; and the needs and desires of the peasants must be the major determinants of the Communist program. The aggregate of new power in China is primarily against feudalism and against the quasi-fascist institutions with which the Kuomintang has tried to bolster feudalism. It is being used to effect what the Communists call the bourgeois-democratic revolution, and what the Communists think this revolution should achieve approximates closely what liberals are working for. This does not mean, of course, that the Communists are just agrarian democrats, as some people still insist; they believe that eventually socialism will appear on the political agenda. To sum up, in China today, as in all revolutionary situations, there is no effective "third choice."

Against the broad coalition of Communists and liberals the Kuomintang is executing two offensives. In its own areas it is using all the familiar instruments of coercion and terror in an effort to destroy all opposition, almost entirely non-Communist. Almost the whole liberal press and many liberal voices have been silenced.

Concurrently, major concentrations of Kuomintang troops are seeking to surround, blockade, and annihilate Communist forces in

---

55. A decade later the Anti-Rightist Campaign of 1957 subjected some 600,000 intellectuals and others to persecution, launching the two decades of intermittent ultra-leftism directed by Mao that cost the Party its liberal allies. Only a small fraction of those charged in 1957 were actually counterrevolutionaries.

particular key or vulnerable areas. The Kuomintang would prefer an undeclared, localized civil war while negotiations go on and on. While its troops attack in one area, it would like the truce maintained in others. Thus the Communists could be destroyed piecemeal, and the United States with less embarrassment could continue to give military aid.

But since this was obvious to the Communists, they have counteracted the Kuomintang offensives with offensives of their own, and so the fighting has spread. At the same time, especially after Chiang Kai-shek's six-point program of August 14, which was virtually a demand for surrender cloaked in the threadbare promise of "constitutional" government, the Communist press and radio became more militant, saying that civil war was an actuality and demanding with new sharpness that the United States cease its intervention. As might be expected, this enabled part of the American press to claim that the Communists had rejected Chiang's conciliatory offer and that the new party line was all-out civil war. A *New York Times* editorial on August 18, for example, declared that the Communists were "in revolt" and "burning their bridges behind them and inviting chaos."

Chiang apparently believes that the worst that can happen to him is not to win. If he destroys or decisively weakens the Communists, only the Soviet Union will be unhappy, and General Marshall can go home, a gallant and patient soldier who did his best. But if the Kuomintang should suffer defeats, Chiang thinks that American power will be used to prevent the Communists from exploiting them.

The cornerstone of Kuomintang policy is the conviction that the United States will not tolerate a revolution in China, even the sort of revolution called for in Mao Zedong's *New Democracy*. In truth, the grounds for this conviction are ample. In the Philippines, Korea, and Japan the United States obviously is supporting conservative and reactionary forces. In China, while purporting to be an honest mediator, the United States has given vast military and economic aid to the Kuomintang. The most compelling motive of American policy seems to be restriction of Soviet influence in Asia, which means that the United States must play a counterrevolutionary role. There are no indications that the United States will change its policy in China, even if full-scale civil war strips away the pretenses used to conceal intervention. In the editorial referred to above, the *New York Times* implied plainly that the prime issue in China is "Soviet imperialism," which requires "a firm attitude" on the part of the United States—that is, continued intervention. The *Times* must consider it truly fortunate that by chance the United States has been maintaining troops in China to assist in the repatriation of the Japanese forces.

Results of the fighting thus far, however, bear out the conclusion that despite the Kuomintang's sixty American-trained and American-equipped divisions, its substantial air force of American planes, its small American-built navy, and its supply base in the United States, the position of the Communists is by no means weak. As the Japanese learned the hard way, military power is difficult to apply in China. In an industrial society the rural areas tend to be dependent on the urban areas, and when a city falls, the nearby countryside falls with it. The economic attraction of the urban commercial market, plus the existence of good roads, which permit a city garrison to fan out over the countryside, makes military control relatively simple. In semi-feudal, non-industrialized China, however, with its subsistence agriculture and lack of communications, the countryside can exist independent of the towns and the capture of the county seat does not entail the capture of the county.

The Japanese never held much of the countryside of north China for any length of time. They were obliged to maintain large garrisons in every city and town and to defend constantly every mile of road and railway. They could not prevent the Communists from building armies and organizing almost self-sufficient governments in the rural areas. At least half a million Japanese troops were always tied down in "conquered" north China.

The Kuomintang has now inherited the Japanese military problem, which is essentially how to hold too much hostile territory with too few men. If the Kuomintang puts a company in every village, the companies will be destroyed separately; if it puts in a battalion—even if a battalion were adequate—there are not enough of them to go around. The Kuomintang will certainly use large-scale terror, but a fair presumption is that it will prove no more effective for Chiang than for the Japanese. The situation is different from the old days in Jiangxi, where the Communists could be contained and slowly squeezed. Now the large Communist armies have the breadth of China in which to fight their particular type of mobile warfare. Now the Communists are entrenched in what may be a decisive number of villages. Now they have well-tested political, economic, and military institutions with which to counteract the traditional weaknesses of peasant rebellions. Perhaps most important, in the dynamics of revolution, power often is created in an incredibly short time, and armies are born in a fortnight.

Every American will be a factor in the bitter struggle ahead, for American-made arms are adding thousands of new names to the long roster of Chinese revolutionary dead: the United States is intervening in China to the same effect that it non-intervened in Spain—the frustration of a revolution.

19. China and the Ruination of MacArthur

> Show me a hero, and I will write you a tragedy.
> F . S C O T T   F I T Z G E R A L D

Douglas MacArthur was in the class of 1903 at West Point and his impressionable years as a cadet and a young army careerist coincided with the American turn to imperialism. His father, General Arthur MacArthur, commanded the counterinsurgency effort in the Philippines, helping to create the alliance between the American and Philippine elites which has held the archipelago in subjection, and Douglas' filial respect for him added to his disposition to accept the rhetoric of Senator Albert J. Beveridge, Brooks Adams, and the others in the chorus prophesying an American destiny which assured an important role for the American military.[56]

Arthur MacArthur was himself an early advocate of U.S. imperialist expansion in East Asia. In a forty-four-page report titled *Chinese Memorandum and Notes* written when Douglas was a three-year-old toddler, the elder MacArthur wrote that unless the U.S. established a powerful presence in Asia, "we cannot attain our natural growth, or even continue to exist as a commanding and progressive nationality. . . . " China, he said, was "the real stepping stone to supremacy throughout the commercial world," and he argued that

---

56. At a time when MacArthur was making news and John Gunther's *The Riddle of MacArthur* was frequently quoted, Tom O'Connor, managing editor of the *Daily Compass* (New York), instructed me to write a comprehensive criticism of Gunther's portrayal. The first of a series of seventeen articles titled "MacArthur Is No Riddle" appeared on April 15, 1951, shortly after the general's recall. In the concluding article I wrote: "Step by step, decision following hard upon decision, as events widened the gap between his illusions and reality, as the revolution in Asia spread in the face of counter-revolution, threatening what he believed to be his own and U.S. destiny in Asia, he moved from evil to evil and error to error." I have drawn on this series of articles in preparing this section.

both strategic and economic reasons summoned an American policy of advance. Upset at having to help break railroad strikes in 1877, he foresaw increasing domestic unrest and concluded: "We must have new and ever-increasing markets to meet our ever-increasing powers of production; and these seem to lie principally in the Far East, and there we naturally and inevitably must go." He specifically urged that "competent Army officers" be sent to keep watch on military developments in China.

In a celebrated address to the Senate in 1900, which Douglas MacArthur is recorded as having read, Senator Beveridge orated: "The Philippines are ours forever. . . . And just beyond the Philippines are China's illimitable markets. . . . The power that rules the Pacific is the power that rules the world. . . . Westward the Star of Empire takes its way. . . . "

In speeches that filled the newspapers, Beveridge spoke of Manifest Destiny, the "imperialism of righteousness," and "Anglo-Saxon civilization."

A half-century later, Douglas MacArthur, then SCAP (the Supreme Commander for the Allied Powers), told Hearst correspondent Bob Considine in a Tokyo interview that a thousand years from now historians will say that the "truly momentous event" of this era was "the bringing by the vital and wonderful United States of America, of Anglo-Saxon civilization to Asia, through Japan."

A year earlier, in summer 1949, MacArthur told another Hearst reporter, David Sentner of the *New York Journal-American,* that "the western march of America did not stop when we reached the edge of the Pacific. A vast new opportunity for trade and commerce dwarfing anything in our past history could be over the Pacific horizon. A billion people . . . are in Asia, hungering for American initiative. . . ."

MacArthur was an admirer of Commodore Matthew Perry and he recalled him when he took the Japanese surrender aboard the battleship *Missouri* on September 2, 1945: "We stand in Tokyo reminiscent of our countryman, Commodore Perry, ninety-two years ago. His purpose was to bring Japan an era of enlightenment."

Perry had a grandiose concept of history. He viewed the opening up of Japan to U.S. trade and influence as but a preliminary to the creation of a vast American sphere of influence in Asia. Japan itself, Perry believed, could be reduced to a subordinate American ally, and Okinawa and Formosa (China's Taiwan) could be seized. Advocating a policy of American "friendship and protection" in Indochina, Thailand, and Indonesia, Perry argued that "we cannot expect to be free from the ambitious longings of increased power which are the natural concomitants of national success."

Perry's imperial dream did not immediately materialize because, though practical as far as supine Asia was concerned, it evoked no great response in the U.S., which had a continent to fill out and the slavery issue to settle. But five decades later, when the frontier had reached the Pacific, when industry looked urgently for export markets, the dream was reborn. And in 1945, standing on the decks of a battleship in the waters of prostrate Japan, his sense of the dramatic struggle on the continent very dim, MacArthur was able to believe that Perry's Pacific was an American moat. "To the Pacific basin has come the vista of a new emancipated world," he said then. "In the Philippines, America has evolved a model for the free world. . . . The history of our sovereignty there has now the full confidence of the East."

MacArthur was twenty when Beveridge orated at the turn of the century. Just out of West Point, MacArthur was sent to the Philippines, where his father had fought Aguinaldo, and in 1905, as an aide to his father, he went on an extended tour of Asia. He discovered that Japan had not gone the subordinate way Perry had envisaged, and he made his first and only visit to China, inspecting military installations and academies and being entertained by Chinese officers. The itinerary included Beijing, Tianjin, Qingdao, Hankou, Shanghai, and Guangzhou. Years later he wrote in his *Reminiscences* that the trip "was without doubt the most important factor of preparation in my entire life. . . . It was crystal clear to me that the future and, indeed, the very existence of America, was irrevocably entwined with Asia and its island outposts. It was to be sixteen years before I returned to the Far East, but always was its mystic hold on me."[57]

At the time of the Japanese surrender aboard the *Missouri* in 1945, MacArthur evidently did not believe that the Chiang Kai-shek regime was in any danger; he rejected a request by General Wedemeyer that seven of his divisions be sent to bolster Chiang's armies. But in later years, looking occasionally from the Dai Ichi bank building to the turbulent mainland, he found American policy in grave error and saw disaster the consequence. According to an aide, "Chagrin turned to near pathological rage as he helplessly watched Chiang Kai-shek's regime being systematically overrun." While indeed generally helpless, his headquarters later cooperated with the

---

57. (New York: McGraw-Hill, 1964), 31–32.

State Department in placing obstacles in the way of trade with the triumphant People's Republic.

At a time when American diplomats in China were very largely united in the view that Chiang's chances of survival were undercut by the oppressive, dictatorial, and corrupt nature of his regime, MacArthur insisted that American efforts to bring about modest reforms in the Kuomintang government were a distracting irrelevancy. He compared reform efforts to plans to change the structural design of a house on fire. He told China lobbyist Walter Judd of Minnesota that "for the first time in our relations with Asia, we have endangered the paramount interests of the United States by confusing them with an internal purification problem."

MacArthur's pessimism presumed the continuance of what he described as Communist-coddling policies. He long saw victory over the Reds as possible if his own counsel were heeded. As late as February 1948 he told the Indian ambassador and other astonished diplomats at lunch that American bombers and quantities of small arms could turn the tide of battle. But "unfortunately," he even cabled the House Committee on Foreign Affairs, the Chinese problem "has become somewhat clouded by demands for internal reform."

To extend Clausewitz, revolutionary war continues politics and economics, but MacArthur had no sense of this. Neither the injustices of China's pyramidal society nor the national humiliations inflicted on China by the powers had a presence in his assessment of the struggle on the mainland. This reversal of the realities appeared in his *Reminiscences*, written after his recall:

In China, Generalissimo Chiang Kai-shek was gradually pushing the Communists back, being largely aided and supplied by the United States. For some unaccountable reason, the Communists were not looked upon with disfavor by the State Department, who labelled them "agrarian reformers." Instead of pushing on to the victory that was within the Generalissimo's grasp, an armistice was arranged, and General Marshall was sent to amalgamate the two opponents. . . .

After months of fruitless negotiation, he withdrew without tangible results, and the war for China resumed. But in this interval a decisive change had taken place. The Generalissimo had received no munitions or supplies from the United States, but the Soviets, working day and night, reinforced the Chinese Communist armies. . . . They pressed their advantage to the fullest, and finally drove the

Generalissimo's forces out of continental Asia onto Formosa.[58] The
decision to withhold previously pledged American support was one of
the greatest mistakes ever made in our history. At one fell blow, everything that had been so laboriously built up since the day of John
Hay was lost.[59]

The flight of the Generalissimo and his entourage, laden with
gold, pilfered art treasures, and other movable loot, to Taiwan was
viewed unhappily in Washington. Anxious to keep the rich island
out of Red hands, and at the same time avoid the opprobrium of bla-
tant intervention, Washington's gambit was to go for an independent
Taiwan. But an investigation of independence sentiment by knowledgeable officials revealed weakness. An alternative, a coup to oust
Chiang and replace him with an untainted leader of the Kuomintang, also came to nothing. The U.S. was stuck with the Generalissimo.

MacArthur, too, briefly kept open the option of an independent
Taiwan. With major help from General Willoughby, MacArthur's
Assistant Chief of Staff for G-2, a Formosan independence organization advocating U.S. occupation of the island surfaced in Tokyo and
held a press conference in December 1949 at which expensive
brochures in admirable English were handed out as a G-2 officer
watched. Thomas Liao (Liao Wenyi) took over as head in January
and the next month a Formosan Independence Party was born—still-
born actually. It gained a handful of members out of the twenty
thousand Taiwanese in Japan. Liao later defected to the Kuomintang.

As early as July 1949 MacArthur sent a private message of support
to Chiang through Howard Handleman, a top Hearst correspondent
in Tokyo. Five months later he used Handleman, Ernest Hobericht of
the United Press, and other favorites to publicize and challenge an
internal State Department memorandum aimed at minimizing the
impact of what it thought was the imminent fall of Taiwan to the
Communists.

In his broad statement at the outset of the Korean war in July
1950, President Truman interposed the Seventh Fleet between Taiwan
and the mainland, instructing it to oppose assault from either direction. But when the war was a month old MacArthur made a dramatic
flight to Taiwan and there issued a communique which implied an

---

58. Formosa, Peiping, Asiatics—not only MacArthur but the entire American
establishment invariably used such words, symbols of the unrealities in their thinking.
They thought well of Confucius, but ignored his doctrine of the rectification of names.
59. MacArthur, *Reminiscences*, 320.

alliance with Chiang against the mainland. He said that Chiang's "indomitable determination" to resist the Communists "parallels the common interest and purpose of Americans that all peoples in the Pacific area shall be free—not slaves." Arrangements had been made, he said, "for effective coordination between the American and Chinese forces the better to meet any attack." A jubilant declaration by Chiang reinforced the interpretation that American power would be committed to a crusade to restore the Kuomintang to authority on the mainland.

A month later, at the end of August, MacArthur put his Formosan view in ripest rhetoric. "Nothing could be more fallacious," he told the Veterans of Foreign Wars, "than the threadbare argument" that "if we defend Formosa we alienate continental Asia." Those who think so "do not understand the Orient. They do not grasp that it is the pattern of Oriental psychology to respect and follow aggressive, resolute, and dynamic leadership—to turn quickly from a leadership characterized by timidity or vacillation. . . . Nothing has so inspired the Far East as the American determination to preserve the bulwarks of our Pacific Ocean strategic position."

Among those bulwarks was the "unsinkable carrier-tender" of Formosa. "The geographic location of Formosa is such that in the hands of a power unfriendly to the United States it constitutes an enemy salient in the very center" of the American lineup of island bases. It was essential to counter "the lustful thrusts of those who stand for slavery as against liberty, for atheism against God."[60]

On that same day, making a "mistake," American planes crossed the Yalu and dropped bombs on Chinese territory.

In Washington the chain of islands from the Philippines north was usually seen in terms of defense. But MacArthur had another vision: of the islands as bases from which the United States could bring enormous pressure to bear on mainland Asia.

Chicago Sun correspondent Mark Gayn, after interviewing a member of MacArthur's inner circle in 1946, reported that to MacArthur Japan "is, above all, an air base from which our bombers could range all of Siberia." In an estimate in *Uncertain Years*,[61] an academic study of the period, MacArthur saw the islands as a line of defense "and, more distantly, as a series of bases from which to launch offensive operations aimed at regaining the mainland. . . . "

---

60. William Manchester, *American Caesar: Douglas MacArthur 1880–1964* (Boston: Little, Brown, 1978), 568.
61. Dorothy Borg and Waldo Heinrichs, eds., *Uncertain Years: Chinese-American Relations, 1947–50* (New York: Columbia University Press, 1980), 77.

In his message to the Veterans of Foreign Wars MacArthur gained wide publicity for his view that from its island bases the United States could "dominate with air power every Asiatic port from Vladivostok to Singapore."

Time magazine attributed to a reliable source in the Dai Ichi building, MacArthur's conviction that the U.S. should fight Communism wherever it arose in Asia, which meant support for Chiang, the British in Hongkong, the anti-Communists in Indochina, Thailand and Burma. The general was said to believe that, "Anything else than this firm, determined action would incite Communism to sweep over all Asia."

MacArthur's brilliant envelopment at Inchon reversed the course of the Korean war. Seoul, gutted by American artillery fire, fell on September 28, 1950. Both Truman and Acheson gave unequivocal support to MacArthur's demand that what was left of the People's Army be pursued across the 38th Parallel. Such qualms as were expressed were blunted by allowing South Korean units to cross the parallel first and by an American promise that crossings would be for tactical purposes and would not affect a decision by the United Nations on whether or not the north should be occupied. The South Koreans crossed on October 1, and on that day MacArthur called for the unconditional surrender of his enemy. On the seventh the First Cavalry crossed and on that day the U.N. Assembly declared that the objective was "a unified, independent and democratic government" of all Korea.

As the Eighth Army moved fast on Pyongyang and the Tenth Corps occupied Wonsan and environs, China protested frontier violations by American bombers and said with increasing sharpness that it would not remain aloof as the imperialists invaded North Korea. When Truman met MacArthur on Wake Island on October 14, he asked him what he thought of the likelihood of Chinese intervention. MacArthur saw little chance of that. "Had they intervened in the first or second month it would have been decisive," he said. "We are no longer fearful. . . . We no longer stand hat in hand." In his estimate, only 50,000 to 60,000 Chinese troops could be got across the Yalu. "They have no air force. Now that we have bases for our air force in Korea, if the Chinese tried to get down to Pyongyang, there would be the greatest slaughter."[62]

When Pyongyang fell on October 20, the northward advance raised the question of how far. Should the United Nations forces proceed to

---

62. Manchester, *American Caesar,* 592.

the Yalu, on the banks of which utilities served both Korea and China? Washington's allies and some Washington officials had misgivings, and on September 28, looking ahead, the Administration directed that only South Korean troops would go to the Yalu, a restriction that was thought sufficient to reassure a China plagued with internal weaknesses.

An exuberant MacArthur told reporters that the war was just about over. He informed the Pentagon that he would need no more reinforcements, that ships en route to Pusan could be diverted to Hawaii or Japan, and that transports to shift the Second Division to Europe could be made ready. On October 24, flouting the restriction on operations near the Yalu, MacArthur ordered the Eighth Army and Tenth Corps to push to the frontier "with all speed and full utilization of their forces." When the Chiefs of Staff expressed concern, MacArthur responded that the September 28 restriction had not been a "final directive" and that he had ignored it for "tactical reasons." When Truman said at a press conference that he had understood that only Korean forces were to go to the Yalu, MacArthur contradicted him: "The mission of the United Nations forces is to clear Korea." Certain of MacArthur's allies and political friends went further. "The war cannot stop at the Yalu," orated Syngman Rhee, president of the Seoul regime, in his head a vision of a Great Korea that included parts of Manchuria. Senator William Knowland of California (known as "the Senator from Formosa") demanded a neutral zone ten miles into Chinese territory.

The first Chinese moved into Korea on or about October 16. But Tokyo minimized reports of clashes and of prisoners taken—as if, I. F. Stone observed in his *The Hidden History of the Korean War*,[63] MacArthur was fearful that the "Chicoms," as they were now called, would pull out and deny him a wider war and an opportunity for "great slaughter." Early in November the Chinese moved up into the hills after inflicting some blows on advanced South Korean and U.S. units, evidently waiting to see if Washington would take heed. A succession of MacArthur's statements were reassuring, equivocal, alarming, then reassuring again: Only Chinese of Korean origin were involved in a limited operation; It was "impossible" to assess Chinese intentions; The Chinese were guilty of an outrageous act of aggression; The situation was well in hand.

---

63. (New York: Monthly Review Press, 1952). American media coverage of the Korean war was mediocre at its best. Stone's columns in the *New York Compass* and his book exposed some of the fabrications.

While the Chinese hid in the hills, MacArthur ordered the Eighth Army and Tenth Corps, including reserves, to drive north on what he described to reporters on November 24 as a "home-by-Christmas offensive." That same day the CIA assured Truman that "there is no evidence that the Chinese Communists plan major offensive operations in Korea." Should, contrary to his expectations, the move on the Yalu fail, MacArthur told a diplomatic aide, he "saw no alternative to bombing key points in Manchuria."

The Pentagon hesitantly tried again to rein in MacArthur, proposing that his forces halt short of the border, seize heights commanding it, and station Korean troops on them. MacArthur replied that his intention was to consolidate positions "along the Yalu." A "request for information" from the Joint Chiefs, an expression of disquiet, went unanswered.

The advance went well. "The giant pincer moved according to plan," a communique announced. Then the hidden Chinese—now and from then on "hordes"—struck from mountains that MacArthur earlier had described as too precipitate to shelter troops. The Koreans in the center and then the split U.S. forces were hard hit, though saved from heavier losses by the inadequate Chinese firepower; some Chinese units carried knife-tipped spears. MacArthur did not face up to reality for four days, ordering troops forward even after the center had collapsed and some American units enveloped. Then he ordered a retreat which did not end until after Seoul had again fallen.

The four lost days were the first evidence of a shaken, nearly distraught MacArthur. From arrogant confidence he went to dispirited pessimism. On November 30 he thought that holding the line against the Chinese was "quite impractical." A few days later he thought the military outlook so bleak that some or all Americans might have to be evacuated from Japan. At the same time he lashed out at critics and defended his actions, without exception. The home-by-Christmas offensive he now called a "reconnaissance in force" which had provoked the Chinese into premature action. Correspondents whose dispatches irked him belonged to "the disaster school of war reporting."

General Matthew Ridgway, taking over the Eighth Army, stabilized the front with the aid of an air force instructed to scorch the earth; the war stalemated. But MacArthur, smarting under the sharpest criticisms of his career, some by those he had thought of as friends (the Luce publications, for example), would not accept what he called a "No Man's Land of Indecision." He was for upping the ante. War with China, that would be his salvation. Turned down again and again as he sought permission to bomb a road junction in Manchuria or a supply depot near the Soviet border, he argued that he could not save his army without it. The general was "near panic" and "in a blue funk," Acheson commented. Responding to a request for his views from Washington as the year 1950 ended, MacArthur proposed that he be authorized to blockade the coast of China, destroy China's industrial capacity to wage war through naval gunfire and bombing raids, reinforce his forces in Korea with Chinese Nationalist troops, and end the restrictions on Chiang's use of his armed forces, anticipating a counter-invasion of the mainland. The choice was between such steps, which would cripple China and "save Asia from the engulfment otherwise facing it," and the contraction of the United Nations line in Korea to a Pusan perimeter.

His views were paid scant heed by an administration which saw him as a peevish Cassandra. Yet in February MacArthur came forth with his boldest proposal yet: He would "sever Korea from Manchuria by laying a field of radioactive wastes—the by-products of atomic manufacture—across all the major lines of enemy supply." That would be followed up by a super-Inchon—"simultaneous amphibious and airborne landings at the upper end of both coasts of North Korea, and close a gigantic trap." The Chinese "would soon starve or surrender." The Pentagon's rejection was again swift.

Indicating MacArthur's loss of imperial mandate, two December 6 orders, aimed at him, prohibited military commanders from publicizing views that had not been cleared with the Pentagon or State Department. MacArthur chafed but initially more or less complied; but then began to vent his frustration and wounded pride. Washington ignored a number of minor lapses.

The Chinese and North Koreans withdrew from Seoul in mid-March and a few weeks later the United Nations forces crossed the 38th Parallel for the second time. But as the basic reality of stalemate became evident, pressure for a negotiated settlement grew. Truman reluctantly bowed to it, and by March 19 the Joint Chiefs and the State Department had concurred in a statement favoring a ceasefire. MacArthur, informed that a statement had been prepared and that the President would make it, moved quickly to end the threat of peace. Addressing his enemy commander-in-chief, he coupled an invitation to a meeting with a virtual demand for surrender. Taunting China for military and industrial weakness, he continued: "The enemy, therefore, must by now be painfully aware that a decision by the United Nations to depart from its tolerant effort to contain the war would doom Red China to the risk of imminent military collapse." The truce statement was shelved, but the sentiment in favor of MacArthur's dismissal grew.

Early in April MacArthur thrice exploded—in a response to an inquiry from *The Freeman,* a far-right periodical; in an interview with a British visitor, and, most fatefully, in a message to Joseph Martin, Republican minority leader in the House. In that message MacArthur sonorously endorsed a speech in which Martin had virtually accused the President of the "murder of thousands of American boys" and demanded the opening of a second front on the Chinese mainland. He approved Martin's call for an invasion of China by Chiang's forces as in keeping with the military tradition of invariably "meeting force with maximum counter-force." "There is no substitute for victory."

MacArthur was especially blunt in calling for war with China— and if the Soviet Union intervened, then with it too—in a conversation with the Spanish and Portuguese ambassadors. Their radioed reports to their capitals were monitored by the National Security Agency at the Atsugi Air Force Base and placed on Truman's desk, strengthening Truman's view that MacArthur had to go.

Recalled with bare civility by General Marshall, MacArthur came home for a farewell feting and then took Olympian quarters in the Waldorf Towers. Over and over for the rest of his days he pleaded his case, justifying in virtually every particular his conduct of the war and denouncing the failure to take the war to China as a sell-out and disgrace.

MacArthur's opponents in the State Department, Pentagon, White House, and Congress were as much in collusion as contention with him. They were for wars on the periphery of China; he was for war with China. They thought economic, political, and military pressures short of war would prove the Chinese revolution to be a "passing phase." He was too impatient for that. He talked of the flag, of duty and honor, often of peace, but vanity and arrogance drove him, and ignorance of Asian realities undid him.

20. The Powell/Schuman Case: Truth Was the Defense

In the time of McCarthyism and its complement McCarranism those who defended or even seriously explained the Chinese revolution, those who opposed or even seriously questioned the U.S. policy of counterrevolutionary intervention in China and its neighbors, were targets for slander and persecution.

Among the principal victims were John W. Powell, former editor of the *China Monthly Review* (for many years the *China Weekly Review*), his wife Sylvia, and Julian Schuman, both former associate editors.[64]

In the postwar period the *Review*, published in Shanghai, had become a vigorous critic of the Kuomintang regime and increasingly sympathetic with the Communist alternative in the years of the civil war (1946–49). Continuing to publish after the establishment of the People's Republic, it denounced the U.S. intervention in the Korean war and thoroughly aired and found credible evidence that the U.S. had resorted to bacteriological warfare both in Korea and across the Yalu River in Manchuria. It called on the American people to protest and put an end to this "crime against humanity."

After struggling against financial losses, the *China Monthly Review* ceased publication in June 1953; many U.S. subscribers never received their copies because of American postal censorship. On the voyage home the CIA pumped and tried to recruit John W. (Bill) Powell, and the U.S. customs officials in San Francisco held the *Review's* library because it included publications and films of "a political nature." At the direction of J. Edgar Hoover the FBI tailed Powell everywhere as he visited friends and relatives. In 1954 both Powells and Schuman were summoned to testify before the Senate Internal Security Subcommittee and subjected to provocative questioning.

Then on April 25, 1956, the Powells and Schuman were indicted in San Francisco on thirteen counts of sedition. The count that made the headlines, and that the government came to focus on, was that they had published the germ warfare charge, knowing it to be false. The *Review* was alleged to have sought to subvert the loyalty of American troops and to foster insubordination.

Proceedings dragged on three years. The actual trial began in January 1959 and ended shortly in a mistrial. Federal Judge Louis Goodman, presiding, made the point with considerable emphasis

---

64. Established in 1917 as *Millard's Review of the Far East*, the *Review*, renamed in 1923, was edited by John Benjamin Powell, father of John W. Powell. Edgar Snow, who worked on the *Review* when he first came to China in 1928, described the older Powell as "more patriotic about China than many Chinese." J. B. Powell was imprisoned by the Japanese and ill treated; he lost both feet to gangrene. He was a staunch supporter of the Kuomintang regime until his death in 1947, but his son, who succeeded him as editor, was a vigorous critic of the Kuomintang performance and sympathetic to the revolutionary challenge.

that because of legal definition treason was more applicable to the charges than sedition, and hasty headline writers turned this into assertions that the judge had accused the Powells of treason, thus prejudicing members of the jury. The government then brought the treason charge but that too ran into difficulties and a dilemma. In 1961 Attorney General Robert F. Kennedy, pointing to technical difficulties, announced that the case would not be pursued.

Actually the prosecution faced problems that were a greater obstacle than technicalities. The heart of the defense was that the germ warfare reports in the *Review* were the truth and that this truth could be established by the contents of Pentagon documents and by the testimony of witnesses from China and Korea.

For reasons that have been made clearer by the passage of time, the government could not permit any serious trial probe of the central germ warfare issue. It refused to produce the documents subpoenaed and to permit witnesses to be brought from China and Korea. Professor Stanley I. Kutler of the University of Wisconsin has summed up the government position this way:

> In effect, the government argued that the accused had committed sedition, but it would not allow him to defend himself by proving the truth of what he had said. The government would not produce material other than its contentions that what Powell said was untrue. Putting it another way, the government maintained that sedition consisted of repeating charges that the government denied.[65]

Kutler says that at one point General MacArthur (Bill Powell recollects that it was actually General Mark Clark) asked the Defense Department when biological warfare weapons would be available. "Naturally, the army refused to declassify this information and it feared the materials might be elicited during a trial."[66]

The government also had qualms about the "Sams Report," which revealed that an army doctor, Sams, had planned to enter a North Korean hospital during a commando raid, inject morphine into a patient thought to be suffering from bubonic plague, and abduct him for physical examination. The Communists had charged that Sams and a naval vessel off the North Korean coast were testing biological warfare weapons. The army refused to declassify Sams mission documents.

---

65. Stanley I. Kutler, *The American Inquisition* (New York: Hill and Wang, 1982), 217.
66. Kutler, *American Inquisition*, 234–35.

The Powells and Schuman went free, but the three-year ordeal wrung them out financially and emotionally. The trial cost the Powells $40,000, even though they received a good deal of pro bono legal help. They lived for years with a tapped telephone and the knowledge that visitors were certain to be checked out by FBI agents outside. Bill Powell told Jim Hood of the *San Francisco Sunday Examiner and Chronicle* years later: "We lived off our friends, really—they supplied us with money. During the trial we shipped the children off to stay with friends or relatives. Our mothers rented a cabin near Boulder Creek, near Santa Cruz, and we sent the boys there."

Sylvia Powell lost her job with an infantile paralysis foundation and Bill lost his as a salesman of school supplies. Sylvia told Hood: "It took several years off our lives, but in a way it was fascinating. We made some wonderful, warm friends you could make only when you're under siege that way."[67]

Julian Schuman suffered the same torments as the Powells and was hurt in a particular way—his just published book, *Assignment China*, received a chill reception. Years later, in his introduction to a reprinting of the book (under the title *China: An Uncensored Look*), Schuman recalled:

> By early 1956, a virtually unknown publisher, Whittier Books, agreed to bring the book out. Published at the end of the year it was met, with the exception of a rare review, with silence. That same year, along with John W. Powell and his wife Sylvia, I was indicted for treason by a grand jury. Talk of timely coincidences. Needless to say the first printing of 3,000 copies never sold out.

What the government held were verities that could not be loyally challenged has been made less than certain by new information and dispassionate analysis. North Korea has to be held responsible for the outbreak of fighting on June 25, 1950, but a strong case can be made that the war originated in the U.S. destruction of the People's Republic in the south in 1945–46.[68]

And new light has been shone on germ warfare. Bill Powell was motivated by his ordeal to go after the facts, and with the help of

67. *San Francisco Sunday Examiner and Chronicle*, March 13, 1977.
68. Hugh Deane, "On the Deadly Parallel: A Review with Reminiscence," *Bulletin of Concerned Asian Scholars* 15, no. 3 (July–August, 1983). The review is of Bruce Cumings' *The Origin of the Korean War: Liberation and the Emergence of Separate Regimes, 1945–47* (Princeton, N.J.: Princeton University Press, 1981).

documents obtained under the Freedom of Information Act and revelations in Japan, has made important progress. He has published his findings in four articles.[69]

He has established beyond doubt that at the end of World War II the U.S. and Japan conspired to keep secret Japan's use of biological weapons against China and the Soviet Union. Victor and vanquished struck a deal by which full information about Japanese experience in biological warfare (files, slides and Japanese experts) was sent to Camp Detrick, later Fort Detrick, in Maryland, and the U.S. in return used its commanding influence to keep the issue out of the war crimes trials in Tokyo. "A Faustian bargain," Bill Powell called it.

MacArthur himself assented to a promise of immunity from war crimes charges, and General Charles A. Willoughby, his head of intelligence, had no qualms over accepting a dinner invitation from Lieutenant General Shiro Ishii, the army doctor in charge of Japan's biological warfare program.[70] The U.S. officers were not deterred from the deal by their knowledge that the Japanese used prisoners of war, including Americans, as guinea pigs in germ experimentation. Prisoners who survived painful experiments were put to death— "sacrificed" was the Japanese word—when their usefulness was over.

Biological weapons were used "with moderate success against Chinese troops and civilians and with unknown results against the Russians," Powell wrote in *The Bulletin of Atomic Scientists* in October 1981.

Since China was subject to epidemics, precise data on the biological assaults could not be gathered, but partial evidence indicated that attacks on Ningbo, south of Shanghai, Changde in Hunan Province, and other places killed some seven hundred people. The files of the People's Republic list eleven cities as germ warfare targets.

The principal Japanese biological center, built in the mid-1930s, was near Harbin. Other installations were located near Changchun

---

69. "Japan's Germ Warfare: The U.S. Cover-up of a War Crime," *Bulletin of Concerned Asian Scholars*, October–December 1980; "A Hidden Chapter in History," *The Bulletin of Atomic Scientists*, October 1981; "The Human Guinea Pigs," *San Francisco Chronicle*, November 3, 1985; "The Gap Between the Natural and Social Sciences Sometimes Leaves the Public Poorly Informed," *Bulletin of Concerned Asian Scholars*, July–September, 1986.
70. In his article in the *San Francisco Chronicle*, Powell has this to say about MacArthur's involvement: "Dr. Murray Sanders, a former lieutenant colonel in the U.S. Army Chemical Corps and one of the early investigators sent to Japan, has described a private meeting between himself, Willoughby and MacArthur. The Japanese were stalling. Assurances of safety from unknown officials in Washington were not enough. They wanted something better. Willoughby asked if Sanders could give Ishii MacArthur's promise of immunity from war crimes charges. MacArthur, Sanders states, gave his nod of sanction."

and in Nanjing. At Harbin, Unit 731, which was officially engaged in water purification, killed some three thousand prisoners in experiments. U.S. documents and statements by former members of Unit 731 indicate that some Americans were among them. The human guinea pigs were infected with massive doses of plague, typhus, gas gangrene, typhoid, smallpox, and the like. The arms of some prisoners were frozen and then thawed in experiments which resulted in rotting flesh and protruding bones. Livers of prisoners were destroyed by repeated x-ray exposure. Prisoners' blood was drained and horse blood pumped into them. Surgical vivisections were performed. After infecting a group of prisoners, the Japanese killed them and performed autopsies on them sequentially so that they could measure the progress of the disease. Unit 731 had a productive capacity of eight tons of bacteria per month.

When Soviet troops poured into the Northeast (Manchuria) in the final stage of World War II, the Japanese destroyed the Harbin center and sought to eliminate all traces of it, but they did not wholly succeed. Now China has reconstructed the center as a public exhibit.

Both the Kuomintang government and the Soviet Union offered evidence of Japanese germ warfare crimes, but the United States was the power in occupied Japan and it was used to minimize the impact of the charges. The Russians captured Japanese personnel who had taken part in Unit 731's biological experimentation and warfare, tried them and found them guilty in a trial in Khabarovosk in 1949. But American officials dismissed the Soviet reports as propaganda even though they knew very well that they were accurate.

Powell obtained a series of top secret cables and documents proving American connivance in the concealing of Japan's germ warfare effort and testifying to the great value of the data obtained at little expense for the Fort Detrick researchers. In a 1947 report, a Fort Detrick official expressed hope that cooperating Japanese would "be spared embarrassment" and that all information obtained would be kept in American hands.

Powell observed that when, during the Korean War, China accused the U.S. of employing updated versions of Japan's germ warfare weapons and tactics, "not only were the charges denied, but it was also claimed there was no proof of the earlier Japanese actions." The U.S. Army continued its secretiveness concerning Japan's germ warfare pioneering until a Japanese documentary in 1976 made deceit no longer possible.

Many Unit 731 veterans not only escaped punishment but enjoyed successful careers in civilian life. A Japanese study listed nine medical school professors, four medical institute researchers, twenty-three practicing doctors, thirty-six government employees, four hospital directors, and seven company executives as former Unit 731 members. The doctor who experimented in pumping horse blood into patients became president of a prosperous blood bank company. A doctor who directed human freezing experiments became a "freezing consultant" in the giant Taiyo Fishery Company.

Such evidence as exists that the U.S. took advantage of Japan's germ warfare development and tried biological weapons in the Korean War does not add up to proof, but the grave charge can no longer be dismissed as a "preposterous fraud" as it was at the time.

Shortly after the outbreak of the war in Korea, according to Powell, "a witches' brew of diseases broke out in North Korea." He has set forth the evidence that the still virulent Korean hemorrhagic fever (KHF) "is a transplanted and possibly mutated descendant of Songo fever, which was cultured by Japanese army scientists in their search for exotic biological warfare agents in the 1930s and 1940s." Many hundreds of American soldiers serving in the war were infected and some died.

Bert V. A. Roling, a Dutch jurist who served as a judge at the Tokyo tribunals, wrote in the issue of *The Bulletin of Atomic Scientists* that carried Powell's article that "it is a bitter experience for me to be informed now that centrally ordered Japanese criminality of the most disgusting kind was kept secret from the Court by the U.S. government."

21. Paul Robeson: "Voice of the People of All Lands"

A number of leading American Blacks had intimate China connections. The poet Langston Hughes visited the old Shanghai and was outraged by the discriminatory practices of the YMCA in the International Settlement. His poem "Roar China" is a paean to the unfolding revolution. Dr. W. E. B. DuBois, scholar, educator, founder of the NAACP (National Association for the Advancement of Colored People), saw the old Shanghai in 1936 and twice visited the new China, in 1958 and 1962, with his wife Shirley Graham DuBois. In 1958 they, accompanied by Anna Louise Strong, had a historic interview with Mao in Wuhan. Shirley Graham DuBois, a writer, teacher, and composer, was a frequent China visitor after the death of her husband. She died of cancer in Beijing and is buried in the cemetery for revolutionaries there. James Killens traveled about China and wrote a pamphlet titled *Black Man in New China* published by the US-China Peoples Friendship Association.

Paul Robeson never went to China, but he made an outstanding contribution to the rich history of U.S.-China friendship. The first issue of *New China* (Spring 1975), published by the US-China Peoples Friendship Association, told of this history in an article by L. H. Yeakey and Robert Glassman.

A concert singer and stage and film actor who used his artistry to further people's struggles everywhere, Robeson began to read about China in the late 1920s, stirred by the revolutionary upheaval of those years; read much more and began his long study of the Chinese language in the early 1930s; gave concerts in Europe and the U.S. to raise money for the China invaded by the Japanese; denounced the blockade of the Communist-held areas by the Chongqing regime; called for a cessation of the U.S. counterrevolutionary intervention in the civil war of 1946–49; campaigned for U.S. recognition of the People's Republic and for its admission into the United Nations; and spoke directly to American Blacks about the significance of the triumph of the Chinese revolution.

Robeson was a renaissance man in an era when the true rebirth that comes with revolution was on the global agenda. He was a fine athlete, an All-American end at Rutgers; a holder of a Phi Beta Kappa key, recognition of scholastic achievement; a graduate of Columbia Law School for whom law became too remote from his feelings for people; an actor whose "Othello" was one of the greatest all-time triumphs of the American theater. What took him to the heights, assuring him continuing curtain calls, was an acute sense of the injustices suffered by his people that led him to examine the plight of peoples the world over.

In her preface to the album of Chinese songs (the title song was "Chee Lai") that Robeson made in 1941 with a Chinese chorus conducted by Liu Liangmo, Soong Ching Ling wrote that some of the finest songs created by China's struggle "are being made available to Americans in the recordings of Paul Robeson, voice of the people of all lands."

Robeson sang the songs of the world's peoples in their own tongues—he insisted on it—and he was a serious student of comparative linguistics. He turned to Chinese around 1933, attracted by similarities he perceived with African languages. "I found that Chinese poems which cannot be rendered into English would translate perfectly into African," he wrote in the *London Daily Herald* in January 1935.

Twenty years later, writing in *Spotlight on Africa*, he observed that "both the Chinese and African people make extensive use of tones," and went on to describe the four tones in standard Chinese [the Han language] by variations in the pronunciation of "yes" in English (for example, high level tone—yes in the sense of "What did you say?"). In the language of Calibar in southern Nigeria "use of tone is much more complicated," he noted. Robeson studied written Chinese and sheets on which he practiced writing ideograms have survived.

Biographer Marie Seton recorded that Robeson brought back from a British tour "an interesting reminder of how he spent much of his time before and after concerts—sheets and sheets of hotel stationary—the Queen's Hotel, Birmingham; Grand Hotel, Sheffield; Grand Hotel, Bristol—all of them covered in Chinese grammatical exercises and Chinese characters, carefully written and numbered."[71]

A chance meeting with Jack Chen, son of Eugene Chen, foreign minister in the Hankou government of 1927, added to Robeson's awareness of China:

> In Moscow some years ago I met three young Chinese, a fellow named Jack Chen and his two sisters. Jack was a newspaperman, one of his sisters was a motion picture technician and the other was a dancer. Their father was part Chinese and part Negro. He had lived in the West Indies and had served under Sun Yat-sen. . . .
>
> Jack was a slight chap, medium height and soft-spoken. He spoke beautiful English. He came to my concerts and we sat around many nights and talked of China and its future. That was in 1936 and '37. Later I met him in London and we often appeared there for China Relief.[72]

On May 2, 1941 Robeson sang at a "Stars for China" concert in Philadelphia. On March 12, 1944, when Robeson addressed a gathering in New York City honoring Sun Yat-sen, he used the occasion to denounce the blockade of the Communist areas by Kuomintang troops:

---

71. Paul Robeson (London: Dobson Books, 1958), 195.
72. "Here's My Story," *Freedom*, May 1951. Also in Philip Foner, *Paul Robeson Speaks* (New York: Citadel, 1978). Marie Seton accompanied Paul and Eslanda Robeson when they visited Moscow in 1934 and gives details of the encounter with Jack Chen. Chen was "the embodiment of the culture with which Robeson was so concerned," she wrote.

China today is fighting with one arm tied. The arm that is tied is the Communist-led Eighth Route and New Fourth Armies. Despite the great work which these armies have done in defending China—not only in fighting but in educating and mobilizing the people for defense. . . . The three years' blockade against the Chinese guerrilla forces must be lifted. The entire might and strength of China's 400 millions must be united.

Two years later, as the civil war began, Robeson and Brigadier General Evans Carlson became co-chairmen of the National Committee to Win the Peace, and in September 1946 called a conference aimed at mobilizing American public opinion in support of the withdrawal of U.S. armed forces from China.

Robeson also joined the Committee for a Democratic Far Eastern Policy, of which Carlson was national chairman until his untimely death in 1947. The committee did what it could to oppose U.S. involvement in the civil war, and in 1949 launched a scroll-signing campaign in support of recognition of the new Chinese regime. Robeson was an early signer, photographed as he took pen in hand.

In December of that year Eslanda Robeson went to Beijing to take part in the First Conference of Asian Women but her husband could not accompany her. Addressing a rally of thirty thousand people, Eslanda Robeson said that the changes taking place in China would be understood and appreciated by "every Negro and every woman."

Within days of the outbreak of the Korean war in June 1950, Robeson denounced U.S. intervention in an address to a rally in Madison Square Garden in New York City: "A new wind of freedom blows in the East. The people rise to put off centuries of domination by outside powers, by the robber barons and white supremacists of Europe and America who have held them in contempt and, too long, have crushed their simplest aspirations with the mailed fist. . . . "

Two years later Robeson was invited to Beijing to attend the Peace Congress of the Asian and Pacific Regions, but had to decline because his passport had been denied him. In an article in the Harlem publication *Freedom*, which he edited with Shirley Graham DuBois and others, Robeson saluted China for coming "to the aid of the heroic Korean people" and for becoming "a power for peace." He wrote that the refusal to grant him a passport was especially bitter to him "because, in addition to my deep concern with the world peace movement, I have for a long time felt a close kinship with the Chinese people."

China made plain its esteem in 1958 when Robeson's sixtieth birthday was a global celebration. Sidney Shapiro reported from Beijing that the occasion was viewed there as of major international significance. For two days preceding the birthday as well as on the birthday itself Radio Beijing played recordings of Robeson's songs. On April 9 the entire cultural page of the *People's Daily* was devoted to him. In a message of thanks, Robeson wrote that "one day I hope to greet you on Chinese soil." That hope was not to be realized. After years of declining health, during which he lived in seclusion, Robeson died in 1976, at the age of seventy-eight. But if he did not survive the weakening of the flesh, the admiration and affection felt for him by Blacks and countless others have survived the abuse by all those who scandalized his name.

Unsparing hindsight has revealed that some of the political judgments of Robeson and others of us were unreal. The hopes for the emancipation of all peoples that Robeson fervently shared are still very far from realization. New courses have had to be charted. But Robeson belonged to that all too small band of men and women who shouted protests others only muttered. He bore the burden in the heat of the day.

22. Howard Adams: The Korean War GI with a China Home

Of the twenty-four American soldiers captured during the Korean war who chose to remain in China after the peace agreement, Howard Adams is the one who settled in and made a good life for himself. He has work he finds congenial, teaching English to medical students in Jinan, Shandong. He has a happy family life. His pleasures include gardening and long-distance running. He has had trying experiences in his three decades in China and now looks out on a society he sees making some progress. [73]

He returned to Texas for a visit in 1974, but after some weeks began to long to go home.

Adams grew up in Corsicana, Texas, the son of an oil field worker and sometime farmer. World War II put him in K Company, First Infantry Regiment, Sixth Division. He served in New Guinea and the

---

73. Adams' story here is based on an interview with me in 1984 and subsequent correspondence.

Philippines. He came ashore in the Philippines in the fifth wave, one of those for men with a future.

After the nuclear bombing of Hiroshima and peace, he was sent to Korea. He was a local assistant police chief with the rank of sergeant, and he remembers worrying that the Reds might be infiltrating the police force. That was the period when the U.S. occupation forces were allying themselves with the South Korean right and breaking up the strong left that had formed the People's Republic. After three months, in January of 1946, Adams received his discharge and was shipped back to the U.S.

The next years were a mixture of study and odd jobs. He graduated from the Navarro County Junior College and went on to take courses in science and other subjects at the University of Houston. He pumped gas, sold encyclopedias.

Restive and dissatisfied, army life began to look good. He reenlisted in 1949. The Korean war began in June of the next year and he was soon there, assigned to radio communications in the Twenty-fourth Division.

He remembers the anxious period when the U.S. forces were cooped up in the Pusan perimeter. But then came the end-run landing at Inchon, the recapture of Seoul, and the swift change in the fortunes of war. "We crossed the 38th parallel and went hell bent north, and I remember a guy said to me we're going to get into trouble. He was right."

He was on the switchboard one night when advance units were almost to the Yalu River and picked up a call from a First Cavalry outfit: "We're getting the hell beat out of us. Gotta go."

Soon he had destroyed the switchboard and joined in a general retreat. The jeep he was riding in was ambushed and raking fire killed the driver. He dove for cover, managed to get away, and painfully made his way south.

But his luck ran out when General MacArthur, ignoring the warning China had given by its initial, strictly limited attack, ordered a second drive on the Yalu, his famous "Home by Christmas" offensive.

Adams has indelible memories of forced marches, hasty attempts to throw up roadblocks, mining of bridges, rumors and more rumors, retreats that turned into scrambles for safety.

Made the battalion's message center chief, he could read coded messages and he remembers this one: "Got to go—they're jumping into holes with us."

For him the end came this way: He jumped into a ditch, drawing fire. Safe for the moment, he dug a hole in deep snow and buried the secret communications equipment in his charge. He put code books and secret papers inside his shirt. He was crawling painfully away through the snow when Chinese jumped out in front of him and he was a prisoner. Several other GIs were taken at the same time. "I was sure I would die and tried to prepare myself for it. I only dared hope that napalm wouldn't get me," he said. But hours later Chinese brought him rice and captured jam and a young soldier gave him an overcoat. "I stopped thinking of death."

With hundreds of other prisoners he was marched north to a mining camp, a layover or collecting point for prisoners destined for camps further north. The captives called it the bean camp because of the steady diet of soybeans and millet cakes. "Later I spent a year in a village near Pyongyang, the northern capital, got to swim in a river, read what they gave us. I read the *History of the Communist Party of the Soviet Union.*" The prisoners' hopes soared when the peace talks began. "We thought we'd be free soon. The Chinese thought so too at one point and gave us a feast, but the talks dragged on and on as the U.S. side made ridiculous demands regarding prisoners and other issues."

Adams is still indignant over treatment of Chinese prisoners, who were subjected to heavy pressure to defect. "Many Chinese families still do not know what happened to their sons."

With the negotiations stalemated, the prisoners were moved north to Camp Number 5, at Pyuktong near the Yalu.

There Chinese efforts to win over the prisoners gradually began to have an effect. "A progressive group of PWs emerged. We were getting to like the Chinese running the camp and at the same time we were furious at the negotiating demands of the Americans at Panmunjon and wanted to retaliate."

In November 1952, the Inter-Camp Olympics were held, each PW camp sending contingents of athletes to Pyuktong. Adams served as a broadcaster. According to a souvenir booklet, he "did a very good job keeping everyone informed over the P.A. system all during the Olympics."

When the peace settlement was finally reached, Adams and twenty-three others refused repatriation and chose to stay on in China. "My idea was to protest U.S. policies at Panmunjon and visit China and see how socialism worked, but I had no intention of living there permanently."

The twenty-four were taken to Taiyuan, Shanxi Province, for an orientation program. "We were given talks and such things as the *China Monthly Review* to read. Combined with these were self-criticism sessions, aimed at raising our consciousness. We ate good Western food at noon, Chinese meals at night."

The Taiyuan experience began in February 1954. In September a group of six which included Adams and James Veneris (also still in China) were sent to Jinan, capital of Shandong Province and an industrial, transportation, and educational center.

Over the years the group of two dozen dwindled as some elected to go home and face Army charges and the prospect of opprobrium. The so-called difficult years, the consequence of natural disasters, Great Leap Forward extremism, the Soviet pullout, and the Cultural Revolution launched in 1966 had a devastating effect on the former PWs far from home.

But Adams got married in 1956, soon had a family, and was adjusting well. Food is at the center of his recollections of the difficult years.

> Everything was tightly rationed then. Everyone lacked food of good quality. Those with more children were worse off. I always received special rations—more grain, vegetables and meat, and so my relatives were always knocking at our door. Anyway my family got through it all right, and we managed to pull the families of my two brothers-in-law through too. Now the children of these two families are grown and working, and most are married. But they never forget their uncle. When they come to see me now, they ask what can they do for me, what do I need. That makes me feel good.

In 1963 Adams was chosen to attend People's University in Beijing. The start of the Cultural Revolution three years later put a stop to the studies of the Chinese students, but the foreigners were allowed to continue and Adams graduated.

He was in Beijing part of the time during the Cultural Revolution, spending his time reading and seeing friends. In Jinan he was able to put to good use knowledge he had acquired at the University of Houston and worked as a technician at a paper-making plant. He was half of a technical staff of two, the other technicians having been sent to the countryside to labor.

> I never had any trouble personally, but like everyone was affected by the shortages and inconveniences. In Jinan at the factory I joined the strongest rebel group and wore its red arm band both in Jinan and Beijing. The rebel group was divided into companies and battalions and had all sorts of struggle meetings, study meetings, strategy ses-

sions and protest and support marches. I took part in them but never took any initiative and never joined in any of the violence, of which there was little in our factory.

In Beijing I went wherever I pleased night or day and no one took notice of me. In Jinan I was accepted as one of the guys. In fact, I have never felt more integrated with the Chinese people. Our factory never lost a day of production, though quality suffered some.

During the worst of those years Adams sometimes was tempted to leave, but his family, by then including two daughters, gave him reason to stick it out.

In 1974 he spent four months in Texas. "But I had got used to the pace of life in China. In the U.S. everyone seemed to be in a rush. The violence disturbed me. I witnessed a knife stabbing. Soon my thoughts were on my family and Jinan. Later my wife told me that she had worried a bit that I wouldn't come back. She needn't have."

As Chinese policies again stressed education, Adams got into teaching, first at the Shandong Chemical Research Institute and Shandong University, and later at Shandong Medical College. He had no experience in the teaching of English and teaching materials were hard to come by. He began by relying almost entirely on a single book of sample sentences but gradually gained in expertise.

For Adams, life is satisfying. He lives on the second floor of a comfortable old house built for foreigners on the campus. His eldest daughter is married and has a college job. His youngest daughter is a reporter/editor on the staff of a weekly newspaper devoted to environmental problems.

He gardens. He likes to be with young people and plays volleyball and basketball. He is an enthusiastic member of the Old Men's Long-Distance Running Team, which takes off on long jaunts to historic sites in the mountains. He jogs three or four miles a day. Sometimes he comes to Beijing to look up old friends. Life is getting better for those he cares about, his own family, his wife's relatives, the people he works with. For all the difficulties it faces, the China he sees about him is no longer the desperate nation he knew forty years ago:.

Everywhere you look buildings are going up. The markets are flowing with goods and people are buying everything from good clothes to refrigerators and color TVs. The colleges and universities are filled with students eager to learn. The factories are getting in high-tech machines, and the hospitals are getting all sorts of sophisticated instruments. It's an exciting time to be in China. If you don't go to a particular area of Jinan for a couple of months, you won't recognize it when you do.

23. The CIA's "Contra" Campaign in Tibet

In the fall of 1942 the OSS, the predecessor of the CIA, sent two agents into Tibet—Ilia Tolstoy, emigré grandson of Leo Tolstoy, and Brooke Dolan, another professional adventurer. Their avowed mission was to search out transportation links between India and Yunnan and Sichuan provinces that would at least partially offset the loss of the Burma Road, which had been severed by the Japanese. But they apparently spent more time on another task—to win high-level friendships in an area which OSS chief William J. Donovan predicted "will be strategically valuable in the future." Donovan supported the opening of radio communications with Lhasa by means of a U.S. gift of three long-range transmitters.

The Tibetan oligarchy also had an agenda. When Tolstoy and Dolan reported to the American embassy in Chongqing they made clear they had been won over to the view that the United States should support Tibetan aspirations for independence from China. The Chinese Foreign Ministry (Kuomintang) officially complained. Soon after, the State Department affirmed that the U.S. did not question Chinese suzerainty over Tibet.

Returning from a stay in Lhasa in October 1949, radio commentator Lowell Thomas and his son Lowell Thomas Jr. embraced the cause of Tibetan independence and American support of it. Received by President Truman on November 1, Thomas urged that "modern weapons and sufficient advisers" be sent to Tibet. Thomas reported to the Dalai Lama that the President was non-committal but "sympathetic to your country's problems." Truman said he hoped "to organize the moral forces of the world against the immoral." The mellifluous voice of Lowell Thomas on the radio won converts to the cause of an independent Tibet.[74]

Lacking foreign aid, its small army easily defeated by the PLA, the Lhasa oligarchy was obliged to reach a seventeen-point agree-

---

74. In Tokyo the Thomases were briefed by General MacArthur and General Willoughby, his chief intelligence officer, according to Israel Epstein, *Tibet Transformed* (Beijing: New World Press, 1983). In the December 1960 issue of *Reader's Digest*, Thomas allowed himself to write that "what Buchenwald was to the 1940s, Tibet was to the 1950s." Supreme Court Justice William O. Douglas played a like role, believing that the Communist powers were intent on conquering the "Buddhist world." See Steve Weissman, "Last Tangle in Tibet," *Pacific Research & World Empire Telegram*, July–August 1973.

ment with Beijing under which social changes were to proceed very slowly. But during this period it also sought covert American aid and found U.S. officials receptive. The American intervention in the Korean war in June, 1950 was accompanied by a general intervention in China and East Asia, including Tibet. Indeed, nine days before the Korean war began Secretary of State Dean Acheson said in a cable that the U.S. and the United Kingdom were discussing ways to "encourage Tibetan resistance to Commie control."[75]

Two of the Dalai Lama's older brothers played key roles. Gyalo Thondup, married to a daughter of a Kuomintang official, visited Taiwan where he conferred with Chiang Kai-shek and presumably helped to arrange the extensive Kuomintang subversive efforts in Tibet. He eventually settled in India. The other brother, Thubten Norbu, negotiated with American officials in the Kalimsong-Darjeeling area and later went to the United States under the auspices of the American Committee for Free Asia, a CIA front.

The U.S. responded agreeably to the Dalai Lama's request for help in 1950. According to John F. Avedon, an American associate of the Dalai Lama, "For its part, the United States pledged to support (the Dalai Lama) and his government abroad, reintroduce Tibet's cause in the United Nations, and finance its struggle against China, including, if it developed, a military option." But the "plan never ripened."[76]

In 1951 the U.S. specified its offer in a secret letter to the Dalai Lama, who was then in Lhasa. But the Dalai Lama could not agree to repudiate the 17-Point Agreement and the overture came to nothing. Secret U.S.-oligarchy talks appear to have continued into 1952, failing in part, according to an American diplomat, because Washington's Tibetan allies were "unable to counterbalance the tremendous weight of superstition and selfish officialdom, including delegates from monasteries, oracles of incredible influence, and the misguided wish of the Lhasa government itself to preserve . . . the religious integrity of Tibetan life as personified and symbolized by the Dalai Lama."[77]

The CIA was already in action. Operating in Taiwan under the cover name of Western Enterprises, Inc., it teamed up with Kuomintang units in carrying out intelligence-gathering and sabotage raids on the mainland through the 1950s. Quemoy was the usual jumping-off place for the midget subs and landing craft. CIA agents

---

75. A. Tom Grunfeld, *The Making of Modern Tibet* (Armonk, N.Y.: M. E. Sharpe, 1987), 95.
76. John F. Avedon, *In Exile from the Land of Snows* (New York: Knopf, 1984), 36.
77. Grunfeld, *The Making of Modern Tibet*, 95.

were infiltrated into China, but all or most were rounded up. Later, regular overflights of China by U-2 and other spy planes and drones made use of agents on the ground less important.

Tibet became the main target of opportunity. In 1951, with the cooperation of Brother Gyalo Thondup, then in Darjeeling, the CIA began setting up an intelligence net. A small number of Tibetans were assembled in Pakistan and taken to Guam or Okinawa for training in clandestine operations.

Expansion of the CIA's role seems to have begun in 1955, by which time the ending Korean war freed resources. The basic perspective and goal was explained in 1954 by Walter Robertson, Assistant Secretary of State for Far Eastern Affairs: "Our hope of solving the problem of the mainland of China was not through attack upon the mainland but rather by actions which would promote disintegration from within."[78] Robertson was disclaiming any intent to engage in a general war with China. In 1955, at a four-day meeting with Tibetan rebels in Kalimsong, a top American intelligence official laid out a ten-year scenario that was supposed to end Chinese rule of Tibet.

Beijing kept its promise to move slowly in changing Tibetan society, but pursued reforms in Tibetan-inhabited areas outside the Tibet Autonomous Region. In 1956–57 the smoldering resistance to Chinese authority and reforms in such areas—Amdo (now Qinghai) and the home lands of the Khampas to the south—flared into violence. Armed bands linked in an organization named Four Rivers, Six Ranges (an old name for Amdo and Kham) ambushed convoys on the just-constructed east-west roads and clashed with the PLA. Lamas in the large Lithang monastery and several other monasteries gave the uprising religious fervor and both stored and themselves took up arms. Lithang was captured and demolished by the PLA after a twenty-six-day siege. By 1958 fighting had spread into central Tibet.

The CIA got into it swiftly. Planes based in Thailand (C-54s, PBY5As and later the Lockheed-built C-130s, which had a 2,400-mile range) dropped small arms and other supplies to rebel forces that would today be called "contras." Parachutes were converted into clothing. The intelligence net was expanded and more Tibetans were given short training courses and dropped into the mountains. Two Tibetan agents were dropped near Lhasa and were able to confer with aides of the Dalai Lama in the Norbu Lingka, the summer palace. In the U.S., the CIA and the cooperative media publicized the cause of Tibetan resistance to what was described as brutal Chinese rule.

---

78. Weissman, "Last Tangle.

In June 1958 a rebel force of some thousands—five thousand, according to several accounts—was formed within a hundred miles of Lhasa and counted on the embrace of the CIA. But the Amdo-Khampa contras suffered setbacks as a reinforced PLA secured the roads, and in March[79] an ineptly timed and weakly organized rebellion in Lhasa itself was crushed in three days of bloody fighting. Many lamas and lay members of the elite and much of the old army joined the uprising, but the populace generally did not, assuring the rebellion's collapse. Many shops reopened after forty-eight hours.

The Dalai Lama fled Lhasa on the eve of the rebellion, and with CIA assistance reached India. A CIA radio operator attached to the party arranged for the dropping of crucially needed supplies. In the judgment of Colonel Fletcher Prouty, Air Force liaison with the CIA's Tibet effort, "The Dalai Lama would never have been saved without the CIA."[80]

The expanding CIA role must have encouraged the aides of the Dalai Lama who decided to risk the March rebellion. The suppression of it brought on stepped-up CIA activity. The appraisal was that at least the People's Republic could be seriously harassed, that better planning and substantial material aid could coalesce the surviving contra groups within Tibet and bring Tibetans in exile into the struggle.[81]

These are particulars of CIA operations in 1959 and thereafter:

Propaganda. Through the Committee for a Free Asia, committees set up to raise money for Tibetan refugees and the various organizations and publications it influenced through funding and staff infiltration, the CIA depicted Tibet as a monstrous example of Communist aggression and as a stepping stone toward the planned conquest of India. The *China Quarterly* in London, established by the CIA-financed and staffed Congress of Cultural Freedom, and *Quest*, pub-

---

79. George Ginsburgs and Michael Mathos conclude in their book *Communist China and Tibet: The First Dozen Years* (The Hague: M. Nijhoff, 1964) that "the Tibetan insurgents never succeeded in mustering into their ranks even a large fraction of the population at hand, to say nothing of a majority. As far as can be ascertained, the great bulk of the common people of Lhasa and of the adjoining countryside failed to join in the fighting against the Chinese both when it first began and as it progressed." (118). Bina Roy Burman reached a similar conclusion in his book *Religion and Politics in Tibet* (New Delhi and Bombay: Vikas, 1979).
80. Leroy Fletcher Prouty, *The Secret Team: The CIA and Its Allies in Control of the United States and the World* (Englewood Cliffs, N.J.: Prentice-Hall, 1973), 395. A conversation with Prouty in March 1987 was most helpful.
81. A State Department estimate in the summer of 1959 was that "the Chinese Communists probably have the capability of preventing prolonged rebellion, except in the most isolated areas."

lished in India by the Congress, featured propaganda articles in sophisticated language. The AFL-CIO, the CIA's ally in Central America and elsewhere, took the message to American unions.[82] But the agency's greatest success was the 1960 report of the International Commission of Jurists, which originated as an anti-Communist propaganda mill and agent recruitment organization set up by the CIA and European intelligence agencies. The 1960 report, purportedly the findings of objective and reputable jurists, but in reality a compilation of fractional truths and outright falsifications, concluded that Beijing was guilty of "cultural genocide" in Tibet. But subsequent citations of it often dropped "cultural." The report was widely accepted as the truth at the time and is still described as a respectable source.[83]

Landslides. As PLA reinforcements moved into Tibet, the CIA was persuaded that pinpoint bombing of sites along the new highways west could start landslides that would block them for weeks, even months. Two Canadian officers familiar with the terrain selected the targets. But what was actually attempted has not been revealed and the results appear to have been negligible.

Airdrops. The dropping of supplies and agents from the air increased enormously, especially after the introduction of the C-120s, though the operation was handicapped by the inability of planes to land anywhere in Tibet and thus pick up agents. Fletcher Prouty, in a position to give an informed estimate, later wrote that more than 14,000 Tibetans were armed, equipped and fed by the agency.

Camp Hale. In April of 1959 the CIA launched an ambitious training project. A location in Saipan was first planned, but the climate of that Pacific island was uncomfortable for Tibetan mountain people. Camp Hale, high up in the Rocky Mountains, eighteen miles north of Leadville, Colorado, was the final choice. Ski troops had been trained there in World War II. Some 500 Tibetans were supposed to be trained but less than 200—170 by one count—had graduated by the time the program was halted. The earliest recruits, who arrived packed in a C-124 Globemaster, were invariably chiefs or the sons of chiefs, but with the expansion, eligibility requirements were broad-

---

82. Four years after the Nixon visit the AFL-CIO was still beating the drums—see Harry Goldberg, "Tibet Still Struggles," *AFL-CIO Free Trade Union News,* January 1976. Goldberg, international affairs representative of the AFL-CIO, accused China of genocide in Tibet and claimed that "the Chinese have not been able to crush the guerrilla warfare." Earlier the Dalai Lama gave AFL-CIO President George Meany an autographed copy of his own account of his flight from Lhasa in recognition of AFL-CIO financial contributions to refugee programs.
83. Grunfeld, *The Making of Modern Tibet,* 141–44.

ened. The Tibetans, Khampas most of them, were trained in small arms (M-1s, mortars, bazookas, revolvers with silencers), radio communication (each was provided with a powerful hand-size radio), use of explosives, survival techniques, map reading, coding, precautions in contacting agents, and behavior under hostile interrogation. Training exercises included the killing of deer on the run and living off raw meat for a week. The CIA instructors were spared the necessity of learning Tibetan names. Simple American first names were imprinted on identification badges.

The CIA set up a subsidiary, Intermountain Aviation, as the air arm of the Camp Hale project. Graduates were parachuted into Tibet or assigned to tasks in India or Nepal.

Security was nearly breached when a busload of Tibetan trainees ran into a ditch during a snowstorm. Civilian employees of Peterson Air Base at Colorado Springs caught sight of the late-arriving Asians and were held at gun point until sworn to secrecy. Through a leak in a Colorado newspaper the *New York Times* got wind of the incident. Its Washington bureau inquired at the Pentagon and Secretary of Defense Robert McNamara was soon on the phone asking that the story be killed. The *Times* complied.

A trainee one day found himself alone while sweeping a normally guarded office at Camp Hale. Years later he told John Avedon that, "Looking behind large white sheets that covered a wall in the main room, he discovered a detailed map of Tibet. All across it red pins marked the location of agents."[84]

Mustang Valley. Selected Camp Hale graduates were assigned to a CIA army assembled in Mustang Valley on the Nepal-Tibetan frontier. A vassal state, the area was the home of a Tibetan minority and could be reached only with difficulty from Katmandu, the capital. To handle the logistics, the CIA established Air Nepal, a subsidiary, and set up a fake AID (Agency for International Development) project. Twenty-six buildings, including a four-story headquarters, were constructed. A brother of the Dalai Lama was the paymaster and distributor of CIA largess. One of the raids into Tibet wiped out a small PLA convoy and captured several sacks of classified documents, but most penetrations achieved little or nothing.

Establishment 22. The largest Tibetan force was a secret part of the Indian Army. The CIA and the Research and Analysis Wing of Indian Intelligence created the force in 1962. Called Special Frontier

---

84. Avedon, *In Exile,* 121.

Force (code-named Establishment 22), it gained a peak strength of 10,500. CIA instructors provided parachute and other specialized training, but the CIA role diminished following differences with Indian officers, and more principled differences with the American ambassador, John Kenneth Galbraith.

All the CIA operations in or near Tibet encountered early difficulties—the central one being the indifference of the people—and had failure written all over them by the time that U.S. policy toward China changed under the Nixon administration and the CIA was enjoined from major interventions.[85]

The shooting down of Gary Francis Powers' U-2 in the Soviet Union on May 1, 1960, not only torpedoed the Eisenhower-Khrushchev summit but had a severely limiting effect on the CIA's air drop operations. In advance of the summit, President Eisenhower had directed that overflights everywhere cease but his order was not heeded by those in the CIA handling U-2s over Russia. Eisenhower's response after the international embarrassment was to again forcefully restrict overflights and the supplying of the Tibetan contras fell off drastically. Deprived of help from the skies and with inadequate support from the Tibetan population, the rebel bands in the mountains shriveled and disintegrated. It was "a military disaster," according to one CIA account.[86]

Briefed on CIA activities in India, Nepal, and Tibet following his appointment as ambassador to India by the Kennedy Administration, Galbraith was appalled. To him the Mustang Valley army was a "particularly insane enterprise." He tried to put an end to it but failed.[87] Kept going through the 1960s, the operation was increasingly beset with command rivalries, charges of embezzlement, equipment shortages, and defections. In 1974 the Nepalese army, strengthened with a contingent of Gurkhas, moved into the valley and broke up the remnants. Gyalo Wangdu, the last survivor of the first group trained in Colorado, was killed.

In October–November of 1962 the Indian army suffered humiliating defeats when it tried some territory grabbing across the Tibetan bor-

---

85. A victim of the historic Nixon visit to China was a thirteen-minute documentary film prepared by the United States Information Agency. Titled "Man from a Missing Land," it depicted the Chinese takeover of Tibet and ended with the Dalai Lama's flight to India. It had the bad luck to be ready for screening when Nixon finally changed American policy. It has never been shown.

86. Nine out of ten agents dropped into Tibet were never heard from again, one CIA review states. Israel Epstein observes that the PLA garrisons were dispersed and that many agents were rounded up by the Tibetans themselves (*Tibet Transformed*, 224–25).

87. Galbraith did succeed in quashing CIA plans to spend millions on influencing Indian elections, corrupting officials and financing anti-Communist publications.

der, in the Aksai region in the west where the Chinese had built a road linking it to Xinjiang and a mountainous pocket to the east. The Special Frontier Force of Tibetan exiles was expected to remedy the revealed weaknesses. It scouted the border and established a string of Indian bases. And, according to Avedon, "New Delhi secretly decided that, in the event of war, an attempt to wrest Tibet's liberty could be made, [Establishment] 22 taking the lead."[88] In reality, 22 was never a serious threat to Tibetan security. It was sent into battle against Pakistan at the time of the Bangladesh breakaway. A force of "freedom fighters," the Indian press predictably called it. Indira Gandhi planned to use 22 to crush opposition riots and uprisings, and kept an aircraft on alert at a 22 base to fly her to Mauritius in the event she had to flee the country.

Its interest in Tibet dwindling, the CIA undertook what turned out to be its last significant intervention into Chinese affairs before Nixon changed policy. Using captured Cultural Revolution documents, and with the help of defectors and Taiwan Chinese, it forged leaflets and declarations designed to intensify Cultural Revolution factionalism. It began the effort late in 1967 when factionalism momentarily appeared to be dying down. Balloon drops and other means of delivering the forgeries were supplemented by broadcasts from a clandestine Taiwan radio. A few defectors had copies of the fabrications with them when they arrived in Hongkong, but how effective they were in setting off one group against another is uncertain.

The CIA may have had nothing to do with the disturbances in Lhasa in the late 1980s and early 1990s, but the one-sided reporting of them in the American press and in Congress reflects the continuing influence of past CIA propaganda efforts.

24. China in American Poetry

American poets most often turned to Europe for inspiration when they lifted their eyes from introspection and the American landscape, but some now and again looked the other way, west to China—Cathay, several preferred to call it.

The very beginning of the U.S.-China connection—the voyage of the *Empress of China* in 1784—was celebrated by the poet Philip Freneau (1752–1832) in stanzas that included these lines:

---

88. Avedon, *In Exile*, 129.

To countries plac'd in burning climes
And islands of remotest times
She now her eager course explores,
And soon shall greet Chinesean shores.

From thence their fragrant teas to bring
Without the leave of Britain's King;
And Porcelain ware, encased in gold,
The product of that finer mold.

Henry Wadsworth Longfellow (1807–1882) of Cambridge extolled Chinese porcelain in his *Keramos*, written in 1877, and went on to describe the magnificent pagoda in Nanjing destroyed by the Taiping rebels:

And yonder by Nankin, behold!
The Tower of Porcelain, strange and old,
Uplifting to the astonished skies
Its ninefold painted balconies,
With balustrades of twining leaves,
And roofs of tile, beneath whose eaves
Hang porcelain bells that all the time
Ring with a soft, melodious chime;
While the whole fabric is ablaze
With varied tints, all fused in one
Great mass of color, like a maze
Of flowers illumined by the sun.

Longfellow's fellow New Englander, Oliver Wendell Holmes (1809–1894), wrote this poetic tribute to a visiting Chinese embassy and himself read it to them when they came to Boston in 1868:

Brothers, whom we may not reach
Through the veil of alien speech,
Welcome! welcome! eyes can tell
What the lips in vain would spell,—
Words that hearts can understand,
Brothers from the Flowery Land! . . .

Land of wonders, fair Cathay
Who long hast shunned the staring day,
Hid in mists of poet's dreams

By thy blue and yellow streams,—
Let us thy shadowed form behold,—
Teach us as thou didst of old.

China is in Walt Whitman's *Leaves of Grass*. Whitman (1819–1892) addressed "You Chinaman and you Chinawoman of China, you Tartars of Tartary" and invoked China's rivers, mountains, steppes, and "the swarms of Pekin, Canton" in his "Salut au Monde":

Health to you! good will to you all, from me
              and America sent!
Each of us inevitable,
Each of us limitless—each of us with his or
              her right upon the earth . . .

The Midwestern poet Vachel Lindsay (1879–1931) wrote two long poems about China, "Shantung, or the Chinese Empire Is Crumbling Down" and "The Chinese Nightingale," about a laundryman. "Nightingale" won *Poetry Magazine's* Levinson Prize in 1915. Lindsay described it as his "favorite long poem" and was delighted when Chicago students performed a dance to it.

A young Chinese, Yee Bow, was a resident in Edgar Lee Masters' Spoon River. Masters (1869–1950) tells us in a few strong lines that Yee Bow died when one Harry Wiley "smashed his ribs into his lungs."

The great Tang dynasty poet Li Bai (Li Po in our literature) was translated most successfully by Ezra Pound (see section 7) and was admired in verse by Archibald MacLeish ("Poet's Laughter") and Conrad Aiken ("A Letter from Li Po"), which includes these lines recalling Li Bai's long years in exile:

Exiles are we. Were exiles born. The "far away,"
language of desert, language of ocean, language of sky,
as of the unfathomable worlds that lie
between the apple and the eye,
these are the only words we learn to say.
Each morning we devour the unknown. Each day
we find, and take, and spill, or spend, or lose
a sunflower splendor of which none knows the source.

And MacLeish paid respect to the Chinese and others on the railroad construction gangs in his "Burying Ground by the Ties":

It was we laid the steel to this land from ocean to ocean;
It was we (if you know) put the U.P. through the passes

Bringing her down into Laramie full load,
Eighteen mile on the granite anticlinal,
Forty-three foot to the mile and the grade holding . . .
Who would do it but we and the Irishmen bossing us?
It was all foreign-born men there were in this country:
It was Scotsmen, Englishmen, Chinese, Squareheads,
                Austrians . . .

Not for this did we come out—to be lying here
Nameless under the ties in the clay cuts:

There's nothing good in the world but the rich will
            buy it:
Everything sticks to the grease of a gold note—Even a
           continent—even a new sky!

In our time Paul Engle[89] has looked at the China of today both through his own eyes and those of his Chinese wife, Nieh Hualing, and turned affectionate, wry, empathetic, humanistic and intense impressions into splendid poems. In a few artfully chosen words he has told us much about China's people and landscape.

Engle had the special gift of being unbothered by noise and motion, and he wrote these poems on pads on trains and planes, in taxis and crowded rooms, in halls in which his wife was lecturing in Chinese, and also in the night quiet of hotel rooms.

His wife tells us in the preface that she "would wake up to find Paul at the hotel room desk crouching over a piece of paper, mumbling the words out loud to catch their sound together before writing them on the page. After a long day of meeting people, driving to see old tombs or new farms, he could not sleep until the poem was dragged out of his head the way you drag a snake out of its hole by pulling the tail."

Engle absorbed images in travels from Yan'an to Guangzhou and what unites them is affection for the people and their land. This is a poem titled "The Poor":

---

89. Paul Engle, *Images of China: Poems Written in China, April–June 1980* (Beijing: New World Press, 1981).

Over too many suffering centuries
Poverty was the inherited disease,
Burned on the baby's blind eyes at its birth.
Ugliness on the beautiful Chinese earth.

The rice bowl turned into a begging bowl
For arms too weak to bear a bamboo pole.
Now foreign birds have flown the bitter city,
No more the starving stare at you for pity.
Now they don't beg nor get down on their knees.
China belongs at last to the Chinese.

In Shanghai he wrote about Lu Xun:

Today in Lu Xun's house I breathed his breath.
I hope he is glad to know
His furious writings are read
By us in our funny foreign alphabet.
You do not honor a writer by praise.
You praise a writer by reading his writing.

After a visit to the Ming Tombs he wrought this:

Kings (like kids) are lovers of dark rooms,
Their final hide-outs are their secret tombs.
Self-loving Emperors piled precious things,
Their jade, jewels, flutes against that stupid fate
Meant for ignorant peasants, not for kings.
Buried in ego's sunlike gold deep down,
Defied their dragon-decorated crown
To keep alive their silk-brocaded breath:
No arrogance in mortal life is great
As marble arrogance of kings in death.

The Ming Tombs earlier had inspired a fine poem by another American poet, Witter Bynner:[90]

Blown shadows, through the
grass,

---

90. *Asia Magazine*, May 1920.

Not of the kings,
But of the builders and carriers
It is the kings now who seem
        chained,
And the others free.

Images of China is a demonstration of virtuosity: Engle uses most verse forms—rhymed poems, free verse, the sonnet, and couplets that remind us of China's traditional poetry. His lines achieve instruction by delighting and moving those who read them.

Engle is known both for his extensive and admirable work (he is the author of twenty-five volumes of poems, translations and prose) and his founding and direction for twenty-five years of the Writers Workshop at the University of Iowa. He is a member of the National Council of the Arts. He and his wife, a novelist, collaborated in a translation of Mao's poems.

25. The Long Intervention Continues: The Taiwan Relations Act

Editor's Note: This chapter originated as a speech at a seminar on U.S.-China relations held in Washington, D.C., April 30–May 1, 1984. It was published in the US-China Review, *May–June 1984. The* Review *is the publication of the US-China Peoples Friendship Association.*

On January 1, 1979 the United States extended diplomatic recognition at long last to the People's Republic of China, apparently putting an end to decades of hostility during which the U.S. had done all it practically could first to abort the Chinese revolution and then to prove it was but a "passing phase." But enmity and intervention were not entirely history. Shortly after the establishment of diplomatic ties the Taiwan Relations Act gave them new life. The Act comes close to making Taiwan an American protectorate, and its effect is to reduce the chances for peaceful reunification of the mainland and the island. It deeply affronts a China generally disposed to seek close commercial, scientific, and cultural ties with the United States. "An immense obstacle in Sino-U.S. relations," Deng Xiaoping called the Act in an interview with Mike Wallace of CBS in 1986.

The Act was the key element in the sleight-of-hand by which early in 1979 Washington managed to both recognize the People's Republic and continue its basic two-Chinas policy. In order to achieve normalization of diplomatic relations on January 1, Washington had to sever relations with Taipei and terminate the Mutual Defense Treaty of 1954. It had to affirm in a joint communique that Taiwan is part of the one China. It had to recognize the People's Republic as "the sole legal government of China," adding that, "within this context, the people of the United States will maintain cultural, commercial, and other unofficial relations with the people of Taiwan."

In view of the inescapable fact of a presently separated Taiwan, American legislation was needed to adjust and replace laws governing relations with the island. But the legislation signed into law by President Carter on April 10 was something very different—an act which went even further in some respects than the Mutual Defense Treaty in casting a mantle of American protection over the island the U.S. had just agreed was part of China.

The Act declares that any attempt to change the status of Taiwan by "other than peaceful means" would jeopardize the peace of the western Pacific and be "of grave concern to the United States." It threatens forceful U.S. intervention, stipulating that American capabilities for such intervention must be maintained.

Going beyond the Mutual Defense Treaty, the Act includes boycotts and embargoes in its definition of "other than peaceful means," and it pledges "appropriate action" in the event of any threat to "the social or economic system" of Taiwan.

The Taipei regime officially, though less and less in practice, boycotts goods from the mainland, but the Act ignores, and in effect condones, this policy. The American presumption that the U.S. has the right to pass on how changes in Taiwan's social or economic system are wrought is the most glaring of the contradictions between the Sino-American Joint Communique of January 1, 1979, and the Act of the following April.

The U.S. objective of preserving the Taiwan status quo was underscored by the Act's only slightly disguised treatment of the island province as an independent state. Taiwan retained almost all of its consulates (the People's Republic was allowed but three) and offices and was allowed to maintain staffs at previous levels. Congress struck out the word "unofficial" in the description of relations with the island. The Act retained in force all treaties and agreements reached with Taipei, other than the Mutual Defense Treaty—accords reached when Taiwan was regarded as a state. It provided that all American laws referring to foreign countries should apply to Taiwan. An undersecretary of state said that a major purpose of the legislation was to make possible treatment of Taiwan as a "country."

Pursuant to the Act, the American embassy in Taipei was renamed the American Institute in Taiwan, and the Taiwan embassy in Washington received the alias of Coordination Council for North American Affairs.

The Taiwan Relations Act is not a tangent, but continues a record of proposed and realized interventions that began in the feisty heyday of imperialism.

Commodore Matthew Perry believed that Japan, which he opened up in 1854, could be reduced to a subordinate American ally and as "timely preparation for events which must, in the ordinary course of things, transpire in the East," he advocated seizure of both Okinawa and Formosa. Of the latter, he wrote that "the U.S. alone should take the initiative in this magnificent island."

Townsend Harris, the first U.S. diplomatic representative in Japan, once recommended that the United States deliver an ultimatum to Beijing, demanding that it be allowed to purchase Formosa. If this was rejected, the U.S. should buy the island directly from those he called aborigines, he argued.

In 1857 Dr. Peter Parker, a medical missionary in Canton turned feckless diplomat, declared in a strong recommendation to Washington: "The subject of Formosa is becoming one of great interest to a number of enterprising fellow-citizens. . . . It is much to be hoped that the government of the United States may not shrink from the action which the interests of humanity, civilization, navigation and commerce impose upon it in relation to Taiwan (Formosa)."

John W. Foster, secretary of state under Harrison and grandfather of John Foster Dulles, connived in support of Japan's takeover of Taiwan in 1895 in the expectation that American control of the island would follow.

But the actual intervention took place as a phase of U.S. hostility to the Chinese revolution.

As the People's Liberation Army chewed up Chiang Kai-shek's American-armed divisions and a crossing of the Taiwan Strait seemed close at hand, the State Department and Pentagon were generally agreed on the necessity of keeping the island out of Communist hands. Perforce, to avoid offending the international community, the U.S. had to proceed duplicitously. Secretary of State Acheson declared in a National Security Council paper that "it is a cardinal point in our thinking that if our present policy is to have any chance in Formosa, we must carefully conceal our wish to separate the island from mainland control."

The U.S. flirted briefly with the idea of utilizing the Taiwan independence movement, which was found hardly to exist. It considered plans to bring in the United Nations with the aim of establishing a U.S.-dominated trusteeship of the island. It supported a coup to displace the Generalissimo that never came off. And a few, among them George F. Kennan, called for an outright invasion of Taiwan.

But as 1949 turned into 1950, the State Department concluded that Communist conquest of Taiwan could not be prevented and it leaked information and issued statements calculated to prepare American opinion for it. On December 23, a State Department memo declared that "Formosa, politically, geographically and strategically, is part of China. . . . Although ruled by the Japanese for fifty years, historically it has been Chinese. Politically and militarily it is a strictly Chinese responsibility."

And on January 5, 1950, Secretary of State Acheson said: "The world must believe that we stand for principle and that we are honorable and decent people and that we do not put forward words . . . only to throw them overboard when the change in events makes the position difficult for us. . . . Therefore . . . we are not going to use our forces in connection with the present situation in Formosa. . . ."

But such disclaimers served to arouse and arm the China Lobby and in the following months pressure in behalf of intervention grew. President Truman seized the opportunity offered by the Korean war to send the Seventh Fleet into the Taiwan Strait, ordering it to oppose invasion from either direction. At the same time he increased military aid to the Philippines and stepped up the fateful intervention in Indochina. But the interventionists were already close to victory when Truman acted.

The alliance with Chiang developed swiftly. U.S. economic and military aid poured into Taiwan—enough arms to mislead *Fortune* magazine into describing Taiwan as "The Sword at the Belly of Red China." The U.S. and the Nationalists dispatched scores of spies and saboteurs to the mainland and U.S.-supplied planes made countless overflights. Taiwan became the central base for CIA activities in China and Southeast Asia. American support of the Nationalist hold on the mainland harbor islands of Quemoy and Matsu provoked crises in which the U.S. contemplated use of nuclear weapons.

The Taiwan-mainland relationship is complex, defying trim analysis. But some circumstances plainly favor eventual unification. The economies are complementary. The vast mainland is a continuing alternative for a Taiwan that may not always do well in markets dominated by the U.S. and Japan. The language and culture of China are shared, as is the historical sense that national unity and prosperous times have gone hand in hand.

But the Taiwan Relations Act counters such positive influences. It strengthens those in Taiwan, mainlander or Taiwan-born, who are adamantly opposed to unification. It enables them to keep saying "No," confident that in any crisis they are wards of the United States.

The leadership of the People's Republic has to suppose that the Act may be intended by American conservatives to help bring about an independent Taiwan. Ever since the State Department and General MacArthur in Tokyo briefly patronized the small Taiwanese independence movement, independence has been a U.S. option and fallback position. A continuing refusal to negotiate with Beijing, made possible by the Taiwan Relations Act, coupled with the inevitable decline of the mainlanders now in control of Taiwan, could lead to an organized independence movement certain to be widely acclaimed in the U.S.

Taiwan is not an issue contrived to give the Chinese people something to think about. It is a very rich island which has been the financial beneficiary of Washington's strategic assessments and of the decision of U.S. and Japanese corporations to export jobs. Reunited with the mainland, even loosely, it could give a boost to China's struggling modernization efforts.

But Taiwan is more. It is an emotion which the late Theodore H. White summed up this way:

> Taiwan involved pride, the nation's sense of itself. And in China, after a century and a half of foreign humiliations, pride has ulcerated. Chinese are taught a modern history that runs from humiliation to humiliation, an abused pride that exploded in the Japanese war of 1937–45. For the old soldiers who lead the government only one thing is lacking to fulfill their young dream of liberating all China—the liberation of Taiwan, and over Taiwan, Chinese passion boils. [91]

---

91. "China After the Terror," *Reader's Digest*, October 1983, 254–55. Also published as "China: Burnout of a Revolution," *Time*, September 26, 1983.

And during a visit, John D. Ehrlichman of Watergate notoriety found that the Chinese he talked to about Taiwan all argued that "The United States has no more right to come between China and its island province than China would have to interject itself in a dispute between the United States and California."

China has retained the option of using force against Taiwan. To foreswear it would be to taint its sovereignty. But plainly it would turn to its armed forces only in the event of a major provocation, such as a declaration of Taiwan independence. Nevertheless, selective upgrading of its armed forces, particularly of the navy, appears to be slowly changing the balance of power between the mainland and the island. Jane's Fighting Ships, an authoritative assessor of the world's navies, observed that in manpower the Chinese navy is four times the size of the navy that once ruled the waves, including the waters of the Yangtze. It concluded that the Chinese navy is "an important element in the future balance of power East of Suez." China's steady acquisition of naval prowess has to weigh on decisions affecting the reunification issue.

But Beijing's reunification strategy is pacific. In recent years it has made successive overtures and concessions to the Taipei authorities and now promises virtual autonomy under the "one country, two systems" formula conceived by Deng Xiaoping. And it has given substance to its rhetoric by promoting trade and offering investment opportunities.

Trade is indeed revising the scenario. Indirect trade (mostly by way of Hongkong) totaled U.S. $1.56 billion in 1987. It has increased twenty times since 1978 and the complementary nature of the two economies—Taiwan needs mainland cotton, coal, and all the oil available for export—suggests that increases will continue. Fujian, the province directly across the strait and the ancestral home of many Taiwanese, is trying hard to lure traders and investors from the island. Overall the PRC's commercial regulations give Taiwan compatriots a break. Major Taiwan enterprises are undertaking marketing research and organizing survey missions in the expectation of gaining economic footholds on the mainland.

The Taipei authorities affirm regularly their rejection of the "one country, two systems" concept and restate their hard line, but the trade factor and other pressures have led to pragmatic tolerances and expansion of covert relationships. In 1987 Taiwan permitted those with relatives on the mainland to visit them. Non-political books published on the mainland may now be sold or republished in Taiwan. Mail service through the Red Cross began in April 1988. Several Taiwan journalists have come to the mainland and sent back series of articles. Many civil encounters and exchanges have taken place at academic and other gatherings and in sports. Such encounters are reminders that language and culture are shared.

Beijing sent condolences when Chiang Ching-kuo (Jiang Jingguo), eldest son of Chiang Kai-shek and his successor, died on January 13, 1988, and they were published in leading Taiwan newspapers.

The Reagan Administration was circumspect in its comments on reunification. It rarely mentions the Taiwan Relations Act. But it continues to sell substantial quantities of arms to Taiwan and much of its ultraconservative political base—including such voices as the Reverend Jerry Falwell and William Buckley's *National Review*—reiterate that Taiwan is part of what they call the Free World and must be kept out of Communist hands. Both the Republican and Democratic parties supported the Taiwan Relations Act in their 1984 platforms. A bill calling for Taiwan independence has been introduced in Congress. So Beijing has to view the Taiwan Relations Act as potentially the instrument of a "one China, one Taiwan" policy.

Yet contrary pressures are at work on those influencing America's China policies. The United States is subject to the pragmatic considerations that have drawn East Asia and Europe in the direction of acceptance of eventual reunification. For Washington, too, the Beijing connection has to do with profits and power. It has to review the relative benefits of the Beijing and Taipei ties and reassess its interventionist capabilities.

The Taiwan question is crisscrossed with variables and uncertainties, and judgments about its outcome have to be tentative. Deep-set hostilities of long standing remain undissipated. But while reunification is a somewhat distant prospect, China's new economic strength and its emergence as a regional power have altered the relationship. What is nearly certain is that the number of tacit understandings and various contacts will proliferate, each a strand in a hawser pulling island and mainland together. The energized mainland vastness is a magnet.

Reunification ought to be left to the two parties themselves. American officials have repeatedly said this, but they also accept and treat respectfully the Taiwan Relations Act. This Act is disruptive of the unification process and a blight on the general U.S.-China relationship. Americans who wish China well and who see the importance of good relations between the two great nations facing each other across the Pacific should do what they can to eliminate or minimize the Taiwan Relations Act.

26. China Friendship Has a Rich History

Friendship is very evidently subordinate in the two-century history of U.S.-China relations. In the nineteenth century and well into the twentieth, the United States was a sort of junior partner of the British, insisting that concessions and benefits wrung from a hapless China by the major imperialisms, of which Britain was the strongest, be granted to it. And when the U.S. succeeded Britain, by force of arms in World War II, as the major Western power in East Asia, it did its utmost to defeat revolution in China. In the 1950s and 1960s it still had illusions that the People's Republic could be undone, only coming to terms with it, in the Nixon Presidency, when China seemed an offset to Soviet power and a way of easing the exit from the shambles in Indochina.

But the better side of America—populist and reformist impulses, concern for social justice abroad as well as at home, generous readiness to help those in trouble—has had repeated China manifestations. Among the Americans who crossed the Pacific were some who were not seduced by the pleasures and prejudices of treaty port life and who were drawn to the cause of a likable people struggling against national humiliation and the cruelties of a society in which a few oppressed and fleeced the many.

China has placed a trio of them—Anna Louise Strong, Agnes Smedley, and Edgar Snow—in a pantheon, celebrating them through the SSS Society. Now the New Zealander Rewi Alley [92] has written informatively of these three and three others, Ma Haide (George Hatem), Evans Carlson and General Joseph (Vinegar Joe) Stilwell.

Alley is exceptionally qualified because he is able to enrich biographical narration with revealing reminiscence. He met Edgar Snow in the famine-stricken Northwest in 1929 and got to know him well when, with Helen Foster Snow (Nym Wales) and a group of progressive Chinese cooperators, they launched the Chinese Industrial Cooperatives in 1938. Evans Carlson, who came to China as a Marine officer, was in that circle too—"the Gung Ho kids," Helen Snow called them. Carlson worked for Indusco for a year in 1940, and later

---

92. Rewi Alley, *Six Americans in China* (Beijing: Intercul, 1985), 64. The following quotes from Alley in the section are also drawn from this book.

as commander of the Marine Raiders who won Pacific island victories, made *Gung Ho* part of our language.

Carlson brought to China the usual imperialist conceits but shed them as Chinese realities reeducated him. He and Snow became friends in Shanghai in the late 1920s when Carlson was attached to the Fourth Marines and Snow was on the staff of the *China Weekly Review*. Snow dedicated *People on Our Side,* published in 1944, to Carlson: "So well thy words become thee as thy wounds; They smack of honor both. . . ."

As Alley might have noted, Carlson served, until his untimely death in May 1947, as chairman of the Committee for a Democratic Far Eastern Policy, which opposed U.S. intervention in the civil war of 1946–49 and which later campaigned for recognition of the People's Republic. Agnes Smedley was one of those who spoke movingly of Carlson at a memorial service for him in New York.

Edgar Snow was invited to China in 1970 and stood beside Mao on the reviewing stand at Tiananmen on October 1, a symbol of China's readiness to respond to friendly signals from the Nixon administration. Snow was already ill and died of cancer in his Swiss home in February 1972, even as the Nixon visit to China initiated the U.S.-China conciliation. Half of his ashes were buried on the campus of Beijing University, half by the Hudson.

Alley says this about Snow: "Edgar Snow cared. He thought as a statesman, one of the greatest, he recognized the sweep of history, saw the direction in which revolution led men, and worked to help bring about unalterable world peace. Always, he was driven by total courage and the highest integrity mixed with wisdom and acute sensitivity and compassion. . . ."

Alley got to know Agnes Smedley and George Hatem in Shanghai in the 1930s when they were among the members of a Marxist study group. The friendships proved lasting. Alley followed Smedley's impassioned, tumultuous, and very productive years in China and got to see her in Hongkong in 1941, when she had left China for what turned out to be the last time.

In 1949, a year before her death in London, Smedley was vilified as a Communist espionage agent by General Charles Willoughby, MacArthur's chief of intelligence, who based his charges on Japanese secret police files. Alley writes: "And so the word of the most corrupt secret police in the world at that time was accepted against that of this American altruist, great writer and historian of her age. There was later an official statement and an apology, but the damage had already been done."

Smedley was buried in the Cemetery for Revolutionaries in Beijing, as she requested, and she left her personal possessions to Zhu De, of whom she had written a great biography.

The attachment between Alley and Ma Haide, the young doctor who journeyed to the Red areas in the Northwest with Snow in 1936 and stayed to begin long service to Chinese medicine, was particularly close. Because of that the chapter on Ma is especially good, and that is important because Ma has steadfastly refused to write an autobiography.

In recent years Dr. Ma has devoted himself to the cause of conquering leprosy and he has traveled the world in its behalf. And, Alley adds, "As the most outstanding living American to have been an integral part of the Chinese revolution, having joined one of the armies for the last portion of the Long March at Huining in Gansu before it arrived in Yan'an, his opinion is eagerly sought by visiting Americans in this new period of China's reaching out to the peoples of foreign lands."

Alley and Anna Louise Strong knew each other as neighbors. Rewi lived in the flat above hers in what was once the residence of the Italian ambassador, Count Ciano, Mussolini's son-in-law, in the compound of the China Peace Committee, later the Chinese People's Association for Friendship with Foreign Countries. He moved downstairs into her quarters following her death in March 1970 at the age of eighty-four. The chapter on her draws on his many conversations with her in a relaxed setting.

Strong was born in Nebraska, the daughter of a Congregational minister. She was moved by experience into sharing the aspirations of revolutionaries, and she wrote, as Alley observes, a shelf of books, several about China. *China's Millions* remains a valuable account of the revolutionary upsurge of 1925–27, and in *The Chinese Conquer China*, published for the Committee for a Democratic Far Eastern Policy in the U.S., she wrote of the reversal of the earlier defeat and its portent. Her many *Letters from China*, based on the imperfect information available to her, were a skilled effort to convey a sense of the complicated turns in China to the American people. If she was reticent about some negative aspects of the Chinese and other revolutions, it was because she kept her eye on the main need and the main chance. She wondered, in a reflection quoted by Alley, "if humanity will grow up fast enough to save itself from death." Like Smedley, Anna Louise Strong was buried in the Cemetery for Revolutionaries in the western suburbs. Edgar Snow and his wife Lois were among the many who stood in respect at the grave site.

Rewi had fewer personal contacts with Joseph Stilwell, but learned a good deal about him from such mutual friends as Agnes Smedley. He reproduces several of the salty letters from Stilwell to Smedley found in her effects after her death in 1950. In one, Stilwell said he had just had a "fine letter" from Zhu De and added he had admired him ever since he offered the reward of one dollar for Chiang Kai-shek. "I enjoyed hearing from you. I respect front line soldiers, and the title fits you. Keep your sense of humor and remember 'ILLEGITIMI NON CARBORUNDUM'—Don't let the bastards grind you down."

Stilwell did make one revealing inquiry of Alley, asking him, in Alley's account, "what could be done to provide necessary workshops, small arsenals and other facilities to assist the (Communist) Eighth Route Army to bring its full strength against the enemy at every required point." Alley thought that about three hundred small mechanized shops would improve the situation and Stilwell was for that. But the reactionary strength and intrigue that eventually forced Stilwell's recall prevailed and the project was not realized.

In marked contrast to certain lesser writers on China, Alley does not spice his biographies with gossip and he does not invade privacies. He writes with respect, admiration, and affection, but pays proper attention to faults and weaknesses. His portraits are not cult figures, but real people.

Of course the history of U.S.-China friendship is not that of a sextet. A long list of Americans of all sorts—missionaries, diplomats, soldiers, artists, and physicians and other professionals, as well as journalists—did what they could, revealing by deeds their feelings of caring concern and friendship. And the history of friendship is about organizations as well as individuals. Smedley contributed to *China Today*, publication of the American Friends of the Chinese People in New York City, and Carlson, Strong, Smedley, and Snow served the Committee for a Democratic Far Eastern Policy. The US-China Peoples Friendship Association, formed locally in 1971 and nationally in 1974, was the larger successor of these organizations.

Of course many besides Americans came from afar to serve China and its people, Rewi Alley among them. Some of the best of these old China hands are still living and their recollections are happily preserved in taped and videotaped interviews. It will take an assortment of cassettes, films, books, and articles to do justice to the rich history of China friendship. Alley's *Six Americans* is an invaluable contribution to it.

Postscript   I had the satisfaction of working with Rewi Alley on the task of recreating the International Committee for the Promotion of Chinese Industrial Cooperatives. Every week brought me notes in his very difficult handwriting in which he kept me informed and encouraged. The committee, of which I became a vice chairman, met in October 1987 while I was in Beijing, and soon after Rewi had me to dinner. The only other guest was Ma Haide and this was the last time I saw them. Rewi died in December, shortly after his ninetieth birthday and Dr. Ma died the following October I expressed my admiration for him in an article published in *China Daily* (December 16, 1988) in the *US-China Review* (Spring 1989).

Rewi Alley and Ma Haide can be best memorialized by continued efforts to realize their great causes—Rewi's vision of a multitude of democratically managed industrial cooperatives and Dr. Ma's of a world free of the scourge of leprosy.

III

. . . .

Recollections

1. Reporting from China in the 1940s

Journalists who worked the China beat in the 1940s gathered in Scottsdale, Arizona, November 19–20, 1982, to reminisce and reflect at a memorable conference sponsored by Arizona State University's Center for Asian Studies, with help from three other organizations in the Asian field.

Our pates were baldish or whitening and the flesh had weakened, but our memories were sharp, especially of incidents that revealed our perceptiveness. The conference echoed some past disagreements, but the exchanges were amiable. It produced more nostalgia and anecdotes than carefully considered judgments but, nevertheless preserved before too late some useful recollections that will inform and enliven the work of the historians, a number of whom were participants.

Present in this sunshiny, manicured, luxurious suburb of Phoenix were many of the by-lines familiar to those old enough to have memories of the tumultuous decade of the 1940s—A. T. Steele of the *Chicago Daily News* and *New York Herald Tribune;* F. McCracken (Mac) Fisher of the United Press, later with the Office of War Information; Albert and Marjorie Ravenholt of the *Chicago Daily News Service;* Philip Potter, *Baltimore Sun;* James White, Associated Press; Annalee Jacoby Fadiman, *Time/Life;* and Tillman Durdin, Henry Lieberman, Harrison Salisbury (earlier United Press) and Walter Sullivan of the *New York Times.* Peter Rand, son of the deceased Christopher Rand of the *New York Herald Tribune* and *New Yorker*, presented excerpts from his father's *Chongqing Diary*, kept in the summer of 1943.

Two whose reporting reads well today came from Beijing. Israel Epstein (Eppy to all) reported for United Press and the *New York Times* and wrote *China's Unfinished Revolution* in those years. At the time of the conference he was editor-in-chief of *China Reconstructs*. Julian Schuman, an associate editor of the *China Weekly* (later *Monthly*) *Review* in Shanghai and author of *China: An Uncensored Look,* now happily back in print, is on the editorial staff of the English-language *China Daily.*

Serving as questioners and commentators were some distinguished academicians and former diplomats: John K. Fairbank of Harvard, who drew on his vast experience and knowledge to keep the discussion headed in realistic directions; John S. Service and John Melby, two of the best of the diplomats who served in China, both victims of post-World War II anti-Communist hysteria; and such scholars as Michael Schaller and Allen Whiting (University of Arizona), Dorothy Borg (Columbia), Doak Barnett (Johns Hopkins, Brookings, also a veteran journalist), Tracy Strong (University of California at San Diego), James Thompson (Harvard), and Nancy Tucker (Colgate).

Stephen MacKinnon (historian at Arizona State) was the convener and principal organizer of the conference. He and Janice MacKinnon, his wife, are the biographers of Agnes Smedley, and he contributed an important paper on Smedley.

The proceedings were taped, and a book based on the transcripts and the prepared papers was published by the University of California Press in 1987.

Though no fault of the organizers, the very best of the China journalists—those whose writings, now published in Chinese as well as English, will long continue to draw readers and influence historians—were not there. Edgar Snow, Agnes Smedley and Anna Louise Strong, whose contributions are kept alive in China through the SSS Society, were dead, and Jack Belden, author of *China Shakes the World,* could not come from Paris.

These four were very different, but all four were on the side of the Chinese people as they struggled for national independence and social justice. They were participants as well as reporters. Snow sheltered left-wing students in Beijing, smuggled Deng Yingchao (Madame Zhou Enlai) out of Beijing to safety disguised as an amah, helped to found and raise money for the Chinese Industrial Cooperatives, and quietly did many good deeds in behalf of national resistance and revolution. Smedley was a revolutionary whose heart went out to the victims of the old society—writers and artists persecuted by Chiang's police, wounded soldiers denied decent medical treatment. She and Anna Louise Strong, a partisan from the 1920s on, wrote and spoke for the Committee for a Democratic Far Eastern Policy in the U.S., which opposed American intervention in the 1946–49 civil war and campaigned for U.S. recognition of the People's Republic.

I remember how personally Jack Belden took the Southern Anhui (New Fourth Army) Incident of January 1941. He had gone into the New Fourth areas from Shanghai and written articles on them for the *China Weekly Review* which were collected in a pamphlet. For his lead on his story on the murderous assault on the New Fourth Army he took the opening line of a famous dispatch on the outbreak of the Spanish civil war: "This is the most difficult story I have ever had to write." As I told the conference, he made a half-dozen or more copies of his account and tried to smuggle them out. I don't know if any got through and were published.

It can be taken as a principle that journalists who rise above competence are caught up in the passions of their times and are broadly on the side of efforts to create a more just society. In his paper on Smedley, MacKinnon argued that she was "one of the best-informed journalists covering the Sino-Japanese war precisely because of her partisan or committed stance." And Tracy Strong (grandnephew of Anna Louise Strong) and Helene Keyssar similarly argued in their paper on Anna Louise Strong that " 'advocacy journalism' plays not only a unique role, but is in fact more 'objective' than its supposed more neutral counterparts."

And Jack Belden took on the standard notion of journalistic objectivity in a long letter to the conference. "American journalists are taught objectivity. That's all very fine, quote this leader and that leader, etc. But it often leads to a gross error and that is the interplay of the subjective and the objective." Journalists, Belden went on, often are too fearful of looking into their own hearts. "In the time of falling of nations what ordinary people feel has an effect on events it does not have in quieter times. Into whose poor people's hearts do you and your war reporters look?" The trouble with most reporters "is that they have no poetry in their souls."

My remarks at the conference included this grateful memory of Belden:

> I learned a great deal from Jack Belden. He'd come in from Shanghai having read Trotsky's *The Revolution Betrayed*, from which he had

drawn a series of twenty-eight or thirty or so questions to ask about the internal situation in Kuomintang-ruled China. He wasn't a Trotskyite. He just used Trotsky's works to get some basic knowledge about the nature of revolution and counterrevolution. Belden knew that I was a beginner. He took me in hand. I went with him to interviews, he told me things and pointed me in the right direction. So there is a personal aspect in my recollections of this great correspondent.

Also present only in recollection and references in the papers was Graham Peck, talented with sketching pencil as well as with words, author of two remarkable books, *Through China's Wall* and *Two Kinds of Time*. A shrewd estimate of the overall realities by Peck was read to the gathering:

> I believe the basic fact about recent Chinese history is that the years 1937 to 1941, from the beginning of the Japanese invasion to Pearl Harbor, were the crucial ones. During that time the Communists showed they could exploit the emergencies of invasion in order to expand, while the Kuomintang began to lose strength because it could not or would not adjust to wartime problems. By the time China became our ally the trend toward a reversal of powers was so marked that we could have influenced it only through the use of more strength and knowledge than we had in China then. . . .

But Frederic S. Marquandt, senior editor of the *Arizona Republic* newspaper, and one or two other participants still thought the question was that asked in the era of McCarthyism—Why Did We Lose China? As if China was ours to lose. Marquandt suggested that journalists may have helped to bring about what he called the "collapse" of China.

To Theodore H. White, who in a letter deeply regretted his inability to attend, "China was a mystery to those of us who reported it; it remains a mystery still." And, he added, that China was a mystery to its leaders too.

Of course all of reality is never grasped even by the most diligent of researchers, but mystery is not the word for what eludes us. Happily, those at the conference kept mystification to a minimum and generally strove to broaden understanding.

Too much time was wasted at the conference on vagaries raised by young historians. Did Zhou Enlai ever depart from the Party line, one from Smith insisted on knowing, and that prompted a number to pay their respects, in a few cases disrespects, to Zhou. Two veteran correspondents testified that Zhou was critical of the seizures of machinery in Manchuria by Soviet troops.

The anecdotes added to history. Annalee Jacoby Fadiman, co-author with Teddy White of *Thunder Out of China*, one of the best, non-mysterious books of the period, described in compelling detail a banquet speech by Patrick Hurley, then ambassador to China, which suggested strongly that he was in his dotage—just at the time when he was twisting U.S. policy and destroying the Chinese careers of able diplomats. Hurley had asked Annalee to be hostess at an embassy dinner, attended by T. V. Soong and others up in the Kuomintang hierarchy. Looking at her at the opposite end of the long table, he offered "the most important toast of all—to my goddess of a bride." He went on to reminisce about the wedding night and the children. Annalee froze and the guests listened in consternation.

In the late 1940s and 1950s anyone who described the Chinese Communists as mere "agrarian reformers" (few did) was put down as a Red or a Pinko. Philip Potter, who covered Senator McCarthy's antics for the *Baltimore Sun*, related how one of the Senator's aides had searched the newspaper's morgue in the hope that Potter had used that damning phrase. But he found only one use of it—in a statement by Hurley before he turned to red-baiting.

Potter also told this story: General Watanabe, commander of the surrendered Japanese forces in north China in 1945, suggested to him that the U.S. and Japan should combine forces to attack the Soviet Union. Potter reported this and expressed his outrage to Walter Robertson, who later served the Eisenhower Administration as Assistant Secretary of State for Far Eastern Affairs. "You're just a Goddamn Communist," Robertson told him.

My old friend Eppy recalled that Hollington Tong, who headed the Kuomintang information ministry, argued that correspondents should be barred from visiting the Communist-held areas for humane reasons—for whatever they wrote would be censored and they would feel frustrated.

John W. Powell, called Bill, editor of the *China Weekly* (later *Monthly*) *Review,* had sensible things to say both at the conference and in a post-conference paper about journalist work in China and described succinctly his later ordeal—the protracted trial in San Francisco of Julian Schuman, Sylvia Powell, his wife, and himself on charges of sedition, which were eventually dropped. And on the lighter side he told this anecdote: His father, J. B. Powell, and Agnes Smedley were friends despite vast differences in political perspective and once at a theater stood up together to sing the *Star Spangled Banner*. "My God, Agnes, I didn't know you knew that song," Powell said.

Mary Barrett Sullivan, who worked for the Office of War Information before joining the staff of the *Review*, recalled that General Marshall, in China on his vain mission, did not want the extent of U.S. aid to the Chiang regime known in China. So in distributing the USIS (United States Information Service) file, "we weren't permitted to include one word of what the U.S. was doing. We censored ourselves. We were never neutral in this conflict."

An intimately informed and eloquently phrased luncheon address by John Hersey dealt with Henry Luce and *Time/Life* reporting on China. Like Luce, Hersey was a "Misskid"—a child of missionaries—and for some time enjoyed Luce's favor. But Luce was a bitter-end apologist for the Chiang regime to the extent that he and his editors, notably Whittaker Chambers, altered or spiked dispatches from his China correspondents. Chambers was *Time's* foreign editor and his high-handed revisions of filed copy generally aroused a united protest by *Time* bureau chiefs in major capitals. Annalee Jacoby recalled an interview she had with Chiang Kai-shek which in print included questions she never asked and answers Chiang never gave.

My own reminiscence included this anecdote: When I returned from Chongqing in the spring of 1941, the *Christian Science Monitor* commissioned a series of ten articles under the general title "Inside the War." Charles E. Gratke, the *Monitor's* distinguished foreign editor, sat me down after reading the first two or three scripts and said: "When you write for publications like *The Nation*, you can call a spade a spade, but at the *Monitor* it's a little trowel." I have to add that Gratke's specific criticisms helped the series enormously.

My impression, refreshed at the conference, is that American reporting from China in the turbulent 1940s was superior to, or at least as good as, coverage of other foreign situations. Some competent people jumped ship or escaped from local universities or started with the local press to serve as correspondents for the agencies or the major dailies. They worked hard and tried to get at the facts, and I think attentive readers could have got to the realities from their reports, despite all the trimming and spiking done on the desks. A. T. Steele and Tillman Durdin were perhaps their epitome.

But the conference was a reminder that the "little trowel principle" applied much of the time to the coverage by the major agencies and newspapers. The reporters saw themselves as hard-headed realists, as compared with "ideologues." But their dispatches were shaped by their antipathy to revolution and their close, even intimate ties with various Kuomintang and American informants. They rather often produced finely balanced accounts of ill-balanced situations; the Communists, being in an increasingly strong position, could tell the truth, or a great deal of it.

At the conference, the dictum of Clausewitz that war continues politics was generally ignored by those who had served the major media. They recalled the civil war of 1946–49 almost exclusively in military terms. The Communist triumph was attributed to the original sin of the Japanese invasion, Chiang Kai-shek's wretched generalship, or the unwise dispositions of Kuomintang troops following the Japanese surrender. John S. Service called the attention of the conference to the truth that after all the Communists had done some things right and won their revolution.

I ventured this observation: "Certainly by the end of the anti-Japanese war, the Communists possessed a great deal of power in north China, substantial power in central China, and a certain amount in south China, including Hainan Island. A key development in Mao's strategy was to notch up the agrarian reform. This contributed to the victory in the civil war. Of course the Communists brilliantly transformed political support, popular support, into military power and that power prevailed."

Archibald Steele reminded the conference that "there was a fear of being labeled pro-Communist on the part of the journalists," one consequence of which was a reluctance to describe the Communists as really Communists. That fear deepened as the Cold War developed, and contributed to a kid-gloves handling of American policy. The essential reality of those years was a persistent American intervention in China's internal affairs—an intervention that perforce stopped short of the major use of U.S. armed forces. But in the leading newspapers and agency dispatches, the intervention was never explicit. The unwritten assumption was that the United States had the right to do what it was doing. Questioning had to do with practicality. This journalistic failure contributed to the acceptance in the U.S., initially at least, of the bloody interventions in Korea and Indochina. And to this day, despite international law clarities, the right of the U.S. to try to bring down foreign governments and organize counterrevolutions is seldom questioned in the media.

The conference did not get to the performance of American journalists in covering the new Communist regime, but Julian Schuman did so in a detailed post-conference paper. By August of 1949, two months before the establishment of the People's Republic, American press coverage began to be characterized by biased speculation and gross fabrication. "Fabrication became a way of reporting—hunger and famine stalked China, Moscow had taken over, the Yellow plus Red menace had designs on much, if not all of Asia, Chiang was pledged to retake the mainland, Mao was dying." Thus Schuman summed it up.

As early as January 1, 1950, a *New York Times* editorial thought the end of the Communist regime might be in sight: "Disillusion must have overtaken the multitudes who have waited in vain for long months for the coming of the Communist heaven. The tide may have turned." And three weeks later, on January 22, another editorial accepted as the truth, Secretary of State Dean Acheson's fanciful allegation that "the Soviet Union is detaching the northern provinces of China from China and is attaching them to the Soviet Union." Shanghai is nearly finished, the Associated Press reported from Tokyo: "Mud is choking off the sea approach to what was once the third busiest port in the world . . . within a year Shanghai will be inaccessible to commercial shipping of any importance."

The conference made no effort to reach any sort of consensus, but John K. Fairbank spoke for some of us when he said:

> We have come to terms with the Chinese revolution after about fifty years. It took us forty years to accept history to a certain degree. . . . Although now we have Reagan who accepts the history of an earlier time. So our troubles are of a continuing type, there are no easy solutions. The American experience in China in the '40s was a first-class disaster for the American people. . . . The war in Korea and the war in Vietnam were part of this disaster—it all goes together.

2. Remembering Lingnan, Notes On Zhongshan[1]

While I was unpacking in my room in Luk Yau dormitory at Lingnan University, where I was an exchange student from Harvard in 1936–37, my Chinese roommate made an awesome entrance. He came striding in at the head of a retinue of eight porters—"coolies," we called them—bearing his luggage and gear, including an iron chest. He must be rich, I wrote in my first letter home. He was. His father was a factory owner and Kuomintang official and a former mayor of

---

1. During the reorganization of institutions of higher learning in 1952 Lingnan University became part of the Zhongshan University.

Guangzhou, in which post he was widely believed to have enriched himself.

And across the hall, sharing a room with Melville Jacoby of Stanford, was the heir to even greater riches. His father was one of Guangxi Province's biggest landlords, the owner of a string of villages and possessor of a private army.

My roommate and neighbor were exceptionally well off, but at that time most college and university students in China did come from upper or middle-class families. Tuition and other costs came to 600–800 yuan a year, more than millions of peasants saw in a lifetime. The campuses were islands of privilege in a country in which at least 80 percent of the people were illiterate.

Lingnan, an especially expensive missionary institution in Guangzhou, had a student body of about five hundred when I was an exchange student. Now Zhongshan University, it had an enrollment of 4,500 undergraduates and four hundred graduates at the time of my visit in the fall of 1982. Marks in a competitive national examination, not family means, decide who is admitted. Tuition, books, lodging, and medical care are free. Some financial aid to pay for food, clothing, and incidentals is available to students from poor families. But equal opportunity has yet to be achieved. Rural kids have less chance of admission because their schools are inferior, and some officials use clout to get their own children in. "Using the back door," as they say in China.

The Christian College in China, the beginning of Lingnan, was founded in 1888 by Presbyterians. Later an extensive and exceptionally beautiful campus was put together from cemeteries, rice fields, and vegetable patches across the Pearl River from Guangzhou; the first of its handsome brick buildings arose, and in 1903 the name was changed to Canton Christian College. Changes to make it less missionary and more Chinese were taken in response to the revolutionary upsurge of the 1920s. A Chinese was made president and in 1927 the name was changed to Lingnan University. A conversion strategy helped to persuade the churches to spend very substantial sums on the development of Lingnan and the other Christian colleges and universities in China, some twenty in all. The thought was that if China's future elite could be converted, a top-down momentum would be generated which would help mightily in the effort to win China for Christ. A fund-raising brochure published by the American trustees of Canton Christian College at the end of World War I stated that China needed "the introduction of foreign capital" and that the Christian cause needed student converts: "It is imperative. .

to gain for Christianity its rightful place among the educated men of the rising generation."[2]

A decade later the missionary leadership was distressed by the success of the Communists in turning peasants into revolutionaries and sought to counter it by undertaking a series of prophylactic reforms in the countryside. The main effort in what was called rural reconstruction took place in north China, financed by the Rockefeller Foundation with a grant of $1.9 million. A leading Chinese Christian, appointed by Chiang Kai-shek, directed the rural reconstruction of the former Red areas in Jiangxi. The Lingnan faculty included some advocates of agrarian reform; the university financed serious studies of the plight of the peasantry in Guangdong by Chen Hansheng (Chen Han-seng) and associates.

But the reforms undertaken by the missionaries hardly impeded the course of the revolution. Bound by their close ties with the Chinese establishment, the Christian reformers could not challenge the landlord-peasant status quo, which was central to the injustice. "The rural reconstruction movement in China in the 1930s was basically the same as the Green Revolution in the Third World in the 1960s," Jerome Ch'en observed. "It was technological change without accompanying social and political reform or revolution."[3]

I visited Zhongshan University briefly in May 1973 with a delegation from the US-China Peoples Friendship Association and returned for a less hurried and much more satisfactory visit late in October 1982.

Much was as I remembered it—brick buildings with green or blue glazed-tile roofs and other Chinese architectural features linked by tree-lined walks and attractive plantings. Toward the North Gate by the Pearl River and elsewhere, new brick buildings that well matched the old have arisen. Many are dormitories. Some of the older dormitories have been turned into classrooms or offices because the rooms were large. My old room in Luk Yau, where I posed for a nostalgic photo, is now the office of the head of the geography department.

Lingnan's handsome library—the oldest building on the campus—was still Zhongshan's library. But not for long. A vast new building with a white exterior, with more than enough room to accommodate Zhongshan's collection of 2.4 million books and periodicals, was un-

---

2. *Canton Christian College (Ling Naan Hok Hau): Its Growth and Outlook* (New York: Trustees of the Canton Christian College, 1919), 3.
3. Jerome Ch'en, *China and the West* (Bloomington, Ind.: Indiana University Press, 1979), 137. An informative chapter deals with missionaries and their converts.

der construction. Aesthetically, it is ill matched to the warm brick surrounding it.

The buildings I saw have been well kept up. Luk Yau's trim and balustrades had been freshly painted, and its name, in ideograms and Roman letters, welcomed from the peak. The pavilion in the central rectangle, a landmark, was in mint condition. The lawn in the area had been dug up and planted in vegetables in earlier years, but has been restored.

Not far off is a statue of Sun Yat-sen, one arm outstretched, orating. A fitting pose and site, for in the background is Hui Shi Hall (Swasey in the Lingnan era) where Dr. Sun delivered a memorable anti-imperialist speech to the student body on December 23, 1923. The university's Sun Yat-sen Museum displays artifacts of his long years of revolutionary struggle. "Zhongshan" is Dr. Sun's honorific name. The university was established in 1924 and the name changed after his death from cancer the next year.

Soong Ching Ling, Madame Sun, had her own Lingnan connection. When a general hostile to Sun Yat-sen took control of Guangzhou and her life seemed in jeopardy, Dr. James M. Henry, president of Lingnan in the 1920s and later provost, helped to spirit her to safety. She may have recollected that episode when, in November, 1979, she sent a message congratulating Zhongshan on its fifty-fifth anniversary.

The Lingnan Alumni Association is quartered in a small building that once housed the Lingnan trustees. It publishes a newsletter and holds an annual reunion that attracts between five to six hundred graduates, many coming from abroad. At the request of the alumni the old Chinese names of buildings have been restored, Luk Yau among them. The foreign names of buildings are missionary history.

Students, though privileged, contributed a good deal to China's protracted national and revolutionary struggles. Canton Christian College was not in the thick of student activity, and indeed was viewed as elitist and aloof by students elsewhere. But some of its students got involved. They joined the anti-American boycott of 1905, a protest against the Exclusion Act, and three hundred students, faculty members, and staff workers marched in the historic anti-imperialist parade of June 23, 1925. The marchers moved along the Bund (the river road) toward Shamian (Shameen), the Anglo-French concession. After turning the corner they were fired on by British and French marines from the bridge to the concession. Twelve were killed, among them a Canton Christian College instructor and a student, and many were wounded. The faculty, which generally maintained a friendly and cooperative relationship with the foreign presence, was divided. Some did sign a statement of protest addressed to the British and French. And in 1947–48 Lingnan students took part in demonstrations calling for an end to the civil war and American intervention in it.

The Japanese encroachment was the overriding national issue when I was at Lingnan. Many of the students were silent on politics and some were unquestioning supporters of Chiang Kai-shek, but at least a few were taking part in what became known as the National Salvation Movement. They demanded that the government cease its attacks on the Communists in the northwest and prepare for armed resistance to Japan by a united China.

We exchange students—there were thirty-two of us—were woefully ignorant about China, and much of what we thought we knew was wrong. Lu Xun died in October 1936; we had never heard of him. We had no sense of Chinese politics. But bit by bit we were brought to some notion of what was happening. A student we liked very much disappeared. We learned that he was one of the leaders of the National Salvation Group and had fled to Hongkong to escape arrest. On a trip into the city, a missionary teacher told us about the Canton Commune of 1927 and pointed out the street corners where the bodies had been piled up after it was crushed.

The climactic event of 1936 was the kidnapping of Chiang at Xi'an. A favorite professor, Y. C. Ho, addressed a closed gathering of exchange students and explained the realities behind the heavily censured news. Chiang's release was feted at a student banquet. Some of them were actually celebrating this turn in China's politics toward national unity.

For most of the exchange students, the year at Lingnan was a superficial adventure which did not lead to a lasting China interest or connection. We shopped for ivory and jade and teak chests, visited Hongkong and Macao for a bit of sin, and Buddhist and Daoist monasteries in the Guangdong mountains for climbing and a taste of exotic change. We scattered between semesters. With three companions, I made my way by bus through Hunan, Guangxi and Guizhou to Chongqing, returning by way of the Yangtze and the Hankou-Guangzhou railroad.

The majority of courses at Lingnan by then were taught in Chinese and of those given in English, most were mediocre and of little use. And I was one of those frustrated by a circumstance described discreetly by a Lingnan historian, Charles Hodge Corbett: "Most of the co-eds (women students) at Lingnan turned their eyes downward when they met a man; only a few were at ease in masculine society."[4]

A few of us were caught up by the panorama of struggle in China, tried to understand it, and became involved in one way or another. Melville Jacoby became a *Time* correspondent and I met him again in Chongqing in 1939; he was later tragically killed in an airfield accident. Betty Chandler, an exchange student from Oregon State, married a Chinese surgeon, raised a family in Tianjin, and later joined the staff of Foreign Languages Press in Beijing.[5] Our friendship resumed when I met her in a park there on May Day 1973. Betty Graham, at Lingnan before me, was the original translator, with Chen Jiakang, of Mao's *Talks at the Yan'an Forum on Literature and Art*. A partisan of the revolution, she served with the New Fourth Army in Shandong during the civil war. Soon after Liberation she died under sad circumstances. Upon my return to Harvard I wrote my honors thesis on the Taiping Revolution, and after graduation immediately went back to China as a journalist.

I found in 1982 that exchange students were again on campus—three from the University of California at Los Angeles and two from Australia. Fifteen foreigners were on the faculty, among them a team of English teachers from UCLA. Lingnan graduates who had distinguished themselves academically abroad were being invited back to teach or lecture. Several missionaries who had taught at Lingnan had come back for visits and been warmly welcomed. Many of the decisions about Lingnan had been made in New York. Zhongshan has expanding links with counterparts abroad, but the relationships are between equals.

Beguiled by sunshine, semitropical foliage, and novel encounters, we exchange students had no inkling that the era of missionary Lingnan was approaching its demise. That summer brought the clash at Lugouqiao (Marco Polo Bridge); the long anti-Japanese war and the ensuing civil war crippled and then put an end to Christian education in China. Christianity was to survive, despite persecution during the Cultural Revolution, but education was permanently secularized. When properties were restored to religions in the early 1980s, schools and hospitals were excluded.

Missionary educators contributed a good deal to Chinese knowledge of the West, to the development of the school system, and to the lit-

---

4. *Lingnan University: A Short History Based Primarily on the Records of the University's American Trustees* (New York: Trustees of Lingnan University, 1963).
5. *Living in China* (Beijing: New World Press, 1979), includes a reminiscence by Betty Chandler.

erary use of the vernacular. They did some social pioneering. Foreshadowing the work-study programs of today, Lingnan introduced woodworking as well as agricultural courses that forced the students to get their hands into the soil. But though a handful of missionaries were converted to the idea that China needed a revolution, as a whole they were a hostile force, allies of the warlords and then the Kuomintang (whose head was at least nominally a Methodist) throughout the period of Western presence. That was part of the background to the painful confrontations and changes at Lingnan in the early 1950s.

Changes were made slowly after the Liberation of Guangzhou in December, 1949. The American faculty members at Lingnan continued to teach. But the U.S. intervention in the Korean war abruptly changed the relationship; early in 1951 the foreigners left for home. The reorganization of the national and Christian universities followed the next year. The liberal arts, social sciences, physical sciences, and foreign language departments of Lingnan and Zhongshan merged. Since Zhongshan was more prestigious academically, but inferior in facilities, it moved into Lingnan's spacious and beautiful campus. Some Lingnan professors and students had fled to Hongkong, Taiwan, or more distant places, but others accommodated themselves to the transformation. Lingnan's president became Zhongshan's vice-president.

At Zhongshan, as elsewhere, sad scenes were enacted during the Cultural Revolution, which initially sought to grapple with real problems, including elitism in education, but which went awry. The students and faculty split into two factions, the "Committee" and the "Commune," each relentlessly dogmatic. They fought each other with home-made weapons as well as harsh invective; a biology student, a bystander, was killed. Many professors, teachers and staff members were humiliated and terrorized; eleven committed suicide. An American teacher at Zhongshan, Ruth Earnshaw Lo, has given an intimate account of those calamitous years in a book, *In the Eye of the Typhoon.*

The Ministry of Education was reestablished in 1975 after eight years of non-existence and the new head of it summed up the effect of the Cultural Revolution, no doubt exaggerating somewhat: University standards reduced to those of middle schools, "no more culture, no more theory, no more scientific research," and the danger that "no one actually studies."

China urgently needs more educated persons just as it needs more agricultural and industrial production, and for intertwined reasons.

Not only material advance but social progress requires a much higher educational level. Chinese education seeks to turn out graduates who are socialist-minded as well as knowledgeable, but the obvious stress is on expertise.

Zhongshan is doing its part through fifteen departments, five research institutes, eighteen seminar rooms and 121 laboratories. Of China's ninety-six universities and colleges, seventeen have been designated key institutions, and Zhongshan is one of them. As a key university, Zhongshan enjoys a more generous budget, preferences in selection of faculty members and students, and more opportunities to send students and teachers abroad for study and to receive foreign lecturers.

But circumstances promote the elitism addressd by the Cultural Revolution with negative results. The competition for admission to the universities is individual and fierce, and those who get in, whether by the front or back door, are virtually assured of the best jobs and the privileges that go with them. Political cynicism, self-centered careerism, and even corruption are manifest to the extent that they have brought on well publicized counter measures. Whether such efforts will have a real effect, whether a balance will be struck at last between expertise and "Redness," an outsider can hardly foretell.

I came away from Zhongshan with positive impressions, which I tried to convey in a detailed report of my visit sent to former Lingnan exchange students. A group of us memorialized our year at Lingnan and celebrated the new library by a donation of some specialized French dictionaries, which Zhongshan had requested.

3. A Visit to the Taiping Beginnings

My visit to the Xin Hua (New China) Commune in October 1982 was doubly instructive. My notebook gained a good deal of specific information on rural progress since the 1978 reforms, and I was given graphic reminders of the long history of struggle that laid the foundation for progress.

For Hong Xiuquan, leader of the 1851–64 Taiping Revolution, lived as a child and young teacher in the village of Guanlubu (part of the commune) and he and his first followers began their proselytizing there and in nearby villages.

Their relatives and neighbors paid dearly. Troops of the Qing dynasty burned Guanlubu and killed many members of the Hong clan.

Those who got away settled elsewhere under changed names. Soon after liberation in 1949 a concerted effort was made to collect Taiping artifacts and memories of the movement handed down from generation to generation. Hong's home and the school where he taught, both simple structures of unbaked mud brick, have been carefully reconstructed from the surviving foundations, and the Hong clan center, built in 1911, has been turned into a permanent exhibition of artifacts of the Hong family and the uprising. A longan fruit tree the young Hong planted has somehow survived and is now a handsomely gnarled specimen. Some eight to ten thousand people come every year to see this memorial of the first chapter of China's century of revolutionary struggle.

Hong Xiuquan was born in 1814 in a nearby village that is now covered by a reservoir, and later brought by his parents to Guanlubu. Visitors are shown his small room at the far end of a rectangular dwelling. Here he prepared his lessons, first as a student, later as a teacher. Here he studied hard for the imperial examination, which he nevertheless failed four times. Here he read and was persuaded by "Good Words to Exhort the Age," a set of Christian tracts handed to him in Guangzhou. Here he wrote essays and poems that became part of the Taiping canon, a mix of Christianity, nationalism and social reformism. Here he and companions planned trips to Guangxi, where the Society of God Worshipers he founded turned into a rebellion.

The years of Hong's young manhood were a time of national humiliation, economic decline, and social hardship. The Western powers inflicted crushing defeats on China's primitive armed forces and in 1842 imposed on her the first of a series of unequal treaties. The peasants were burdened with heavy taxation and exorbitant rents and were hurt also by a decline in village weaving brought on by imports of Manchester cloth. Opium, brought in huge quantities by British and American ships, both debilitated the people and drained China's silver.

Hong's family and all the people in the area had more to contend with. They were Hakkas, northern Chinese who had fled south from turmoil centuries earlier and who had clung to their language and own ways. They were discriminated against and harassed by the authorities and neighboring people. Hong's reflections on the problems of the people he encountered in his travels and the sentiments of those he recruited added drastic reform to the Taiping purposes of religious conversion and dynastic overthrow.

An American missionary influenced Hong's religious outlook. The Reverend Issachar J. Roberts, a Southern Baptist in Guangzhou, heard that Hong had seen visions and come to regard himself as a Christian, and invited him to stay at his mission. Accompanied by his cousin, Hong Rengan, Hong arrived in mid-March 1849, and stayed most of two months. He left somewhat precipitately when Roberts withdrew his favor. Two of Roberts' Chinese assistants apparently saw Hong as a rival and persuaded Roberts that he was just another rice Christian.

But the weeks in Guangzhou shaped Taiping beliefs and practices. For the first time, Hong got a copy of the whole Bible as well as various tracts and pamphlets. He took away with him the texts of the ten commandments and doxology, both introduced into the Taiping canon. The list of commandments was expanded to prohibit sorcery, gambling, drinking, and smoking of tobacco and opium, but original texts themselves were little changed. Taiping services, like those Hong attended at the mission, featured hymns, prayers and sermons.

In later years Roberts tried a number of times to reach the Taiping capital, Tianjing (Nanjing), but failed. He succeeded in October of 1860. He was warmly welcomed by Hong and appointed vice-minister of foreign affairs, serving under Hong Rengan, then the chief minister. Roberts' task was to publicize the Taiping cause and he undertook to set up an organization in the United States for this purpose. But Roberts fell out with Hong Rengan and departed in anger on January 20, 1862. According to Lindley (Lin-le), a staunch partisan of the Taipings, Roberts was petty, peevish, and arrogant, but his feelings of disillusion may have been strengthened by the degeneration of the Taiping administration. A feudal hierarchy had replaced the camaraderie of the early years and corruption was widespread.

Roberts' shift from support to hostility was fairly typical of the missionary response to the Taiping upsurge. In the first years, some missionaries and missionary publications were articulate supporters, though others were put off by the Taiping deviations from the various Western religious orthodoxies. Missionaries for whom miracles were Biblical episodes found upsetting a movement for which they were a daily reality. Missionary disaffection grew and disapproval became general as the imperialist powers stepped up their intervention against it. All but a tiny handful of missionaries habitually lined up with the policies of their home countries and with the Chinese authorities with whom the powers were cooperating.

Taiping Christianity was a mass movement; Christianity thereafter was a fringe persuasion. In the wake of the Taiping collapse,
some missionary observers had regrets. W. A. P. Martin wrote in *A
Cycle of Cathay* that "an opportunity was lost such as does not occur
twice in a thousand years."[6] And Robert E. Speer expressed doubt in
his *Missions and Modern History* that "in all her history another
such opportunity as this has been presented to the Christian
Church."[7]

I found that the Taipings' victorious successors had brought about
considerable change for the better in the area where Hong Xiuquan
had thought and dreamed and won his first converts. The worst of
the past has been done away with and the lives of the people improved and extended. In the Xin Hua Commune, 42.5 square miles of
flat land and rolling hills, a hospital, clinics, health care stations,
and primary and junior and senior middle schools had been built over
the years. Old people without children were assured of food, clothing, shelter, medical care and funeral expenses. Electricity was pow-
ering the growing number of television sets and tape recorders and
running machinery doing some of the chores.

The community has had downs as well as ups. The cash and grain
incomes of the peasants rose only slightly over many years. The
decade of the Cultural Revolution saw a greater rise in peasant complaints than in production. But the reforms set in motion by the third
plenary session of the Eleventh Central Committee in December 1978
have brought marked changes for the better. The value of annual
production has more than doubled and the income of the peasants has
mounted steadily.

The adoption of the responsibility system coupled with greater
stress on diversification is credited with the relatively rapid
change. The gist of the system[8] is that compensation is linked to
output, giving the peasants more incentive to work hard and acquire
skills.

---

6. (New York: Fleming H. Revell, 1897), 142. Martin wrote "more than once when the
insurgents were on the verge of success, the prejudices of shortsighted diplomats
decided against them, and an opportunity was lost such as does not occur once in a
thousand years."
7. (New York: Fleming H. Revell, 1904), 65. Speer, who was secretary of the Board of
Foreign Missions of the Presbyterian Church, attributed Taiping errors and faults
largely to a lack of missionary guidance.
8. In 1982 I visited a variety of rural collectives in Sichuan and the Beijing
Municipality, as well as Guangdong. See Hugh Deane, "China's Changing
Countryside," *Far East Reporter*, March 1983.

Hong Xiuquan died in Nanjing after a long illness shortly before the city fell. But if his shade could come back to Guanlubu, he would learn from members of the Hong clan that he and his fellow-rebels hadn't struggled in vain.

My long-standing interest in the Taiping Revolution was gratified again at Nanjing, the rebel capital for twelve years, which I visited in April 1985 on a tour of returning American journalists. The city burned for three days and nights when recaptured by Qing forces under Zeng Guofan in May of 1864. The palace of Hong Xiuquan was spared overnight, so that it could be systematically looted and then put to the torch. A pool, a marble boat, and foundations survived.

Leading provincial and party officials received us in the splendid reconstruction, which earlier served Sun Yat-sen and Chiang Kai-shek as presidential headquarters when Nanjing was the capital. With notebooks full of statistics about Jiangsu's swift economic growth, we walked through the grounds, a dialectic of garden and structure, saw the pool and boat and Taiping artifacts in a pavilion.

The next day, with my old friend Israel Epstein, then editor of *China Reconstructs* (now *China Today*), I visited the Museum of the Taiping Kingdom. The museum occupies what had been the palace of Yang Xiuqing, the Eastern King, one of the ablest of the Taiping chiefs. Yang was killed, perhaps in the garden of this palace, during a period of violent internal dissension in 1856.

The message of the museum, told by graphics, proclamations, and artifacts, was that the Taipings were more than simple rival claimants for dynastic power. Especially in their early years, they pressed for all sorts of social changes.

Augustus F. Lindley (Lin Le) was the closest thing to Edgar Snow in the Taiping era. His two-volume work on the rebellion is its *Red Star Over China*.[9] A respectful recognition of his partisanship features a photo of his restored grave in London.

The American mercenary adventurer Frederick Townsend Ward, who played a contrary role in the revolution, is remembered at the museum also. His gravestone was brought there from the temple memorializing him on the outskirts of Shanghai.

---

9. *Ti-ping Tien-kwoh, The History of the Ti-Ping Revolution, Including a Narrative of the Author's Personal Adventures* (London: Day & Son, 1866).

4. Chongqing Then and Now

Chongqing—Chungking in the pre-pinyin era—became the capital of China after Wuhan fell to the Japanese in October 1938. I was there from September, 1939 into the spring of 1941 and contributed this description of the city to the *Christian Science Monitor* of August 23, 1941:

Chongqing was being bombed when London was still dozing uneasily in the shade of Neville Chamberlain's umbrella. It is being bombed savagely today. When you walk through Chongqing you see shattered buildings, heaps of broken brick and tile, charred timbers, streets meandering meaninglessly through acres of devastation. You look in vain for a building which the bombs have not scarred.

When you watch the young children playing in the streets, you remember that they have no recollection of a life free from the horror of air raids. You wonder how the people have endured, and you sense that in their travails is a tale somehow lost beneath the dramatic politics of a war capital.

If you are in downtown Chongqing on a fine summer day, you hardly see a soul on the streets. Fine weather means bombs. In Chongqing people pray for rain and dull weather. Winter is the favorite season, because it rains much of the time and the sun rarely shines. When the trees begin to sprout in the spring, people shudder, for the Japanese bombers come back with the robins. The people have a new proverb, not quite up to the standard set by Confucius: "When it isn't raining water, it's raining bombs."

Sometimes, though, after a long respite, an air raid alarm catches a city full of people. You are walking along the street when suddenly you notice that everybody is running or walking fast. You look up and see a red canvas ball hoisted on one of the gallows-like structures placed strategically throughout the city. The planes are on the way.

Instantly the city seethes with commotion. Clerks board up the shops. People are hurrying in all directions. A panicky feeling makes them run, even though they know they have plenty of time. Some descend the long flights of stone steps to the Yangtze River and try to get a boat to the South Bank, which is never bombed, because it is mostly foreign property. On the river's edge the people shout and push and overload the boats, and soon a flotilla of sampans and one or two steamboats are heading for the opposite shore.

Meanwhile the roads leading out of the city are jammed with people and conveyances of all sorts, rickshas, carts, wheelbarrows, sedan chairs, bicycles—all moving in a thick cloud of choking dust.

Babies are strapped to the backs of the women, who pull along little children by the hand. The men carry precious belongings, suspended on the two ends of a bamboo pole. Trucks rumble past, a few lucky people clinging to their sides. Shiny new American automobiles, carrying officials and their families, race past the hurrying people.

Then you hear the undulating moan of the siren. The planes are in the province. People in the city move toward the dugouts cut deep in the rocky hills on which Chongqing is built. Chongqing has hundreds of excellent dugouts and more are always being built—all day you hear the sound of chisel on rock and the explosion of dynamite. Inside the dugouts you are safe from bombs. In the dugouts for the ordinary people, however, ventilation is a major problem. Recently 4,000 people suffocated in one huge, mile-long dugout because the authorities had failed to install a ventilating system according to schedule.

The government ministries and departments, the banks and other institutions have private dugouts, and these are by far the best. When you enter your dugout, you show your pass to gendarmes. If you are an official, a foreigner, or an upper-class person, you have a blue pass and go in one entrance. If you are a coolie, you have a brown pass and go in another entrance.

Twenty minutes or a half-hour after the first alarm, the siren moans again. The last stragglers hurry for cover. You hear the pitifully ineffective antiaircraft guns fire a few shells, and if you look up you can see the beautiful silver planes glinting in the sun.

While the bombs are dropping the people in the dugouts stuff their fingers in their ears and open their mouths to lessen the effect of concussion. The explosions send a quaking breeze through the dugouts. The whole earth shakes. The people are calm, but on their faces you can see fear and a trace of bewilderment. They are very still; only the children whimper a bit. . . .

Chongqing in summer is a dreary place. Everyone who can leaves the city. Yet even in the summer people somehow live with few complaints, somehow do their work. And when dull weather sets in with the fall, the heart-warming hum of reconstruction accelerates. Every day when you walk through the city you notice new buildings which have sprung up like mushrooms. Shops which formerly had two or three stories reappear after bombing with one story. The old bricks are simply piled up, coated with plaster, roofed, and the shop is ready for business. Merchants have learned to keep most of their stock outside the city, so losses are minimized. Anyway, so many merchants are making a good thing out of the war that they can afford a new shop occasionally. Profiteering has kept a smile on burgher faces.

Chongqing is like a booming mining town—a city of unweathered planks, ugly, sprawling, alive with activity. It is a city 2,000 years old, and yet today it is all new, except for the worn stone steps that lead up from the Yangtze and the ancient, crenelated walls. And these old walls no longer confine it. Hastily built suburbs stretch for twenty-five miles outside the city. Here you see new factories housing the machinery brought from the East. Here are new arsenals, garages, shops, dwellings, schools where but a few years ago were only rice fields. . . .

Everywhere you see marked inequality and at the same time signs of change. A veneer of modernity has been superimposed on the backwardness of centuries. Sleek, shiny autos throw dust on rickshas. Wide, new streets intersect noisy, twisting narrow alleys. You visit modern shops with plate-glass windows, price tags, and deferential clerks, and yet you still hear the clicking of two hard pieces of bamboo as the traditional pedlar announces his coming. Chinese from the East eat ice cream and cake in the fashionable Yangtze Store; elsewhere the people gather as usual to drink tea and chew watermelon seeds in tea shops. In the street, ladies from Shanghai wear smart dresses and high-heeled shoes, walking briskly past old Sichuanese dames with bound feet.

A column of thin, ragged, dispirited conscript laborers tied together with a rope and guarded by soldiers march past the slogans painted on the walls about China's fight for freedoms. . . .

There is plenty of evidence in Chongqing that when the people demand new rights, they are going to meet tremendous obstacles. Official distrust of the people is manifested everywhere. At every intersection there is a fortified rifle pit or pillbox, officially said to be a defense against a Japanese parachute invasion, but widely believed to be primarily designed to forestall domestic disorder. Talk about democratic reforms is discouraged, and such ideas are "dangerous thoughts" in the minds of some officials. Many leftist and liberal bookshops have been closed, and "subversive" periodicals suppressed. In the newspapers you see many a phrase denoting material deleted by censors. You hear that a large number of outspoken liberals and leftists have been arrested, and that several large dugouts, such as the Eastern Sichuan Normal School, have been converted into political prisons. You notice how reluctantly people discuss politics. [10] Yet a people who have shown such courage and resourcefulness in living through years of air raids will some day secure a real part in the political and cultural life of their country.

Accompanied by Zhang Yan and Li Lailai of *China Reconstructs* I revisited Chongqing in October 1982, and wrote this account for that magazine:

Every morning before breakfast and one long afternoon I walked the streets of Chongqing, mixing nostalgia with curiosity, looking for surviving landmarks of the Chongqing I had known in the years 1939–41 and taking note of the impressive changes. Americans who resided in Chongqing when it was the wartime capital and find themselves again in the old part of the city, on the hilly wedge between the converging Yangtze and Jialing rivers, might initially feel that not so much had changed. Grayish structures often made more somber by drizzle and overcast skies—that is still the Chongqing look. But then the differences begin to redraw the picture.

More of the alleys and lanes have been widened into streets and the rats that once cavorted in the gutters are gone. Caves dug for air raid shelters are warehouses. Interspersed with the gray buildings from the past is much new housing. Trees lining the streets, potted plants on the terraces of the new housing, flower beds at traffic circles and street junctures do relieve the sobriety. The rickshas are gone. So are the sedan chairs that once bore better-off people up the long flights of stone steps from the banks of the Yangtze and Jialing. Bicycles are scarce because of the steep inclines, but what seems to be an adequate bus service—developed, I was told, by an exemplary official who was Zhou Enlai's wartime chauffeur—gets people from one hill to another. The city is much cleaner than it was in the Kuomintang era. Saturday is clean-up day and teams of office workers, students, and neighborhood residents tidy up everything.

Revisitors would see people doing familiar chores and hear familiar street sounds, but the beggars who pleaded for coppers are gone. The people are more colorfully dressed. The markets seem well stocked with the foodstuffs sent in by the increasingly productive state farms and communes on the outskirts; spicy noodles and other dishes cooked in street stalls give off enticing odors. The children are

---

10. I dealt with these and related political events in detail in "Political Reaction in Kuomintang China," *Amerasia*, July 1942.

cherubic—no more of the rheumy eyes, scabs and rickety limbs that were so common in the old days.

The Chongqing once girt by a nine-gated wall is now but a section of an enormously expanded city. The growth began hastily in 1939 when Japanese bombers, guided by the silver ribbon of the Yangtze, unloaded on the wartime capital in an effort to break the morale of the populace. Along the road west fleeing people started life anew. I described the scene this way in an article I wrote for my hometown paper, the *Springfield Republican*, on July 28, 1940:

> Our truck bumped along out of Chongqing. For miles the road is lined with buildings so new that the unpainted boards have not yet weathered. . . . Dozens of new towns have sprung up. . . . They look like boom towns in a gold rush. With mud, bamboo, brick and plaster the Chinese have created new suburban centers. . . .

The jerry-built structures of those years have made way for a planned urban development. A mountain top has made way for a stadium (near where the Press Hostel was) and other hills have been carved to accommodate factories, shops, schools and housing. Greater Chongqing had a population of 6.3 million—14 million if fourteen rural counties it administers are included. Its 3,600 industrial enterprises employ 800,000 workers and produce thirty-six times the 1949 output. Bridges span both the Yangtze and Jialing; railroads, three of them, and highways vie with the rivers in the transport of goods and people.

Chongqing was made a treaty port in 1890. The imperial powers did not insist on territorial concessions, as they did at the major treaty ports, but they did more or less take over much of the hillside on the South Bank. They built enormous brick houses, with high ceilings and generous verandas, in which they were attended by slews of servants headed by Number One Boys (of indeterminate age). In the high-water season, British, French, and American gunboats chugged up through the gorges to show the flag. The officers were feted at a round of parties and joined foreign residents some evenings at the Chongqing Club. The seamen had their own club. For both officers and men horseback excursions into the hills were a frequent pastime.

I lived for some months in 1940–41 in the Shell House on the South Bank. Despite wartime scarcities we lived in comfort. Scotch was in short supply of course and at the Chongqing Club the principal drink was Chongqing Vodka, made by a local Greek dentist named Maliotis. The vodka was also used as aftershave lotion. Available also were the gin, cointreau, and beer made out of oranges by Pop Schwer, a retired U.S. Navy petty officer who also ran the ice house.

The halcyon days of the treaty ports were over, but the portrait of the British sovereign looked down from the club wall on snooker and poker players and signers of chits. Below, the gunboat U.S.S. *Tutuila* rode at anchor. Nearby for some months were H.M.S. *Falcon* and the French gunboat *Balny*.

In those years I got to the South Bank either on a small ferry or by sanpan. This time I made it in a few minutes by the impressive bridge. My hosts and I scrambled up and down the worn steps as I searched for yesterday. I walked about what had been the American Embassy compound, visited the former Chongqing Club and the seamen's club, and looked up at the Butterfield Swire House, where I once interviewed Agnes Smedley. Some of the foreign mansions have been demolished, but most are still there, somewhat rundown and scruffy. But they now serve far more useful social purposes, housing municipal health care services and the like. The huge British Consulate is now a Party headquarters. I imagined irate British ghosts prowling the corridors.

The foreign-built mansions are now hemmed in. The linking of the north and south banks by the bridge has made the southern hills an integral and swiftly developing part of the metropolis.

In 1941 I visited the Chongqing Iron and Steel Plant, which had been moved up river from Wuhan by an arduous effort and reopened just a few months earlier. Its open hearth furnaces made a scene from Dante's *Inferno* but their capacity was just ten tons each and a year's production was less than seven thousand tons.

A tour of the plant forty-one years later gave me graphic evidence of China's enormous advance in industrial capacity since Liberation. Chongqing Iron and Steel Plant is in the medium industry category but is a complex of twenty-two factories employing forty thousand people. It was turning out huge quantities of coke and iron, steel ingots in a variety of dimensions, and many products for the military. An early achievement was to manufacture rails for the Chongqing-Chengdu Railroad, built in the early 1950s.

The plant official who received us recited production statistics with evident satisfaction, stressing the gains since the 1978 reforms. But typically, Chongqing Iron and Steel Plant is responsible for the housing and social needs of its workers and their families, and our hosts seemed to be especially proud of the statistics in this area, which funds generated by expanded production have made even more impressive: 38 apartment buildings, 22 kindergartens and nurseries, 13 primary schools, 3 middle schools, 1 spare-time university, 47 canteens, 5 hospitals and 33 medical stations served by 800 doctors and nurses, 38 reading rooms, three swimming pools.

Like Chinese industry in general, Chongqing Iron and Steel Plant is grappling with the complex problems of meshing market mechanisms with planning (and planning is regional and local as well as central). Once barred even from directly accepting local orders, management has new options. Trials and errors continue as they are exercised. Bureaucracy remains irksome. "We have too many mothers-in-law" is a standard way of voicing the complaint. But intractable as some of the problems seem, they are overshadowed by the fundamental achievement of major gains in production.

Before going to Chongqing I had read with satisfaction that workshop heads, section chiefs, and group leaders at Chongqing Iron and Steel Plant were being elected and that in some cases several candidates vied for the posts. But I found that elections were no longer held. Too many amiable but incapable workers had been elected, and campaigning had revived animosities dating from the Cultural Revolution, I was told. But local journalists I met were critical of the decision to terminate elections. They thought results would have improved as more democratic experience was gained. The *Chongqing Daily* editorialized that the roles and rights of the workers had to be expanded as those of management were expanded.

Chongqing has many revolutionary memories. Zhou Enlai was the Party's chief representative in the wartime capital; serving with him were his wife, Deng Yingchao, Dong Biwu, and Ye Jianying. Their headquarters residence was a hillside compound overlooking the Jialing River named Red Crag Village. In addition to official liaison functions, Zhou and his comrades had a heavy secret responsibility, guiding the proscribed Party underground in Kuomintang-ruled areas. A secret upper floor, unrevealed by the exterior, was the center for this hazardous effort.

The Party published a heavily censored newspaper, *New China Daily*, and this was produced in another hilly compound near the Jialing, closer to the city. Zhou Enlai had a city office and the *New China Daily* a city store front. The newspaper compound no longer exists but the other locations have been restored and opened to Chinese and foreign visitors. Seeing them again and refreshing old memories was an especially rewarding part of my Chongqing stay. Rounding a corner in the museum attached to Red Crag Village I saw my younger self in a group photo of foreign journalists and progressive Chinese, among them Israel Epstein, editor of *China Reconstructs;* Jack Belden, author of the *China Shakes the World;* Graham Peck, author of *Two Kinds of Time;* and Mao Dun, distinguished writer and friend of Lu Xun. If I recollect rightly, the photo was taken by Ye Junjian, who became one of China's most distinguished writers. I identified everyone in the group for the museum guides.

I remembered best the Party's city office. Especially during the period leading up to the "Southern Anhui (New Fourth Army) Incident," I went there several times a week, usually with Jack Belden, to interview Zhou or one of his aides. I sat again on the foyer bench where we had waited to be received and at the table where the interviews were conducted, and looked again at the face of Zhou Enlai, looking down from a photo on the wall. New information about the treacherous attack on the New Fourth Army has come to light over the years, but I remembered that while Zhou of course did not tell us everything he knew, what he did tell us was the essential truth.

Visiting the *New China Daily* store front, I remembered the first issue published after news of the attack reached Chongqing. Waiting until the censor had cleared the contents and departed, Zhou inserted a memorial statement and a four-line poem and later joined staff members in hawking the paper on the streets. The police soon confiscated what copies they could find. My copy, printed on coarse green paper, was stolen from my room in the Press Hostel during an air raid, presumably by a police agent.

5. Three Visions of the Yangtze

I. The Lindberghs and the Yangtze in Flood. In 1931 Charles Lindbergh and his wife, Anne Morrow Lindbergh, flew to East Asia by the Great Circle Route in a small plane fitted with pontoons. The Orient was alluring and they felt something akin to the adventurous impulse that had taken Lindbergh on his historic flight across the Atlantic to Paris. They also had a mission—to determine the practicality of the route for Pan-American Airlines, which had decided to try to be the first to inaugurate trans-Pacific service. Ultimately Pan-American chose an island-hopping route to the south, but Northwest and Japan Airlines were among the carriers that adopted the Great Circle route, with a stopover at Anchorage.

On the flight from Tokyo to China, the Lindberghs met the Yangtze (also called the Changjiang River) before the land, its silt

darkening the sea for miles. Anne Lindbergh commented in her book
North to the Orient:

> What a river this must be to make itself felt so far from land, to so
> impress its personality on its overlord, the sea, I made obeisance to it
> in my mind, for I felt in the presence of a great monarch. And I was
> not mistaken. The Yangtze River, as we followed its smooth course
> up through the immense stretches of flat farm lands of coastal
> China, was one of those rivers which give the impression of being
> the only true and permanent rulers of the earth. [11]

But quickly they found that the river was not a friend, but in raging revolt. It had broken dykes, inundated the nurtured fields, destroying some villages, turning others into islands, creating the sorrow of homelessness and starvation. In the center of the devastation
was a roaring torrent, Anne Lindbergh observed, "the very heart of
the river gone mad with power, carrying all in front of it: houses,
trees, boats, livestock and coffins."

The plane, named *Sirius,* had been specially fitted for long-range
flights, and the Lindberghs volunteered its services to the National
Flood Relief Commission in Nanjing. That city, then the capital, was
inspected appreciatively from the air by the Lindberghs. Purple
Mountain and the river seemed to vie with each other, Anne Lindbergh wrote, and the city wall threw "its gray rope around hills and
fields, railroads and canals, mud huts and tiled roofs, pointed eaves
and towers, crowded streets and shaded gardens drawing them altogether. . . . A walled city has an unmistakable quality of majesty. It
stands isolated as an island, self-sufficient as a ship, unassailable as
a mountain."

Taking off from Lotus Lake, just outside Nanjing, the Lindberghs
conducted surveillance flights over the flooded areas and mapped
them as best they could, so that relief efforts could be rationalized.
Anne Lindbergh sent back terse reports by wireless.

And they undertook a medical relief mission to a walled city
wholly isolated by the rising waters. Anne Lindbergh stayed in
Nanjing and her husband took two doctors and supplies of medicines
to the area. But a swarm of sanpans converged on the plane as it
landed. The people in them thought the boxes of medical supplies
were food. They cupped their hands and made chopstick eating motions to say they were starving. When one boat reached a pontoon

---

11. (New York: Harcourt, Brace, 1935), 200.

and a man stepped on it and others began to scramble aboard, Lindbergh fired a 38 revolver over their heads and the plane made a perilous takeoff.

On one flight the Lindberghs looked down on a magnificent pagoda, "an embodiment of all peace and stillness," which also by the climbing progression of its stories suggested growth. The *Sirius* flew around it three times. After two weeks of flights the *Sirius* landed in the river off Hankou and was hauled aboard the British aircraft carrier *Hermes*. But the later lowering was mishandled in a strong wind and current. Anne Lindbergh jumped into the Yangtze before the plane sank.

The *Sirius* was raised, sent to Lockheed Aircraft in California for repair, and is now in the American Museum of Natural History in New York City.

II. Cruising Down the Yangtze and Playing Gin. In the winter of 1980 a cotton-jacketed crowd watched in silence as three mink coats boarded the Lindblad-chartered *East Is Red No. 39* in Chongqing. Lurabelle Laughlin was wearing a golden coat made of thirty-five minks of the touraline variety. Ami Ver Bryck's was a rich glossy mahogany. Bea Bratman hadn't brought her best mink. "This is the one I wear at all the football games," she said.

The three ladies were on a passenger list of thirty-three, all rich enough to pay $10,000 for a ride to Shanghai, many millionaires, some multis. "If you have only two or three million you're not a millionaire," one observed. "If you have twenty-five million, you can get by."

The richest on board was Lurabelle Laughlin of Pasadena, who had inherited $50 million in oil money.

Accompanying the group was a note taker and scribe, Paul Theroux, who turned out a small book,[12] an alternative title for which could be "Cruising Down the Yangtze and Playing Gin."

Theroux reports that some of his companions were "very smart about Chinese history or porcelain and talked intelligently about why they disliked Norman Mailer," while others read cowboy novels, called Mao "Mayo," and mixed up Taiwan and Thailand. They played and drank a lot of gin and cheated at scrabble.

A not overly kind Boswell, Theroux has preserved these utterances along the way:

—"I've been everywhere and didn't have to walk. I pay money so I don't have to walk."

---

12. *Sailing Through China* (Boston: Houghton Mifflin, 1984).

—"Do you know the Chinese couldn't care less if the Rams are playing tomorrow."

—"I'm going to make goddam sure my granddaughter is spoiled rotten."

—An exclamation at the Yellow Cat Gorge—"What a place to build a condominium!"

—On Chinese food—"Once a month maybe. But every damned day? I can't eat the stuff."

—"Of course I'm happier than you. I have more money."

—"It's about time the world started to be afraid of America again."

One of the Chinese questioned a rich lady, "What about food? You must spend ten or twenty dollars a week on food."

"Twenty dollars is nothing," the woman replied.

Asked what kind of a car she drove, she said, "Actually, I have four."

"Comrade Tao seemed to swallow something very large," Theroux wrote.

Fortunately he hadn't put the question to the passenger from Connecticut whose auto possessions included twenty Cadillacs.

Theroux played gin with a sore loser who stomped away after a string of defeats, insisted later on a rematch, played until he had won three nights in a row, and then said Theroux was a waste of his time.

So Theroux played gin with ladies from New York "who proved exhausting opponents." But Scrabble was exasperating since the players cheated, there being no dictionary aboard. "Of course yo is a word—as in yo-ho-ho."

A huge Chinese shore sign declaring that "the world belongs to the people" was challenged by the Cadillac owner. Not true, he said, "the world belongs to some of the people."

Theroux, a confirmed misanthrope, could find no solace when he looked up from his gin and Scrabble games. He was appreciative of the gorges, as everyone is, but otherwise the landscape depressed him. Chongqing "stank like poison." Wanxian was "dreary" and Chang Shou "one of the nightmare cities of the river." All river cities looked like Pittsburgh. Fengdu "was a sullen agglomeration of scorched factories and workers' flats under a weeping corona of smog." Shanghai's air was "dark brown."

Nothing at all of the river as perceived by generations of Chinese poets came through to those on *East Is Red No. 39.*

To Theroux, China was a dismal failure. "In a hundred years or so, under a cold, uncolonized moon, what we call the civilized world will all look like China, muddy, senile and old-fangled, no trees, no birds, and shortages of fuel and metal and meat, but plenty of push-carts, cobblestones, ditchdiggers, and wooden inventions."

Any change in China would be for the worse, he thought, "which is a pity because it seemed so bad when I sailed through it."

The Yangtze just keeps rolling along.

III. Notes of a Revisiting Journalist. I first took ship down the Yangtze in February 1937 when I was an exchange student at Lingnan University in Guangzhou. My three companions and I, on a between-semester swing through southwest China, traveled second or third class, ate quantities of tangerines and peanuts, and conversed in bumbling Latin with a Catholic-educated soldier—Quod nomen habetis?

My wife and I made the trip more comfortably aboard a Butter-field & Swire ship in the summer of 1940, our attention divided between tallish tales of the treaty port days told by Captain Paul, a Scot who had been sent to sea at fourteen with a Bible and a silver coin, and the magnificence of the gorges, an unfolding of successive splendors.

Yichang, where the riverfront street was still called the Bund by foreigners, fell to the Japanese not long after our departure. Our stay with Canadian missionaries left pleasant memories, but I remember best the Anglican father who worked tirelessly to ease the deaths of Sichuan soldiers ill with tuberculosis and malnutrition. No medicines were within his reach, but with money he begged for, he and Chinese assistants built mat shelters for the dying and gave them water, gruel, and such comfort as they could, trusting that God would take into consideration the pain, bewilderment and innocence of their passing.

A luxurious voyage down the Yangtze was a memorable part of a look around China by revisiting veteran journalists in the spring of 1985. The river had been at least partially tamed and I had learned something of its history.

The most perilous places, where whirlpools had sucked down many a craft, had been made safe or nearly so by the dynamiting of rocks, and at every bend in the river what had been blind turns had been given advance sight by hill-top signals. Radar was coming soon, we were told by a young official who gave us a two-session, five-hour briefing on the great river. He's married to it, I thought. When he finished a superb presentation, we gave him an ovation. The gangs of coolies who, straining at hawsers, had pulled junks up the river against the current were gone, but the paths they had trod memorialize their pain.

At Baidicheng (White King Town) at the entrance to the first of the gorges, Qutang Gorge, we climbed what we were told would be nine hundred steps (fortunately a long count) to a splendid view and a temple full of history. Great drama was enacted here in the period of the Three Kingdoms and some fifteen hundred years later leaders of the Taiping Rebellion climbed and conferred, sitting in ornate chairs now displayed.

The brilliant Tang dynasty poet Du Fu lived in a thatched hut near here for two years (A.D. 766–768). I hoped I might be standing close to where he looked down at the rushing river and the canyons of the first gorge and in his head began to write his poem on Baidicheng:

> Above the city of the White King
> the clouds leave by the city gate;
> Below the city wall, the rain pours down
> as if from an upturned bucket.
> In the swelling river and gulping gorges,
> thunders battle. . . .

Du Fu was in ill health, just a few years from death and no doubt drinking too much, but the river, nearby Wushan (Witch Mountain) and raging winds and gray skies inspired him to write the fine series on Autumn Thoughts. A few lines:

> On Witch Mountain, in Witch Gorge,
> the air is somber, desolate.
> Billowy waves from the river roar
> and rush toward the sky. . . .
> To cut winter clothes, women everywhere
> ply their scissors and rulers—
> Below the White King's tall city wall
> is heard the urgent pounding of the evening wash.

Du Fu's great friend and fellow poet Li Bai (Li Po) also traveled down the Yangtze in the closing years of his life and left us a poem about Baidicheng:

> We bid farewell to Baidi in morning glow. . .
> Our vessel floats past ten thousand mountains.

A GENERAL CHRONOLOGY

1784   Voyage of *Empress of China* to Guangzhou (Canton) inaugurates trade between the U.S. and Chinese. Americans soon join British in the opium trade.

1839–42   Chinese efforts to halt the opium traffic in Guangzhou are used as an excuse to start the First Opium War, in which British land and sea forces overwhelm the armed forces of the Qing (Manchu) dynasty.

1842   The Treaty of Nanjing, the first of the unequal treaties, cedes Hongkong to Britain and opens up five ports to trade and local imperialist control.

1844   The Treaty of Wangxia, the first of the "Me Too" treaties, gives the U.S. the benefits won by British arms and then some.

1851–64   The Taiping Revolution, headed by Hong Xiuquan, sweeps south-central China. It is finally suppressed as a result of its own weaknesses and foreign intervention.

1860   Frederick Townsend Ward, American adventurer, organizes a Shanghai-based mercenary force to fight against the Taipings. Ward is killed near Ningpo in August 1862 and succeeded by a British officer, Charles George Gordon, with the approval of his government.

1856–60   The Second Opium War legalizes the opium trade and greatly extends imperialist rights and influence. British and French troops sack and burn the old Summer Palace, Yuan Ming Yuan, in Beijing.

1868   Burlingame Treaty stipulates free immigration of Chinese laborers into the United States.

1872   The first Chinese students are sent to the U.S. as the Qing dynasty undertakes limited reform efforts—the "self-strengthening" movement.

1877   Riots against Chinese workers break out in California and other parts of the West Coast after the completion of the transcontinental railway.

233

1879	Harvard University offers a course in the Chinese language.
1882	Chinese Exclusion Act passed by U.S. Congress.
1894–95	Japan swiftly defeats China in a war ended by the Treaty of Shimonoseki. Japan is given Taiwan and control of Korea.
1894	Sun Yat-sen organizes the Xing Zhong Hui (Society for the Survival of China), a revolutionary group in Hawaii. Committed to the overthrow of the Qing dynasty, it is one of a number of antecedents of the Kuomintang.
1898	The reform of the Hundred Days, supported by Emperor Guang Xu, is crushed by Empress Dowager Ci Xi. The imperialist powers wrest spheres of influence and investment concessions from a weak China. The U.S. occupies the Philippines.
1899	U.S. Secretary of State John Hay proclaims the Open Door policy in notes to the powers, asserting American insistence on access to China trade and investment opportunities.
1899–1900	The Boxer movement against foreign intrusions and humiliations is put to a bloody end by the intervention of the troops of eight nations, including the U.S.
1905	A new Chinese Exclusion Act passed by the U.S. Congress leads to a boycott of American goods in many Chinese cities.
1911	1911 Revolution brings down the effete Qing dynasty and creates a republic. Sun Yat-sen serves briefly as provisional president but is succeeded by a reactionary militarist, Yuan Shikai, favored by the U.S. and other foreign powers.
1913	The U.S. formally recognizes the republic in May.
1914	World War I breaks out. Japan occupies Qingdao, German-leased territory on the Shandong peninsula.
1915	Japan issues the Twenty-One Demands, signaling its ambition of gaining *de facto* control of China.
1917	China enters the war on the side of the Allies and sends laborers to France. The October Revolution in Russia. By the Lansing-Ishii agreement, the U.S. recognizes Japan's claim of predom-inant interests in Manchuria and Shandong Province due to geographical contiguity.
1919	Students take to the streets in Beijing and other cities to protest against the Versailles Treaty, which gives Japan the right to occupy Qingdao and inherit German privileges in Shandong Province. The Chinese delegation in Paris refuses to sign it. This develops into the May Fourth

Movement, which makes far reaching demands for literary and social reforms and national regeneration.

1921   The Chinese Communist Party is formed in Shanghai by Mao Zedong and twelve others.

1922   The Washington Conference and Nine-Power Treaty reflects the increased global muscle of the U.S. and China's continuing subservience.

1924   The first Kuomintang-Communist United Front is formed.

1925   China's patriotic statesman, Sun Yat-sen, dies, leaving what he calls "an unfinished revolution."

1925–27   Trade and peasant unions are organized in a revolutionary up-surge and a northern expedition is launched from Guangzhou (Canton) against the warlords. But in April 1927, Chiang Kai-shek turns against the revolution and thousands of union members, Communists, and others are massacred in Shanghai.

1927   Armed forces organized by the Communist Party rise up in Nanchang on August 1, later designated Army Day. Communist bases are established in the Jinggang Mountains in Jiangxi Province and the countryside.

1928   The U.S. is the first nation to recognize Chiang's Nanjing regime.

1931–32   Japan seizes the northeast and sets up the puppet state of "Manchukuo." The 19th Route Army staunchly defends Shanghai against a Japanese attack. The Communists set up a government in Ruijin, Jiangxi Province, in the southeast.

1934–36   The Communist forces make their Long March to the northwest, eventually making Yan'an in Shaanxi Province their capital.

1936   The Xi'an Incident: In December Chiang Kai-shek is abducted by his own officers motivated by anti-Japanese sentiments, and forced to agree to a policy of resistance and the Second Kuomintang-Communist United Front.

1937   Edgar Snow's *Red Star Over China* is published, illuminating the drama of the revolution.

1937–45   The Japanese invade China and capture many cities and towns, but are denied control of the countryside by a partisan war conducted by the rapidly expanding Communist forces, organized into the Eighth Route and New Fourth armies. The war becomes part of World War II and ends in Japan's surrender in August 1945.

1941   The Southern Anhui Incident: A Kuomintang attack on the New

Fourth Army in January foretells the civil struggle to come. Pearl Harbor is bombed in December and the U.S. declares war on Japan.

1943   The Exclusion Act is repealed and a token number of Chinese permitted to immigrate annually.

1944   The recall of General Joseph Stilwell, at Chiang Kai-shek's insistence, points to a firm U.S. policy of alliance with the Kuomintang regime and hostility toward the Communists.

1945–47   The tainted mediation effort of the Marshall Mission, intended to keep the Kuomintang in power, fails.

1946–49   The renewed civil war: Despite their vast quantities of American arms, the Kuomintang armies are defeated by the Communist forces, renamed the People's Liberation Army.

1949   The People's Republic is proclaimed on October 1. It invites recognition by the powers. The U.S. refuses and allies itself with the remnant Kuomintang regime on Taiwan.

1950   The Korean war begins in June. President Truman seizes the occasion to order the Seventh Fleet to patrol the Taiwan Strait in support of Chiang Kai-shek. Chinese "Volunteers" intervene in the war when General MacArthur sends American forces to the Yalu River, the border with China. The war is stalemated, ending in what is generally a return to the prewar status quo.

1950   Agnes Smedley dies in London. She leaves her personal possessions to General Zhu De, whose biography she has written. She is buried in the cemetery for revolutionaries in Beijing.

1955–56   Socialist collectivization is rapidly carried out in China's countryside and cities.

1956–57   The period of free discussion of the Hundred Flowers is abruptly halted and followed by an anti-rightist campaign, which victimizes a large number of intellectuals.

1958–59   Rural cooperatives are greatly enlarged into communes. A drive for swift economic progress, the Great Leap Forward, turns extremist and has disastrous consequences, including famine.

1958   Quemoy-Matsu crisis: China begins bombardment of Quemoy, heavily garrisoned by Kuomintang troops. U.S. naval vessels escort supply ships from Taiwan to the offshore islands. Mutual restraint dissolves the confrontation.

1959   The Tibetan upper class undertakes a quickly suppressed revolt against Chinese rule. The CIA steps up its intervention in Tibet.

1960   Beijing and Moscow split; the Soviet Union withdraws its technicians from China and ends aid projects.

1962   Indian troops try to slice off segments of Chinese territory but suffer quick defeat.

1964   China explodes its first atomic bomb. It states that "China will never . . . be the first to use nuclear weapons."

1965–66 The U.S. eases restrictions on travel to China by professionals.

1966–76 The Great Proletarian Cultural Revolution begins with the promise of "new socialist things" and a closer relationship between people and government, but degenerates into a disastrous mixture of extreme factionalism, dogmatic rhetoric and gross violations of human rights.

1970   Anna Louise Strong dies in Beijing and is buried in the cemetery for revolutionaries. She, along with Snow and Smedley, are later honored in China through the SSS Society.

1971   An exchange of positive signals, the China visit of an American ping-pong team and a secret visit by Henry Kissinger. The People's Republic enters the United Nations.

1972   President Nixon visits China. The Shanghai Communique is signed. Edgar Snow dies of cancer in Switzerland on February 15 even as the U.S.-China conciliation he helped to bring about is realized. His ashes are divided between the grounds of Beijing University and a glade by the Hudson River.

1976   Zhou Enlai, Zhu De, and Mao Zedong die. The death of Mao is followed shortly by the arrest of the Gang of Four and the formation of a transitional regime headed by Hua Guofeng.

1978   In December the Third Plenum of the 11th Central Committee begins far-reaching economic and political reforms associated with Deng Xiaoping. China embarks on a course of socialist modernization accompanied by an opening to foreign nations.

1979   Full diplomatic relations between the U.S. and China are established on January 1. But enactment of the Taiwan Relations Act soon after continues the American Two-Chinas policy.

1981   The Party leadership takes a close look at the recent past in its "Resolution on Certain Questions in the History of Our Party Since the Founding of the People's Republic of China." It draws a distinction between Mao's important contributions during the years of the struggle for power and his "mistakes in his later years."

1982   The 12th Party Congress sets goals to be reached by the year 2000—a quadrupling of annual production and raised living standards. The census shows that China had a population of 1.008 billion people, an 85 percent increase since 1949. China and the U.S. reach an agreement that U.S. sales of arms to Taiwan are to be gradually reduced.

1983   Widespread instances of crime and corruption in the Party and state are publicized. Concern over the negative effects of the influence of foreign culture leads to an Oppose Spiritual Pollution Campaign, which is short-lived because of excesses.

1984   Economic development zones are created in fourteen coastal cities as China seeks export-oriented advances and access to world technology. Premier Zhao Ziyang visits the U.S.

1985   Wage and price reforms begin to increase the role of the market. The overheating of the economy leads to counter-measures. The goal of reducing the size of the army by a million men is announced and is achieved in two years.

1986   The reforms of the economic mechanisms and the global opening are pressed forward. Discussion of political reform begins. Corruption is a paramount concern.

1987   Student demonstrations, begun late in 1986, continue and are bluntly criticized as a threat to order and the Party. A campaign against "bourgeois liberalization" is launched. Hu Yaobang resigns as Party general secretary, though continuing as a member of the Politburo. Three leading intellectuals are expelled from the Party for advocating· "bourgeois liberalization." But no change in basic policies follows. The 13th Party Congress affirms reforms, describes China as in the primary stage of socialism, and elects a younger leadership. Demonstrations in Tibet point to social unrest and serious continuing problems.

1988   Lively sessions of the National People's Congress and the Chinese People's Political Consultative Conference are evidence of gains in democratic practice. More disturbances in Tibet take place.

1989   Reports early in the year point to a steady inflation fueled by an excess of demand. Industrial growth continues but such problems as corruption, energy and transport shortages and environmental destruction remain unsolved. A resurgence of student demonstrations in April and May raises demands for party reform, more democracy and corrective action on corruption and inflation. Some workers and others participate in demonstrations in eighty cities; in Beijing hundreds go on a hunger strike at Tiananmen. On June 4 troops move against the protesters, killing or wounding thousands in the streets of Beijing as television cameras whirl and reporters jot down notes. The regime says that a counterrevolutionary rebellion has been crushed but the response abroad generally is outrage. Zhao Ziyang, accused of softness on bourgeois liberalism, is ousted as party secretary and replaced by Jiang Zemin, a Shanghai cadre. President Bush moderates the official U.S. reaction to the turn in China out of consideration of the importance of U.S.-China relations.

A TAIWAN CHRONOLOGY

230   The Kingdom of Wu (A.D. 222–265) tries to occupy Taiwan militarily.

1200– 1600 Pirates and trickles of fishermen, farmers, and small traders established bases and small settlements on the island.

1601–42   The Japanese, Spanish and Dutch establish small colonies, but the Japanese withdraw and in 1642 the Dutch succeed in ousting the Spanish. Taiwan is known in the West by the name given it by the Portuguese—Formosa, Beautiful Island.

1662   A harsh Dutch policy of maximizing profits and exploiting the Chinese inhabitants brings about its undoing. Zheng Cheng-gong (Koxinga), of mixed Chinese and Japanese parentage, leads an expedition of two-hundred-fifty ships and twenty-five thousand men from Xiamen (Amoy) in 1661 which captures Fort Zeelandia and ends Dutch rule after a nine-month siege.

1700s   About the same time that Europeans are settling the Atlantic seaboard, Chinese from Fujian and Guangdong (most of these Hakkas or "guest people") arrive in Taiwan in increasing numbers. Especially after the defeat of the Dutch, settlers ditch, dike, and terrace the western plain. They reproduce the villages they came from, making the landscape thoroughly Chinese. The population is approximately 250,000 at the end of the seventeenth century. A century later it swells to 1,300,000.

1850s   As a consequence of the British victory over the Chinese in the First

Opium War (1840–42), Britain, France, and the U.S. show acquisitive interest in Taiwan. Commodore Matthew Perry (whose fleet ended Japanese isolation), Townsend Harris (New York merchant and first diplomatic representative in Japan), and Peter Parker (medical missionary who became the U.S. commissioner to China), are among those who urge the U.S. to seize Taiwan. However, domestic conflict which led to civil war discourages such foreign adventures. Years later, John W. Foster (Secretary of State in the Harrison cabinet) supports Japanese annexation of Taiwan in the belief that U.S. control would follow.

1884   The French invade Taiwan and hold an enclave for a year, withdrawing when unable to extend their control of the island.

1885   The alarmed Imperial Court makes Taiwan a province and begins an effort to modernize the island's economy and infrastructure and strengthen its defenses. The capital is moved from Tainan in the south to Taipei in the north, near the best harbors.

1895   Japan acquires Taiwan as one of the spoils of its easy conquest of China in the war of 1894–95, but its troops have to suppress a series of uprisings in the early years of its rule. The republic proclaimed by a handful of Taiwanese is short-lived.

1895–1945   Japan systematically develops and commercializes much of the agriculture, gearing it to the Japanese market. Infrastructural improvements such as roads, railroads, power plants and communications spur economic progress. Some advances in education and health care are achieved. The population doubles to over six million. The Taiwanese are subjected to Japanization campaigns and are exploited and discriminated against; resentment of Japanese rule increases.

1943   The Cairo Declaration of the United Kingdom, China, and the U.S. states that Formosa, the Pescadores (Penghu Islands) and other territories stolen from China by Japan are restored to China.

1945   The Potsdam Declaration of the same three allies affirms the Cairo decisions. In August, Japan surrenders. Chinese troops occupy Taiwan and are greeted as liberators by the people.

1947   On February 28, the population rises up against the Nationalist authorities, provoked beyond endurance by plundering, corruption, and oppression. The beleaguered authorities temporize and make promises while awaiting the arrival of fifty thousand troops from the mainland. The revolt is drowned in blood; some ten thousand people are killed.

1949   As the Chiang Kai-shek regime crumbles, an average of five thousand a day flee to Taiwan. Altogether some two million mainlander troops, functionaries, and upper-class families take refuge on the island, bringing with them art treasures and gold. In December, Taipei is declared capital of a regime which claims to be the government of China.

1949–50   On December 23, 1949 an internal State Department memo declares: "Formosa is politically, geographically and strategically part of China. . . . Although ruled by the Japanese for fifty years, historically it has been Chinese. Politically and militarily it is strictly a Chinese responsibility." And on January 5, 1950, Secretary of State Acheson states: "The world must believe that we stand for principle and that we are honorable and decent people and that we do not put forward words . . . only to throw them overboard when the change in events makes the position difficult for us . . . therefore . . . we are not going to use our forces in connection with the present situation in Formosa. . . ." During the U.S. intervention in the Korean war, President Truman sends the Seventh Fleet into the Taiwan Strait, ordering it to oppose invasion from either direction. At the same time he increases U.S. military aid to the Philippines and to the French in Indochina. "The occupation of Formosa by Communist forces would be a direct threat to the security of the Pacific area and to the U.S. forces . . . in the area"—Truman. In one of many statements over the years, Zhou Enlai, China's foreign minister, declares " . . . the fact that Taiwan is a part of China will remain unchanged forever." He pledges an unceasing struggle to regain the island.

1954   On December 2, the U.S. and Taiwan regime conclude the Mutual Defense Treaty, which Zhou denounces as illegal, null and void. Earlier, President Eisenhower "unleashed Chiang Kai-shek"—rescinding the order to the Seventh Fleet to oppose an invasion of the mainland.

1958   The second and most acute of two crises centered on Quemoy and Matsu, islands in mainland harbors, develops as the U.S. sends destroyers and supplies in their defense to the Nationalist garrisons. The U.S. military prepares to use nuclear weapons based on Taiwan, but the U.S. disclaims any intention of taking part in an invasion of the mainland, and the crisis subsides.

1965   The U.S. ends economic aid to Taiwan's increasingly prosperous export-oriented economy after having provided it with $2 billion in such aid. Military aid continues in the billions. Meanwhile, the U.S. and Taipei cooperate in overflights of the mainland and in dispatching to the mainland hundreds of spies and saboteurs. Taiwan becomes a principal CIA base.

1971   The People's Republic of China is seated in the United Nations as the representative of China while Taiwan is ousted. Admission of the P.R.C. to most international bodies follows.

1972   The U.S.-China reconciliation culminates in President Nixon's visit. The Shanghai Communique, signed on February 28 by Nixon and Zhou, includes this unilateral U.S. statement: "The United States acknowledges that all Chinese on either side of the Taiwan Strait maintain there is but one China and that Taiwan is part of China. The United States does not challenge that position."

1978   The third plenum of the 11th Central Committee, meeting in December, launches major domestic reforms and alters policy toward Taiwan. Policy drops the word "liberation" in favor of "reunification" which states it can be achieved on the basis of consultations and negotiations.

1979   As of January 1, the U.S. severs official relations with Taipei, terminates the Mutual Defense Treaty and recognizes the P.R.C. as the official representative of China. In April, the Taiwan Relations Act provides for extensive unofficial relations with Taipei and extends protection with American armed forces. China denounces the act as a violation of their agreement.

1981   In a major statement amplified several times, Ye Jianying, Chairman of the Standing Committee of the National People's Congress, declares "Taiwan can enjoy a high degree of autonomy as a special administrative region and it can retain its armed forces. The central government will not interfere with local affairs on Taiwan." He further promises "Taiwan's current socio-economic system will remain unchanged, so will its way of life and its economic and cultural relations with foreign countries."

1982   In a Joint Communique dated August 17, the U.S. says it intends to gradually reduce sales of arms to Taiwan " . . . leading over a period of time to a final resolution." A statement by President Reagan expressed " . . . an abiding interest and concern" that any resolution of the Taiwan issue ". . . be peaceful."

1984   In February, Deng Xiaoping tells a U.S. delegation that Taiwan can still practice capitalism after a reunification with the People's Republic of China. In September, the agreement providing for the restoration of Hongkong to China is reached and several weeks later Deng elaborates his concept of the "one country, two systems" principle which was applied to Hongkong. He says retention of capitalism in Taiwan for an extended period is consonant with the goal of modernization and of building socialism with Chinese characteristics.

1985   New Year's statements in Beijing are optimistic regarding peaceful re-unification with Taiwan. Trade between the mainland and Taiwan grows to approximately $1 billion, reflecting China's general economic expansion. China's strengthened regional role leads to an increasing number of tacit understandings and quiet exchanges. This leads some observers to believe that reunification may be the eventual result of past efforts.

1986   In an interview with Mike Wallace of CBS, Deng Xiaoping recalls with regret that " . . . the U.S. Congress adopted the Taiwan Relations Act, which has become an immense obstacle in Sino-American relations." He says also that mainland-Taiwan contacts can increase understanding and create the conditions for negotiation of the reunification issue.

1987   The Taiwan authorities permit those with relatives on the mainland to visit them. The Taiwan Red Cross Society is swamped with applications and thousands soon make the trip. Among them are businessmen who look into trade and investment possibilities. A growing number of non-political books published on the mainland are reprinted or sold in Taiwan.

1988   Taiwan President Chiang Ching-kuo (Jiang Jingguo) dies on January 13. Messages of condolence from Party General Secretary Zhao Ziyang and the Central Committee are published in major Taiwan newspapers. Chiang is succeeded by Taiwan-born Lee Tsung-hui, who restates the regime's negative attitude toward reunification, but also warns against advocating the island's independence. Meanwhile, trade between the island and the mainland continues to grow, with a $2 billion total for the year very likely. Bilateral trade is twenty times what it was in 1978. Other exchanges and contacts expand.

1989   A March report shows expanding relations with Taiwan. Economic and trade ties were valued at $2.4 billion in 1988, up from $1.6 billion in 1987. Mainland post offices received 1.48 million letters from Taiwan, and nearly 450,000 Taiwanese visited the mainland. Some one hundred Taiwan journalists covered mainland events, and four Taiwan troupes performed on the mainland. But an immediate consequence of the violent suppression of the student-worker demonstrations on June 4 was a widening of Taipei-Beijing differences.

BIBLIOGRAPHY

Alley, Rewi. *At 90: Memoirs of My China Years*. Beijing: New World Press, 1986.

Alley, Rewi. *Six Americans in China*. Beijing: Intercul, 1985.

Ambrose, Stephen E. *Eisenhower: Volume Two, The President*. New York: Simon and Schuster, 1984.

Amerasia Papers. Washington, D.C.: U.S. Government Printing Office, 1970.

Avedon, John F. *In Exile from the Land of Snows*. New York: Knopf, 1984.

Bachrack, Stanley D. *The Committee of One Million: "China Lobby" Politics*. New York: Columbia University Press, 1976.

Borg, Dorothy, and Waldo Heinrichs, eds. *Uncertain Years: Chinese American Relations, 1947–50*. New York: Columbia University Press, 1980.

Belden, Jack. *China Shakes the World*. New York: Monthy Review Press, 1977.

Braeman, John. *Albert J. Beveridge, American Nationalist*. Chicago: University of Chicago Press, 1975.

Burman, Bina Roy. *Religion and Politics in Tibet*. New Delhi and Bombay: Vikas, 1979.

Burner, David. *Herbert Hoover, a Public Life*. New York: Knopf, 1979.

Cahill, Holger. *A Yankee Adventurer: The Story of Ward and the Taiping Rebellion*. New York: The Macauley Company, 1930.

Caldwell, Oliver J. *A Secret War: Americans in China, 1944–1945*. Carbondale, Ill.: Southern Illinois University Press, 1972.

Chen Han-seng. *Gung-ho! The Story of the Chinese Cooperatives*. New York: American Institute of Pacific Relations, 1947.

Ch'en, Jerome. *China and the West*. Bloomington Ind.: Indiana University Press, 1979.

Chu, Limen. *The Images of China and the Chinese in the Overland Monthly, 1868–1875, 1883–1935.* Durham, N.C.: Duke University Press, 1965.

Crane, Stephen. *The Blood of the Martyr.* Mount Vernon, N.Y.: Peter Pauper Press, 1940.

Cumings, Bruce. *The Origin of the Korean War: Liberation and the Emergence of Separate Regimes, 1945–47.* Princeton, N.J.: Princeton University Press, 1981.

Cunningham, Isabel Shipley. *Frank N. Meyer: Plant Hunter in Asia.* Ames, Iowa: Iowa State University Press, 1984.

Dayer, Roberta Allbert. *Bankers and Diplomats in China, 1917–1925: The Anglo-American Relationship.* Notawa, N.J.: F. Cass, 1981.

Deane, Hugh, ed. *Remembering Koji Ariyoshi: An American GI in Yenan* (Los Angeles: US-China Peoples Friendship Association, 1978).

———. *MacArthur Is No Riddle.* Series of seventeen articles published in the *New York Daily Compass*, April–May 1951.

Epstein, Israel. *From Opium War to Liberation.* Hongkong: Joint Publishing Co., 1980).

———. *Tibet Transformed.* Beijing: New World Press, 1983.

Esherick, Joseph W., ed. *Lost Chance in China: The World War II Despatches of John S. Service.* New York: Random House, 1974.

Fairbank, John King. *Chinese-American Interactions: A Historical Summary.* New Brunswick, N.J.: Rutgers University Press, 1975.

———. *China Perceived: Images and Policies in Chinese-American Relations.* New York: Knopf, 1976.

———. *Chinabound: A Fifty-Year Memoir.* New York: Harper & Row, 1982.

Feis, Herbert. *The China Tangle.* New York: Atheneum, 1966.

Foner, Philip S. *Mark Twain: Social Critic.* New York: International Publishers, 1958.

———. *Paul Robeson Speaks.* New York: Citadel, 1978.

Galbraith, John Kenneth. *A Life in Our Times: Memoirs.* Boston: Houghton, Mifflin, 1981.

Geismar, Maxwell, ed. *Mark Twain and the Three R's: Race, Religion, Revolution and Related Matters.* Indianapolis and New York: Bobbs-Merrill, 1973.

Ginsburgs, George, and Michael Mathos. *Communist China and Tibet: The First Dozen Years.* The Hague: M. Nijhoff, 1964.

Glubok, Shirley. *See* Tamarin, Alfred.

Grayson, Benson Lee, ed. *The American Image of China, with a History of Sino-American Relations by Benson Lee Grayson.* New York: Ungar, 1979.

Greenberg, Michael S. *British Trade and the Opening of China, 1840–1842.* Cambridge: Cambridge University Press, 1969.

Griswold, A. Whitney. *The Far Eastern Policy of the United States.* New York: Harcourt, Brace, 1938.

Grunfeld, A. Tom. *The Making of Modern Tibet.* Armonk, N.Y.: M. E. Sharpe, 1987.

Hake, A. Egmont. *Events of the Taeping Rebellion.* London: W. H. Allen, 1891.

Hamill, John. *The Strange Career of Mr. Hoover under Two Flags.* New York: William Faro, 1931.

Inglis, Brian. *The Opium War.* London: Hodder and Stoughton, 1976.

Jacoby, Annalee. *See* White, Theodore H.

Jen Yu-wen, with the editorial assistance of Adrienne Suddard. *The Taiping Revolutionary Movement.* New Haven and London: Yale University Press, 1973.

Kahn, E. J., Jr. *The China Hands: America's Foreign Service Officers and What Befell Them.* New York: Viking, 1975.

Kinderman, Katherine S. *See* Lo, Ruth Earnshaw.

Kirker, James. *Adventures to China: Americans in the Southern Oceans, 1792–1812.* New York: Oxford University Press, 1970.

Kutler, Stanley I. *The American Inquisition.* New York: Hill and Wang, 1982.

Lindbergh, Anne Morrow. With maps by Charles A. Lindbergh. *North to the Orient.* New York: Harcourt, Brace, 1935; 1966.

Lingnan University. *Canton Christian College, Ling Naan Hok Hau: Its Growth and Outlook.* New York: Trustees of the Canton Christian College, 1919.

Lingnan University: A Short History, Based Primarily on the Records of the University's American Trustees. New York: n.p., 1963.

Lin-le [Augustus F. Lindley]. *Ti-Ping Tien-Kwoh: The History of the Ti-Ping Revolution, Including a Narrative of the Author's Personal Adventures.* 2 vols. London: Day & Son, 1866.

Lo, Ruth Earnshaw, and Katherine S. Kinderman; John K. Fairbank, intro. *In the Eye of the Typhoon.* New York and London: Harcourt, Brace, Jovanovich, 1980.

Lockwood, Stephen C. *Augustine Heard and Company, 1858–1862.* Cambridge, Mass.: Harvard University Press, 1971.

Luo Guangbin and Yang Yiyang. *Red Crag.* Beijing: Foreign Languages Press, 1978.

MacArthur, Douglas. *Reminiscences*. New York: McGraw-Hill, 1984.

MacKinnon, Janice R., and Stephen R. MacKinnon. *Agnes Smedley—The Life and Times of an American Radical*. Berkeley, Ca.: University of California Press, 1988.

McLaughlin, Charles Capen, ed. *The Papers of Frederick Law Olmsted*, vol. 1. *The Formative Years: 1822–1852*. Baltimore and London: Johns Hopkins University Press, 1977.

Manchester, William. *American Caesar, Douglas MacArthur: 1880–1964*. Boston and Toronto: Little, Brown: 1978.

Martin, W. A. P. *A Cycle of Cathay*. New York: Fleming H. Revell, 1897.

Mathos, Michael. *See* Ginsburgs, George.

Meadows, Thomas Taylor. *The Chinese and Their Rebellions*. London: Smith, Elder, 1856).

Miles, Milton E. *A Different Kind of War*. New York: Doubleday, 1967.

Nash, George H. *The Life of Herbert Hoover: The Engineer, 1874–1914*. New York: W. W. Norton, 1983.

Prouty, Leroy Fletcher. *The Secret Team: The CIA and Its Allies in Control of the United States and the World*. Englewood Cliffs, N.J.: Prentice-Hall, 1973.

Reinsch, Paul S. *An American Diplomat in China*. New York and Toronto: Doubleday, Page, 1922; Taipei: Ch'eng Wen Publishing Co., 1967.

Schaller, Michael. *The U.S. Crusade in China, 1938–1945*. New York: Columbia University Press, 1979.

———. *The United States and China in the Twentieth Century*. New York: Oxford University Press, 1979.

Schuman, Julian. *China: An Uncensored Look*. Sagaponack, NY: Second Chance Press, 1979.

Seton, Marie. *Paul Robeson*. London: Dobson Books, 1958.

Shen Zui. *A KMT War Criminal on New China*. Changsha and Beijing, 1986.

Service, John S. *See* Esherick, Joseph W.

Shewmaker, Kenneth E. *Americans and Chinese Communists, 1927–1945: A Personal Encounter*. Ithaca, N.Y.: Cornell University Press, 1971.

Smedley, Agnes. *Battle Hymn of China*. New York, 1943; reprinted New York: Da Capo Press, 1975, and as *China Correspondent*, London: Methuen, 1984.

Smith, Janet, ed. *Mark Twain on the Damned Human Race*. New York: Hill and Wang, 1962.

Smith, R. Harris. *OSS: The Secret History of America's First Central Intelligence Agency.* Berkeley, Ca.: University of California Press, 1972.

Snow, Edgar. *Red Star Over China.* New York: Random House, 1938; first revised and enlarged edition, New York: Grove Press, 1968.

————. *Journey to the Beginning.* New York: Random House, 1958.

Snow, Helen Foster. *China Builds for Democracy.* New York: Modern Age Books, 1941.

Snow, Helen Foster, and Margaret Stanley, comps. *The Gung Ho Papers.* Madison, Conn.: Bookmark Limited Press, 1985.

Snow, Helen Foster. *My China Years: A Memoir.* New York: William Morrow, 1984.

Snow, Lois Wheeler. *Edgar Snow's China.* New York: Random House, 1981.

Speer, Robert E. *Missions and Modern History.* New York: Fleming H. Revell, 1904.

Spence, Jonathan D. *To Change China: Western Advisers in China, 1620–1960.* Boston: Little, Brown, 1969.

Stevenson, Elizabeth. *Park Maker: A Life of Frederick Law Olmsted.* New York and London: MacMillan, 1977.

Stilwell, Joseph Warren. *See* White, Theodore H..

Stone, I. F. *The Hidden History of the Korean War.* New York: Monthly Review Press, 1952; a later edition as *The Hidden History of the Korean War, 1950-1951,* with a preface by Bruce Cumings. Boston: Little, Brown, 1988.

Strong, Tracy B., and Helene Keysarr. *Right in Her Soul: The Life of Anna Louise Strong.* New York: Random House, 1983.

Su Kaiming. *Modern China: A Topical History.* Beijing: New World Press, 1985.

Tamarin, Alfred, and Shirley Glubok. *Voyaging to Cathay: Americans in the China Trade.* New York: Viking, 1976.

Taylor, Bayard. *A Visit to India, China and Japan in the Year 1853.* New York: G. P. Putnam, 1855.

Tolley, Kemp. *Yangtze Patrol: The U.S. Navy in China.* Annapolis, Md.: Naval Institute Press, 1976.

Tuchman, Barbara. *Stilwell and the American Experience in China, 1911–45.* New York: MacMillan, 1970.

Twain, Mark. *Mark Twain's Letters,* vol. 2. Edited by Harriet Elinor Smith and Richard Bucci. Berkeley, Ca.: University of California Press, 1990.

Wales, Nym. *See* Snow, Helen Foster.

Ward, Geoffrey C. *Before the Trumpet: Young Franklin Roosevelt, 1882–1905*. New York: Harper & Row, 1985.

White, Theodore H. *In Search of History: A Personal Adventure*. New York: Harper & Row, 1978.

———, ed. *The Stilwell Papers*. New York: W. Sloane Associates, 1948; Shocken, 1972; Harper & Row, 1978.

White, Theodore H., and Annalee Jacoby. *Thunder Out of China*. New York: William Sloane Associates, 1946.

Williams, William Appleman. *The Tragedy of American Diplomacy*. Cleveland and New York: World Publishing, 1959; second revised and enlarged edition: New York: Dell, 1972.

———. *The Contours of American History*. Cleveland and New York: World Publishing, 1961.

INDEX